T0257999

Data Structures and Algorithms in Computer Science

Data Structures and Algorithms in Computer Science

Edited by Joe Oswald

CLANRYE
INTERNATIONAL
www.clanryeinternational.com

Clanrye International,
750 Third Avenue, 9th Floor,
New York, NY 10017, USA

ISBN: 978-1-63240-703-0

Cataloging-in-Publication Data

Data structures and algorithms in computer science / edited by Joe Oswald
    p. cm.
Includes bibliographical references and index.
ISBN 978-1-63240-703-0
1. Data structures (Computer science). 2. Computer algorithms. 3. Computer science.
I. Oswald, Joe.
QA76.9.D35 D38 2018
005.73--dc23

For information on all Clanrye International publications
visit our website at www.clanryeinternational.com

Contents

Preface

Data structure refers to the assimilation of data in a way so that it can be used efficiently. The important types of data structures are the record, the array, the table, the file, the tree, the class, the union, etc. Data structures are designed by using different intricate algorithms in any computer program. Algorithms are a sequence of actions used for data processing along with calculation and reasoning tasks. This book is compiled in such a manner, that it will provide in-depth knowledge about the theory and practice of data structures and algorithms with respect to computer science. It unfolds the innovative aspects of this subject, which will be crucial for the holistic understanding of this area. This textbook is an essential guide for both academicians and those who wish to pursue this discipline further.

A detailed account of the significant topics covered in this book is provided below:

Chapter 1- Data structure is systematic way of arranging data to maximize efficiency. Types of data structures include array, record, linked test, stack, etc. The information setting can be understood by binary number system, real number, binary coded decimal, and character string. This is an introductory chapter which will introduce briefly all the significant aspects of date structure and its types.

Chapter 2- A calculating method that takes in data or inputs and produces outputs is referred to as algorithm. It contains specifications, body of algorithm, pre-conditions, and post-conditions. The chapter also delves deep into the concept of sorting algorithm that organizes a list of elements in an order. This section has been carefully written to provide an easy understanding of the varied facets of algorithms.

Chapter 3- The major categories of trees in data structure are dealt with great details in the section. It focuses on binary tree, its operation, representation and transversal. Binary tree is a type of tree that has a distinct node and can have a maximum of two children. Other type of tree discussed here is the search tree. It helps in finding out specific keys from a set. The chapter strategically encompasses and incorporates the major components and key concepts of data structures, providing a complete understanding.

Chapter 4- The chapter serves as a source to understand program development and the processes related to it. Software development is crafting a software product that involves processes such as programming, testing, bug-fixing etc. In the development stage, source code is written and maintained as well. The section also sheds light on concepts of programming language, source code, debugger, etc. This chapter is an overview of the subject matter incorporating all the major aspects of program development.

Chapter 5- Science and technology has undergone rapid developments in the past decade which has resulted in the discovery of significant techniques in the field of search algorithms and hashing. Search algorithm helps in recovering information from data structures. Hashing is a method to optimize searching, inserting, deleting, and sorting functions by storing data in an array. Two notable techniques of hashing are chaining and rehashing. This chapter will provide an integrated understanding of search algorithms.

I would like to make a special mention of my publisher who considered me worthy of this opportunity and also supported me throughout the process. I would also like to thank the editing team at the back-end who extended their help whenever required.

Editor

An Overview of Data Structures

Data structure is systematic way of arranging data to maximize efficiency. Types of data structures include array, record, linked test, stack, etc. The information setting can be understood by binary number system, real number, binary coded decimal, and character string. This is an introductory chapter which will introduce briefly all the significant aspects of data structure and its types.

Data Structure

1. A *data structure* is a systematic way of organizing and accessing data.

2. A *data structure* tries to structure data.

   - Usually more than one piece of data

   - Should define legal operations on the data

   - The data might be grouped together (e.g. in an linked list)

3. When we define a data structure we are in fact creating a new data type of our own.

   - i.e. using predefined types or previously user defined types.

   - Such new types are then used to reference variables type within a program

In computer science, a data structure is a particular way of organizing data in a computer so that it can be used efficiently.

Usage

Data structures can implement one or more particular abstract data types (ADT), which specify the operations that can be performed on a data structure and the computational complexity of those operations. In comparison, a data structure is a concrete implementation of the specification provided by an ADT.

Different kinds of data structures are suited to different kinds of applications, and some are highly specialized to specific tasks. For example, relational databases commonly use B-tree indexes for data retrieval, while compiler implementations usually use hash tables to look up identifiers.

Data structures provide a means to manage large amounts of data efficiently for uses such as large databases and internet indexing services. Usually, efficient data structures are key to designing efficient algorithms. Some formal design methods and programming languages emphasize data structures, rather than algorithms, as the key organizing factor in software design. Data structures can be used to organize the storage and retrieval of information stored in both main memory and secondary memory.

Implementation

Data structures are generally based on the ability of a computer to fetch and store data at any place in its memory, specified by a pointer—a bit string, representing a memory address, that can be itself stored in memory and manipulated by the program. Thus, the array and record data structures are based on computing the addresses of data items with arithmetic operations; while the linked data structures are based on storing addresses of data items within the structure itself. Many data structures use both principles, sometimes combined in non-trivial ways (as in XOR linking).

The implementation of a data structure usually requires writing a set of procedures that create and manipulate instances of that structure. The efficiency of a data structure cannot be analyzed separately from those operations. This observation motivates the theoretical concept of an abstract data type, a data structure that is defined indirectly by the operations that may be performed on it, and the mathematical properties of those operations (including their space and time cost).

Examples

There are numerous types of data structures, generally built upon simpler primitive data types:

- An *array* is a number of elements in a specific order, typically all of the same type. Elements are accessed using an integer index to specify which element is required (Depending on the language, individual elements may either all be forced to be the same type, or may be of almost any type). Typical implementations allocate contiguous memory words for the elements of arrays (but this is not always a necessity). Arrays may be fixed-length or resizable.

- A *linked list* (also just called *list*) is a linear collection of data elements of any type, called nodes, where each node has itself a value, and points to the next node in the linked list. The principal advantage of a linked list over an array, is that values can always be efficiently inserted and removed without relocating the rest of the list. Certain other operations, such as random access to a certain element, are however slower on lists than on arrays.

- A *record* (also called *tuple* or *struct*) is an aggregate data structure. A record is a value that contains other values, typically in fixed number and sequence and typically indexed by names. The elements of records are usually called *fields* or *members*.

- A *union* is a data structure that specifies which of a number of permitted primitive types may be stored in its instances, e.g. *float* or *long integer*. Contrast with a record, which could be defined to contain a float *and* an integer; whereas in a union, there is only one value at a time. Enough space is allocated to contain the widest member datatype.

- A *tagged union* (also called *variant, variant record, discriminated union,* or *disjoint union*) contains an additional field indicating its current type, for enhanced type safety.

- A *class* is a data structure that contains data fields, like a record, as well as various methods which operate on the contents of the record. In the context of object-oriented programming, records are known as plain old data structures to distinguish them from classes.

Language Support

Most assembly languages and some low-level languages, such as BCPL (Basic Combined Programming Language), lack built-in support for data structures. On the other hand, many high-level programming languages and some higher-level assembly languages, such as MASM, have special syntax or other built-in support for certain data structures, such as records and arrays. For example, the C (a direct descendant of BCPL) and Pascal languages support structs and records, respectively, in addition to vectors (one-dimensional arrays) and multi-dimensional arrays.

Most programming languages feature some sort of library mechanism that allows data structure implementations to be reused by different programs. Modern languages usually come with standard libraries that implement the most common data structures. Examples are the C++ Standard Template Library, the Java Collections Framework, and the Microsoft .NET Framework.

Modern languages also generally support modular programming, the separation between the interface of a library module and its implementation. Some provide opaque data types that allow clients to hide implementation details. Object-oriented programming languages, such as C++, Java, and Smalltalk, typically use classes for this purpose.

Many known data structures have concurrent versions which allow multiple computing threads to access a single concrete instance of a data structure simultaneously.

Why Data Structures?

1. Data structures study how data are stored in a computer so that operations can be implemented efficiently

2. Data structures are especially important when you have a large amount of information

3. Conceptual and concrete ways to organize data for efficient storage and manipulation.

Methods of Interpreting Bit Setting

1. Binary Number System

   - Non Negative

- Negative
  - o Ones Complement Notation
  - o Twos Complement Notation
2. Binary Coded Decimal
3. Real Number
4. Character String

Non-Negative Binary System

In this System each bit position represents a power of 2. The right most bit position represent 2^0 which equals 1. The next position to the left represents $2^1 = 2$ and so on. An Integer is represented as a sum of powers of 2. A string of all 0s represents the number 0. If a 1 appears in a particular bit position, the power of 2 represented by that bit position is included in the Sum. But if a 0 appears, the power of 2 is not included in the Sum. For example 10011, the sum is $2^0 + 2^1 + 2^4 = 19$.

Ones Complement Notation

Negative binary number is represented by ones Complement Notation. In this notation we represent a negative number by changing each bit in its absolute value to the opposite bit setting. For example, since 001001100 represent 38, 11011001 is used to represent -38. The left most number is reserved for the sign of the number. A bit String Starting with a 0 represents a positive number, where a bit string starting with a 1 represents a negative number.

Twos Complement Notation

In Twos Complement Notation is also used to represent a negative number. In this notation 1 is added to the Ones Complement Notation of a negative number. For example, since 11011001 represents -38 in Ones Complement Notation 11011010 used represent -38 in Twos Complement Notation.

Binary Coded Decimal

In this System a string of bits may be used to represent integers in the Decimal Number System . Four bits can be used to represent a Decimal digit between 0 and 9 in the binary notation. A string of bits of arbitrary length may be divided into consecutive sets of four bits. With each set representing a decimal digit. The string then represents the number that is formed by those decimal digits in conventional decimal notation. For example, in this system the bit string 00110101 is separated into two strings of four bits each: 0011 and 0101. The first of these represents the decimal digit 3 and the second represents the decimal 5, so that the entire string represents the integer 35.

In the binary coded decimal system we use 4 bits, so this four bits represent sixteen possible states. But only 10 of those sixteen possibilities are used. That means, whose binary values are 10 or larger, are invalid in Binary Coded Decimal System.

Real Number

The Floating Point Notation use to represent Real Numbers. The key concept of floating-point notation is Mantissa, Base and Exponent . The base is usually fixed and the Mantissa and the Exponent vary to represent different Real Number. For Example, if the base is fixed at 10, the number -235.47 could be represented as $-23547 * 10^{-2}$. The Mantissa is 23547 and the exponent is -2. Other possible representations are $-23547 * 10^3$ and $-235.47 * 10^0$.

In the floating-point notation a real number is represented by a 32-bit string. Including in 32-bit, 24-bit use for representation of Mantissa and remaining 8-bit use for representation of Exponent .Both the mantissa and the exponent are twos complement binary Integers. For example, the 24-bit twos complement binary representation of -23547 is 111111111010010000000101, and the 8-bit twos complement binary representation of -2 is 11111110. So the representation of 235.47 is 111111111010010000 00010111111110. It can be used to represent extremely large or extremely small absolute values.

Character Strings

In computer science, information is not always interpreted numerically. Item such as names, address and job title must also be represented in some fashion with in computer. To enable the representation of such nonnumeric objects, still another method of interpreting bit strings is necessary. Such information is usually represented in character string form. For example, in some computers, the eight bits 11000000 is used to represent the character "A" and 11000001 for character "B" and another for each character that has a representation in a particular machine. So, the character string "AB" would be represented by the bit string 1100000011000001.

Types of Data Structures

Array Data Structure

In computer science, an array data structure, or simply an array, is a data structure consisting of a collection of *elements* (values or variables), each identified by at least one *array index* or *key*. An array is stored so that the position of each element can be computed from its index tuple by a mathematical formula. The simplest type of data structure is a linear array, also called one-dimensional array.

For example, an array of 10 32-bit integer variables, with indices 0 through 9, may be stored as 10 words at memory addresses 2000, 2004, 2008, ... 2036, so that the element with index i has the address $2000 + 4 \times i$.

The memory address of the first element of an array is called first address or foundation address.

Because the mathematical concept of a matrix can be represented as a two-dimensional grid, two-dimensional arrays are also sometimes called matrices. In some cases the term "vector" is used in computing to refer to an array, although tuples rather than vectors are more correctly the mathematical equivalent. Arrays are often used to implement tables, especially lookup tables; the word *table* is sometimes used as a synonym of *array*.

Arrays are among the oldest and most important data structures, and are used by almost every program. They are also used to implement many other data structures, such as lists and strings. They effectively exploit the addressing logic of computers. In most modern computers and many external storage devices, the memory is a one-dimensional array of words, whose indices are their addresses. Processors, especially vector processors, are often optimized for array operations.

Arrays are useful mostly because the element indices can be computed at run time. Among other things, this feature allows a single iterative statement to process arbitrarily many elements of an array. For that reason, the elements of an array data structure are required to have the same size and should use the same data representation. The set of valid index tuples and the addresses of the elements (and hence the element addressing formula) are usually, but not always, fixed while the array is in use.

The term *array* is often used to mean array data type, a kind of data type provided by most high-level programming languages that consists of a collection of values or variables that can be selected by one or more indices computed at run-time. Array types are often implemented by array structures; however, in some languages they may be implemented by hash tables, linked lists, search trees, or other data structures.

The term is also used, especially in the description of algorithms, to mean associative array or "abstract array", a theoretical computer science model (an abstract data type or ADT) intended to capture the essential properties of arrays.

History

The first digital computers used machine-language programming to set up and access array structures for data tables, vector and matrix computations, and for many other purposes. John von Neumann wrote the first array-sorting program (merge sort) in 1945, during the building of the first stored-program computer.[p. 159] Array indexing was originally done by self-modifying code, and later using index registers and indirect addressing. Some mainframes designed in the 1960s, such as the Burroughs B5000 and its successors, used memory segmentation to perform index-bounds checking in hardware.

Assembly languages generally have no special support for arrays, other than what the machine itself provides. The earliest high-level programming languages, including FORTRAN (1957), Lisp (1958), COBOL (1960), and ALGOL 60 (1960), had support for multi-dimensional arrays, and so has C (1972). In C++ (1983), class templates exist for multi-dimensional arrays whose dimension is fixed at runtime as well as for runtime-flexible arrays.

Applications

Arrays are used to implement mathematical vectors and matrices, as well as other kinds of rectangular tables. Many databases, small and large, consist of (or include) one-dimensional arrays whose elements are records.

Arrays are used to implement other data structures, such as lists, heaps, hash tables, deques, queues, stacks, strings, and VLists. Array-based implementations of other data structures are frequently simple and space-efficient (implicit data structures), requiring little space overhead, but may have poor space complexity, particularly when modified, compared to tree-based data structures (compare a sorted array to a search tree).

One or more large arrays are sometimes used to emulate in-program dynamic memory allocation, particularly memory pool allocation. Historically, this has sometimes been the only way to allocate "dynamic memory" portably.

Arrays can be used to determine partial or complete control flow in programs, as a compact alternative to (otherwise repetitive) multiple IF statements. They are known in this context as control tables and are used in conjunction with a purpose built interpreter whose control flow is altered according to values contained in the array. The array may contain subroutine pointers (or relative subroutine numbers that can be acted upon by SWITCH statements) that direct the path of the execution.

Element Identifier and Addressing Formulas

When data objects are stored in an array, individual objects are selected by an index that is usually a non-negative scalar integer. Indexes are also called subscripts. An index *maps* the array value to a stored object.

There are three ways in which the elements of an array can be indexed:

- 0 (*zero-based indexing*): The first element of the array is indexed by subscript of 0.
- 1 (*one-based indexing*): The first element of the array is indexed by subscript of 1.
- n (*n-based indexing*): The base index of an array can be freely chosen. Usually programming languages allowing *n-based indexing* also allow negative index values and other scalar data types like enumerations, or characters may be used as an array index.

Arrays can have multiple dimensions, thus it is not uncommon to access an array using multiple indices. For example, a two-dimensional array A with three rows and four columns might provide access to the element at the 2nd row and 4th column by the expression A[1, 3] in the case of a zero-based indexing system. Thus two indices are used for a two-dimensional array, three for a three-dimensional array, and *n* for an *n*-dimensional array.

The number of indices needed to specify an element is called the dimension, dimensionality, or rank of the array.

In standard arrays, each index is restricted to a certain range of consecutive integers (or consecutive values of some enumerated type), and the address of an element is computed by a "linear" formula on the indices.

One-dimensional Arrays

A one-dimensional array (or single dimension array) is a type of linear array. Accessing its elements involves a single subscript which can either represent a row or column index.

As an example consider the C declaration `int anArrayName [10];`

Syntax : datatype `anArrayname[sizeofArray];`

In the given example the array can contain 10 elements of any value available to the int type. In C, the array element indices are 0-9 inclusive in this case. For example, the expressions anArrayName and anArrayName are the first and last elements respectively.

For a vector with linear addressing, the element with index i is located at the address $B + c \times i$, where B is a fixed *base address* and c a fixed constant, sometimes called the *address increment* or *stride*.

If the valid element indices begin at 0, the constant B is simply the address of the first element of the array. For this reason, the C programming language specifies that array indices always begin at 0; and many programmers will call that element "zeroth" rather than "first".

However, one can choose the index of the first element by an appropriate choice of the base address B. For example, if the array has five elements, indexed 1 through 5, and the base address B is replaced by $B + 30c$, then the indices of those same elements will be 31 to 35. If the numbering does not start at 0, the constant B may not be the address of any element.

Multidimensional Arrays

For multi dimensional array, the element with indices i,j would have address $B + c \cdot i + d \cdot j$, where the coefficients c and d are the *row* and *column address increments*, respectively.

More generally, in a k-dimensional array, the address of an element with indices $i_1, i_2, ..., i_k$ is

$$B + c_1 \cdot i_1 + c_2 \cdot i_2 + ... + c_k \cdot i_k.$$

For example: int a [2][3];

This means that array a has 2 rows and 3 columns, and the array is of integer type. Here we can store 6 elements they are stored linearly but starting from first row linear then continuing with second row. The above array will be stored as $a_{11}, a_{12}, a_{13}, a_{21}, a_{22}, a_{23}$.

This formula requires only k multiplications and k additions, for any array that can fit in memory. Moreover, if any coefficient is a fixed power of 2, the multiplication can be replaced by bit shifting.

The coefficients c_k must be chosen so that every valid index tuple maps to the address of a distinct element.

If the minimum legal value for every index is 0, then B is the address of the element whose indices are all zero. As in the one-dimensional case, the element indices may be changed by changing the base address B. Thus, if a two-dimensional array has rows and columns indexed from 1 to 10 and 1 to 20, respectively, then replacing B by $B + c_1 - - 3 c_1$ will cause them to be renumbered from 0 through 9 and 4 through 23, respectively. Taking advantage of this feature, some languages (like FORTRAN 77) specify that array indices begin at 1, as in mathematical tradition while other languages (like Fortran 90, Pascal and Algol) let the user choose the minimum value for each index.

Dope Vectors

The addressing formula is completely defined by the dimension d, the base address B, and the increments c_1, c_2, ..., c_k. It is often useful to pack these parameters into a record called the array's *descriptor* or *stride vector* or *dope vector*. The size of each element, and the minimum and maximum values allowed for each index may also be included in the dope vector. The dope vector is a complete handle for the array, and is a convenient way to pass arrays as arguments to procedures. Many useful array slicing operations (such as selecting a sub-array, swapping indices, or reversing the direction of the indices) can be performed very efficiently by manipulating the dope vector.

Compact Layouts

Often the coefficients are chosen so that the elements occupy a contiguous area of memory. However, that is not necessary. Even if arrays are always created with contiguous elements, some array slicing operations may create non-contiguous sub-arrays from them.

There are two systematic compact layouts for a two-dimensional array. For example, consider the matrix

$$\mathbf{A} = \begin{bmatrix} 1 & 2 & 3 \\ 4 & 5 & 6 \\ 7 & 8 & 9 \end{bmatrix}.$$

In the row-major order layout (adopted by C for statically declared arrays), the elements in each row are stored in consecutive positions and all of the elements of a row have a lower address than any of the elements of a consecutive row:

1	2	3	4	5	6	7	8	9

In column-major order (traditionally used by Fortran), the elements in each column are consecutive in memory and all of the elements of a column have a lower address than any of the elements of a consecutive column:

1	4	7	2	5	8	3	6	9

For arrays with three or more indices, "row major order" puts in consecutive positions any two elements whose index tuples differ only by one in the *last* index. "Column major order" is analogous with respect to the *first* index.

In systems which use processor cache or virtual memory, scanning an array is much faster if successive elements are stored in consecutive positions in memory, rather than sparsely scattered. Many algorithms that use multidimensional arrays will scan them in a predictable order. A programmer (or a sophisticated compiler) may use this information to choose between row- or column-major layout for each array. For example, when computing the product $A \cdot B$ of two matrices, it would be best to have A stored in row-major order, and B in column-major order.

Resizing

Static arrays have a size that is fixed when they are created and consequently do not allow elements to be inserted or removed. However, by allocating a new array and copying the contents of the old array to it, it is possible to effectively implement a *dynamic* version of an array. If this operation is done infrequently, insertions at the end of the array require only amortized constant time.

Some array data structures do not reallocate storage, but do store a count of the number of elements of the array in use, called the count or size. This effectively makes the array a dynamic array with a fixed maximum size or capacity; Pascal strings are examples of this.

Non-linear Formulas

More complicated (non-linear) formulas are occasionally used. For a compact two-dimensional triangular array, for instance, the addressing formula is a polynomial of degree 2.

Efficiency

Both *store* and *select* take (deterministic worst case) constant time. Arrays take linear ($O(n)$) space in the number of elements n that they hold.

In an array with element size k and on a machine with a cache line size of B bytes, iterating through an array of n elements requires the minimum of ceiling(nk/B) cache misses, because its elements occupy contiguous memory locations. This is roughly a factor of B/k better than the number of cache misses needed to access n elements at random memory locations. As a consequence, sequential iteration over an array is noticeably faster in practice than iteration over many other data structures, a property called locality of reference (this does *not* mean however, that using a perfect hash or trivial hash within the same (local) array, will not be even faster - and achievable in constant time). Libraries provide low-level optimized facilities for copying ranges of memory (such as memcpy) which can be used to move contiguous blocks of array elements significantly faster than can be achieved through individual element access. The speedup of such optimized routines varies by array element size, architecture, and implementation.

Memory-wise, arrays are compact data structures with no per-element overhead. There may be a per-array overhead, e.g. to store index bounds, but this is language-dependent. It can also happen that elements stored in an array require *less* memory than the same elements stored in individual variables, because several array elements can be stored in a single word; such arrays are often called *packed* arrays. An extreme (but commonly used) case is the bit array, where every bit represents a single element. A single octet can thus hold up to 256 different combinations of up to 8 different conditions, in the most compact form.

Array accesses with statically predictable access patterns are a major source of data parallelism.

Comparison with Other Data Structures

Comparison of list data structures						
	Linked list	Array	**Dynamic array**	**Balanced tree**	**Random access list**	**hashed array tree**
Indexing	$\Theta(n)$	$\Theta(1)$	$\Theta(1)$	$\Theta(\log n)$	$\Theta(\log n)$	$\Theta(1)$
Insert/delete at beginning	$\Theta(1)$	N/A	$\Theta(n)$	$\Theta(\log n)$	$\Theta(1)$	$\Theta(n)$

Insert/delete at end	$\Theta(1)$ when last element is known; $\Theta(n)$ when last element is unknown	N/A	$\Theta(1)$ amortized	$\Theta(\log n)$	$\Theta(\log n)$ updating	$\Theta(1)$ amortized
Insert/delete in middle	search time + $\Theta(1)$	N/A	$\Theta(n)$	$\Theta(\log n)$	$\Theta(\log n)$ updating	$\Theta(n)$
Wasted space (average)	$\Theta(n)$	0	$\Theta(n)$	$\Theta(n)$	$\Theta(n)$	$\Theta(\sqrt{n})$

Growable arrays are similar to arrays but add the ability to insert and delete elements; adding and deleting at the end is particularly efficient. However, they reserve linear ($\Theta(n)$) additional storage, whereas arrays do not reserve additional storage.

Associative arrays provide a mechanism for array-like functionality without huge storage overheads when the index values are sparse. For example, an array that contains values only at indexes 1 and 2 billion may benefit from using such a structure. Specialized associative arrays with integer keys include Patricia tries, Judy arrays, and van Emde Boas trees.

Balanced trees require O(log n) time for indexed access, but also permit inserting or deleting elements in O(log n) time, whereas growable arrays require linear ($\Theta(n)$) time to insert or delete elements at an arbitrary position.

Linked lists allow constant time removal and insertion in the middle but take linear time for indexed access. Their memory use is typically worse than arrays, but is still linear.

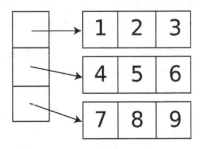

An Iliffe vector is an alternative to a multidimensional array structure. It uses a one-dimensional array of references to arrays of one dimension less. For two dimensions, in particular, this alternative structure would be a vector of pointers to vectors, one for each row. Thus an element in row i and column j of an array A would be accessed by double indexing ($A[i][j]$ in typical notation). This alternative structure allows jagged arrays, where each row may have a different size — or, in general, where the valid range of each index depends on the values of all preceding indices. It also saves one multiplication (by the column address increment) replacing it by a bit shift (to index the vector of row pointers) and one extra memory access (fetching the row address), which may be worthwhile in some architectures.

Dimension

The dimension of an array is the number of indices needed to select an element. Thus, if the array is seen as a function on a set of possible index combinations, it is the dimension of the space of which its domain is a discrete subset. Thus a one-dimensional array is a list of data, a two-dimensional array a rectangle of data, a three-dimensional array a block of data, etc.

This should not be confused with the dimension of the set of all matrices with a given domain, that is, the number of elements in the array. For example, an array with 5 rows and 4 columns is two-dimensional, but such matrices form a 20-dimensional space. Similarly, a three-dimensional vector can be represented by a one-dimensional array of size three.

Linked List

In computer science, a linked list is a linear collection of data elements, called nodes, each pointing to the next node by means of a pointer. It is a data structure consisting of a group of nodes which together represent a sequence. Under the simplest form, each node is composed of data and a reference (in other words, a *link*) to the next node in the sequence. This structure allows for efficient insertion or removal of elements from any position in the sequence during iteration. More complex variants add additional links, allowing efficient insertion or removal from arbitrary element references.

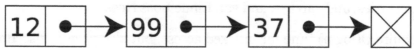

A linked list whose nodes contain two fields: an integer value and a link to the next node. The last node is linked to a terminator used to signify the end of the list.

Linked lists are among the simplest and most common data structures. They can be used to implement several other common abstract data types, including lists (the abstract data type), stacks, queues, associative arrays, and S-expressions, though it is not uncommon to implement the other data structures directly without using a list as the basis of implementation.

The principal benefit of a linked list over a conventional array is that the list elements can easily be inserted or removed without reallocation or reorganization of the entire structure because the data items need not be stored contiguously in memory or on disk, while an array has to be declared in the source code, before compiling and running the program. Linked lists allow insertion and removal of nodes at any point in the list, and can do so with a constant number of operations if the link previous to the link being added or removed is maintained during list traversal.

On the other hand, simple linked lists by themselves do not allow random access to the data, or any form of efficient indexing. Thus, many basic operations — such as obtaining the last node of the list (assuming that the last node is not maintained as separate node reference in the list structure), or finding a node that contains a given datum, or locating the place where a new node should be inserted — may require sequential scanning of most or all of the list elements. The advantages and disadvantages of using linked lists are given below.

Advantages

- Linked lists are a dynamic data structure, which can grow and be pruned, allocating and deallocating memory while the program is running.

- Insertion and deletion node operations are easily implemented in a linked list.

- Dynamic data structures such as stacks and queues can be implemented using a linked list.

- There is no need to define an initial size for a linked list.

- Items can be added or removed from the middle of list.

- Backtracking is possible in two way linked list.

Disadvantages

- They use more memory than arrays because of the storage used by their pointers.

- Nodes in a linked list must be read in order from the beginning as linked lists are inherently sequential access.

- Nodes are stored incontiguously, greatly increasing the time required to access individual elements within the list, especially with a CPU cache.

- Difficulties arise in linked lists when it comes to reverse traversing. For instance, singly linked lists are cumbersome to navigate backwards and while doubly linked lists are somewhat easier to read, memory is consumed in allocating space for a back-pointer.

History

Linked lists were developed in 1955–1956 by Allen Newell, Cliff Shaw and Herbert A. Simon at RAND Corporation as the primary data structure for their Information Processing Language. IPL was used by the authors to develop several early artificial intelligence programs, including the Logic Theory Machine, the General Problem Solver, and a computer chess program. Reports on their work appeared in IRE Transactions on Information Theory in 1956, and several conference proceedings from 1957 to 1959, including Proceedings of the Western Joint Computer Conference in 1957 and 1958, and Information Processing (Proceedings of the first UNESCO International Conference on Information Processing) in 1959. The now-classic diagram consisting of blocks representing list nodes with arrows pointing to successive list nodes appears in "Programming the Logic Theory Machine" by Newell and Shaw in Proc. WJCC, February 1957. Newell and Simon were recognized with the ACM Turing Award in 1975 for having "made basic contributions to artificial intelligence, the psychology of human cognition, and list processing". The problem of machine translation for natural language processing led Victor Yngve at Massachusetts Institute of Technology (MIT) to use linked lists as data structures in his COMIT programming language for computer research in the field of linguistics. A report on this language entitled "A programming language for mechanical translation" appeared in Mechanical Translation in 1958.

LISP, standing for list processor, was created by John McCarthy in 1958 while he was at MIT and in 1960 he published its design in a paper in the Communications of the ACM, entitled "Recursive Functions of Symbolic Expressions and Their Computation by Machine, Part I". One of LISP's major data structures is the linked list.

By the early 1960s, the utility of both linked lists and languages which use these structures as their primary data representation was well established. Bert Green of the MIT Lincoln Laboratory published a review article entitled "Computer languages for symbol manipulation" in IRE Transactions on Human Factors in Electronics in March 1961 which summarized the advantages of the linked list approach. A later review article, "A Comparison of list-processing computer languages" by Bobrow and Raphael, appeared in Communications of the ACM in April 1964.

Several operating systems developed by Technical Systems Consultants (originally of West Lafayette Indiana, and later of Chapel Hill, North Carolina) used singly linked lists as file structures. A directory entry pointed to the first sector of a file, and succeeding portions of the file were located by traversing pointers. Systems using this technique included Flex (for the Motorola 6800 CPU), mini-Flex (same CPU), and Flex9 (for the Motorola 6809 CPU). A variant developed by TSC for and marketed by Smoke Signal Broadcasting in California, used doubly linked lists in the same manner.

The TSS/360 operating system, developed by IBM for the System 360/370 machines, used a double linked list for their file system catalog. The directory structure was similar to Unix, where a directory could contain files and other directories and extend to any depth.

Basic Concepts and Nomenclature

Each record of a linked list is often called an 'element' or 'node'.

The field of each node that contains the address of the next node is usually called the 'next link' or 'next pointer'. The remaining fields are known as the 'data', 'information', 'value', 'cargo', or 'payload' fields.

The 'head' of a list is its first node. The 'tail' of a list may refer either to the rest of the list after the head, or to the last node in the list. In Lisp and some derived languages, the next node may be called the 'cdr' (pronounced *could-er*) of the list, while the payload of the head node may be called the 'car'.

Singly Linked List

Singly linked lists contain nodes which have a data field as well as a 'next' field, which points to the next node in line of nodes. Operations that can be performed on singly linked lists include insertion, deletion and traversal.

Link – Each link of a linked list can store a data called an element.

Next – Each link of a linked list contains a link to the next link called Next.

Linked List – A Linked List contains the connection link to the first link called First.

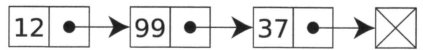

A singly linked list whose nodes contain two fields: an integer value and a link to the next node.

Doubly Linked List

In a 'doubly linked list', each node contains, besides the next-node link, a second link field pointing to the 'previous' node in the sequence. The two links may be called 'forward('s') and 'backwards', or 'next' and 'prev'('previous').

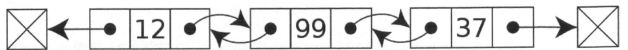

A doubly linked list whose nodes contain three fields: an integer value, the link forward to the next node,
and the link backward to the previous node

A technique known as XOR-linking allows a doubly linked list to be implemented using a single link field in each node. However, this technique requires the ability to do bit operations on addresses, and therefore may not be available in some high-level languages.

Many modern operating systems use doubly linked lists to maintain references to active processes, threads, and other dynamic objects. A common strategy for rootkits to evade detection is to unlink themselves from these lists.

Multiply Linked List

In a 'multiply linked list', each node contains two or more link fields, each field being used to connect the same set of data records in a different order (e.g., by name, by department, by date of birth, etc.). While doubly linked lists can be seen as special cases of multiply linked list, the fact that the two orders are opposite to each other leads to simpler and more efficient algorithms, so they are usually treated as a separate case.

Circular Linked List

In the last node of a list, the link field often contains a null reference, a special value used to indicate the lack of further nodes. A less common convention is to make it point to the first node of the list; in that case the list is said to be 'circular' or 'circularly linked'; otherwise it is said to be 'open' or 'linear'.

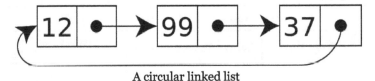

A circular linked list

In the case of a circular doubly linked list, the only change that occurs is that the end, or "tail", of the said list is linked back to the front, or "head", of the list and vice versa.

Sentinel Nodes

In some implementations an extra 'sentinel' or 'dummy' node may be added before the first data record or after the last one. This convention simplifies and accelerates some list-handling algorithms, by ensuring that all links can be safely dereferenced and that every list (even one that contains no data elements) always has a "first" and "last" node.

Empty Lists

An empty list is a list that contains no data records. This is usually the same as saying that it has zero nodes. If sentinel nodes are being used, the list is usually said to be empty when it has only sentinel nodes.

Hash Linking

The link fields need not be physically part of the nodes. If the data records are stored in an array and referenced by their indices, the link field may be stored in a separate array with the same indices as the data records.

List Handles

Since a reference to the first node gives access to the whole list, that reference is often called the 'address', 'pointer', or 'handle' of the list. Algorithms that manipulate linked lists usually get such handles to the input lists and return the handles to the resulting lists. In fact, in the context of such algorithms, the word "list" often means "list handle". In some situations, however, it may be convenient to refer to a list by a handle that consists of two links, pointing to its first and last nodes.

Combining Alternatives

The alternatives listed above may be arbitrarily combined in almost every way, so one may have circular doubly linked lists without sentinels, circular singly linked lists with sentinels, etc.

Tradeoffs

As with most choices in computer programming and design, no method is well suited to all circumstances. A linked list data structure might work well in one case, but cause problems in another. This is a list of some of the common tradeoffs involving linked list structures.

Linked Lists Vs. Dynamic Arrays

Comparison of list data structures						
	Linked list	Array	Dynamic array	Balanced tree	Random access list	hashed array tree
Indexing	$\Theta(n)$	$\Theta(1)$	$\Theta(1)$	$\Theta(\log n)$	$\Theta(\log n)$	$\Theta(1)$
Insert/delete at beginning	$\Theta(1)$	N/A	$\Theta(n)$	$\Theta(\log n)$	$\Theta(1)$	$\Theta(n)$
Insert/delete at end	$\Theta(1)$ when last element is known; $\Theta(n)$ when last element is unknown	N/A	$\Theta(1)$ amortized	$\Theta(\log n)$	$\Theta(\log n)$ updating	$\Theta(1)$ amortized
Insert/delete in middle	search time + $\Theta(1)$	N/A	$\Theta(n)$	$\Theta(\log n)$	$\Theta(\log n)$ updating	$\Theta(n)$
Wasted space (average)	$\Theta(n)$	0	$\Theta(n)$	$\Theta(n)$	$\Theta(n)$	$\Theta(\sqrt{n})$

A *dynamic array* is a data structure that allocates all elements contiguously in memory, and keeps a count of the current number of elements. If the space reserved for the dynamic array is exceeded, it is reallocated and (possibly) copied, which is an expensive operation.

Linked lists have several advantages over dynamic arrays. Insertion or deletion of an element at a specific point of a list, assuming that we have indexed a pointer to the node (before the one to be removed, or before the insertion point) already, is a constant-time operation (otherwise without this reference it is O(n)), whereas insertion in a dynamic array at random locations will require moving half of the elements on average, and all the elements in the worst case. While one can "delete" an element from an array in constant time by somehow marking its slot as "vacant", this causes fragmentation that impedes the performance of iteration.

Moreover, arbitrarily many elements may be inserted into a linked list, limited only by the total memory available; while a dynamic array will eventually fill up its underlying array data structure and will have to reallocate — an expensive operation, one that may not even be possible if memory is fragmented, although the cost of reallocation can be averaged over insertions, and the cost of an insertion due to reallocation would still be amortized $O(1)$. This helps with appending elements at the array's end, but inserting into (or removing from) middle positions still carries prohibitive costs due to data moving to maintain contiguity. An array from which many elements are removed may also have to be resized in order to avoid wasting too much space.

On the other hand, dynamic arrays (as well as fixed-size array data structures) allow constant-time random access, while linked lists allow only sequential access to elements. Singly linked lists, in fact, can be easily traversed in only one direction. This makes linked lists unsuitable for applications where it's useful to look up an element by its index quickly, such as heapsort. Sequential access on arrays and dynamic arrays is also faster than on linked lists on many machines, because they have optimal locality of reference and thus make good use of data caching.

Another disadvantage of linked lists is the extra storage needed for references, which often makes them impractical for lists of small data items such as characters or boolean values, because the storage overhead for the links may exceed by a factor of two or more the size of the data. In contrast, a dynamic array requires only the space for the data itself (and a very small amount of control data). It can also be slow, and with a naïve allocator, wasteful, to allocate memory separately for each new element, a problem generally solved using memory pools.

Some hybrid solutions try to combine the advantages of the two representations. Unrolled linked lists store several elements in each list node, increasing cache performance while decreasing memory overhead for references. CDR coding does both these as well, by replacing references with the actual data referenced, which extends off the end of the referencing record.

A good example that highlights the pros and cons of using dynamic arrays vs. linked lists is by implementing a program that resolves the Josephus problem. The Josephus problem is an election method that works by having a group of people stand in a circle. Starting at a predetermined person, you count around the circle n times. Once you reach the nth person, take them out of the circle and have the members close the circle. Then count around the circle the same n times and repeat the process, until only one person is left. That person wins the election. This shows the strengths and weaknesses of a linked list vs. a dynamic array, because if you view the people as connected nodes in a circular linked list then it shows how easily the linked list is able to delete nodes (as it only has to rearrange the links to the different nodes). However, the linked list will be poor at finding the next person to remove and will need to search through the list until it finds that person. A dynamic array, on the other hand, will be poor at deleting nodes (or elements) as it cannot remove one node without individually shifting all the elements up the list by one. However, it is exceptionally easy to find the nth person in the circle by directly referencing them by their position in the array.

The list ranking problem concerns the efficient conversion of a linked list representation into an array. Although trivial for a conventional computer, solving this problem by a parallel algorithm is complicated and has been the subject of much research.

A balanced tree has similar memory access patterns and space overhead to a linked list while permitting much more efficient indexing, taking O(log n) time instead of O(n) for a random access. However, insertion and deletion operations are more expensive due to the overhead of tree manipulations to maintain balance. Schemes exist for trees to automatically maintain themselves in a balanced state: AVL trees or red-black trees.

Singly Linked Linear Lists Vs. Other Lists

While doubly linked and circular lists have advantages over singly linked linear lists, linear lists offer some advantages that make them preferable in some situations.

A singly linked linear list is a recursive data structure, because it contains a pointer to a *smaller* object of the same type. For that reason, many operations on singly linked linear lists (such as merging two lists, or enumerating the elements in reverse order) often have very simple recursive algorithms, much simpler than any solution using iterative commands. While those recursive solutions can be adapted for doubly linked and circularly linked lists, the procedures generally need extra arguments and more complicated base cases.

Linear singly linked lists also allow tail-sharing, the use of a common final portion of sub-list as the terminal portion of two different lists. In particular, if a new node is added at the beginning of a list, the former list remains available as the tail of the new one — a simple example of a persistent data structure. Again, this is not true with the other variants: a node may never belong to two different circular or doubly linked lists.

In particular, end-sentinel nodes can be shared among singly linked non-circular lists. The same end-sentinel node may be used for *every* such list. In Lisp, for example, every proper list ends with a link to a special node, denoted by nil or (), whose CAR and CDR links point to itself. Thus a Lisp procedure can safely take the CAR or CDR of *any* list.

The advantages of the fancy variants are often limited to the complexity of the algorithms, not in their efficiency. A circular list, in particular, can usually be emulated by a linear list together with two variables that point to the first and last nodes, at no extra cost.

Doubly Linked Vs. Singly Linked

Double-linked lists require more space per node (unless one uses XOR-linking), and their elementary operations are more expensive; but they are often easier to manipulate because they allow fast and easy sequential access to the list in both directions. In a doubly linked list, one can insert or delete a node in a constant number of operations given only that node's address. To do the same in a singly linked list, one must have the *address of the pointer* to that node, which is either the handle for the whole list (in case of the first node) or the link field in the *previous* node. Some algorithms require access in both directions. On the other hand, doubly linked lists do not allow tail-sharing and cannot be used as persistent data structures.

Circularly Linked Vs. Linearly Linked

A circularly linked list may be a natural option to represent arrays that are naturally circular, e.g. the corners of a polygon, a pool of buffers that are used and released in FIFO ("first in, first out") order, or a set of processes that should be time-shared in round-robin order. In these applications, a pointer to any node serves as a handle to the whole list.

With a circular list, a pointer to the last node gives easy access also to the first node, by following one link. Thus, in applications that require access to both ends of the list (e.g., in the implementation of a queue), a circular structure allows one to handle the structure by a single pointer, instead of two.

A circular list can be split into two circular lists, in constant time, by giving the addresses of the last node of each piece. The operation consists in swapping the contents of the link fields of those two nodes. Applying the same operation to any two nodes in two distinct lists joins the two list into one. This property greatly simplifies some algorithms and data structures, such as the quad-edge and face-edge.

The simplest representation for an empty *circular* list (when such a thing makes sense) is a null pointer, indicating that the list has no nodes. Without this choice, many algorithms have to test for this special case, and handle it separately. By contrast, the use of null to denote an empty *linear* list is more natural and often creates fewer special cases.

Using Sentinel Nodes

Sentinel node may simplify certain list operations, by ensuring that the next or previous nodes exist for every element, and that even empty lists have at least one node. One may also use a sentinel node at the end of the list, with an appropriate data field, to eliminate some end-of-list tests. For example, when scanning the list looking for a node with a given value x, setting the sentinel's data field to x makes it unnecessary to test for end-of-list inside the loop. Another example is the merging two sorted lists: if their sentinels have data fields set to $+\infty$, the choice of the next output node does not need special handling for empty lists.

However, sentinel nodes use up extra space (especially in applications that use many short lists), and they may complicate other operations (such as the creation of a new empty list).

However, if the circular list is used merely to simulate a linear list, one may avoid some of this complexity by adding a single sentinel node to every list, between the last and the first data nodes. With this convention, an empty list consists of the sentinel node alone, pointing to itself via the next-node link. The list handle should then be a pointer to the last data node, before the sentinel, if the list is not empty; or to the sentinel itself, if the list is empty.

The same trick can be used to simplify the handling of a doubly linked linear list, by turning it into a circular doubly linked list with a single sentinel node. However, in this case, the handle should be a single pointer to the dummy node itself.

Linked List Operations

When manipulating linked lists in-place, care must be taken to not use values that you have invalidated in previous assignments. This makes algorithms for inserting or deleting linked list nodes somewhat subtle. This section gives pseudocode for adding or removing nodes from singly, doubly, and circularly linked lists in-place. Throughout we will use *null* to refer to an end-of-list marker or sentinel, which may be implemented in a number of ways.

Linearly Linked Lists

Singly Linked Lists

Our node data structure will have two fields. We also keep a variable *firstNode* which always points to the first node in the list, or is *null* for an empty list.

```
record Node

{

    data; // The data being stored in the node

    Node next // A reference to the next node, null for last node

}

record List

{

    Node firstNode // points to first node of list; null for empty list

}
```

Traversal of a singly linked list is simple, beginning at the first node and following each *next* link until we come to the end:

```
node := list.firstNode

while node not null

    (do something with node.data)

    node := node.next
```

The following code inserts a node after an existing node in a singly linked list. The diagram shows how it works. Inserting a node before an existing one cannot be done directly; instead, one must keep track of the previous node and insert a node after it.

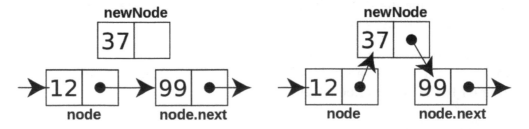

```
function insertAfter(Node node, Node newNode) // insert newNode after node

    newNode.next := node.next
```

```
    node.next     := newNode
```

Inserting at the beginning of the list requires a separate function. This requires updating *firstNode*.

```
function insertBeginning(List list, Node newNode) // insert node before current
first node

    newNode.next    := list.firstNode

    list.firstNode := newNode
```

Similarly, we have functions for removing the node *after* a given node, and for removing a node from the beginning of the list. The diagram demonstrates the former. To find and remove a particular node, one must again keep track of the previous element.

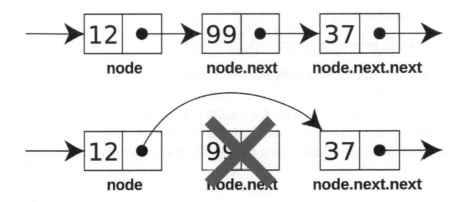

```
function removeAfter(Node node) // remove node past this one

    obsoleteNode := node.next

    node.next := node.next.next

    destroy obsoleteNode

function removeBeginning(List list) // remove first node

    obsoleteNode := list.firstNode

    list.firstNode := list.firstNode.next // point past deleted node

    destroy obsoleteNode
```

Notice that `removeBeginning()` sets `list.firstNode` to `null` when removing the last node in the list.

Since we can't iterate backwards, efficient `insertBefore` or `removeBefore` operations are not possible. Inserting to a list before a specific node requires traversing the list, which would have a worst case running time of O(n).

Appending one linked list to another can be inefficient unless a reference to the tail is kept as part of the List structure, because we must traverse the entire first list in order to find the tail, and then append the second list to this. Thus, if two linearly linked lists are each of length n, list appending has asymptotic time complexity of $O(n)$. In the Lisp family of languages, list appending is provided by the append procedure.

Many of the special cases of linked list operations can be eliminated by including a dummy element at the front of the list. This ensures that there are no special cases for the beginning of the list and renders both `insertBeginning()` and `removeBeginning()` unnecessary. In this case, the first useful data in the list will be found at `list.firstNode.next`.

Circularly Linked List

In a circularly linked list, all nodes are linked in a continuous circle, without using *null*. For lists with a front and a back (such as a queue), one stores a reference to the last node in the list. The *next* node after the last node is the first node. Elements can be added to the back of the list and removed from the front in constant time.

Circularly linked lists can be either singly or doubly linked.

Both types of circularly linked lists benefit from the ability to traverse the full list beginning at any given node. This often allows us to avoid storing *firstNode* and *lastNode*, although if the list may be empty we need a special representation for the empty list, such as a *lastNode* variable which points to some node in the list or is *null* if it's empty; we use such a *lastNode* here. This representation significantly simplifies adding and removing nodes with a non-empty list, but empty lists are then a special case.

Algorithms

Assuming that *someNode* is some node in a non-empty circular singly linked list, this code iterates through that list starting with *someNode*:

```
function iterate(someNode)

  if someNode ≠ null

    node := someNode

    do

      do something with node.value

      node := node.next

    while node ≠ someNode
```

Notice that the test "while node ≠ someNode" must be at the end of the loop. If the test was moved to the beginning of the loop, the procedure would fail whenever the list had only one node.

This function inserts a node "newNode" into a circular linked list after a given node "node". If "node" is null, it assumes that the list is empty.

```
function insertAfter(Node node, Node newNode)

    if node = null
```

```
     newNode.next := newNode

   else

     newNode.next := node.next

     node.next := newNode
```

Suppose that "L" is a variable pointing to the last node of a circular linked list (or null if the list is empty). To append "newNode" to the *end* of the list, one may do

```
insertAfter(L, newNode)

L := newNode
```

To insert "newNode" at the beginning of the list, one may do

```
insertAfter(L, newNode)

if L = null

  L := newNode
```

Linked Lists using Arrays of Nodes

Languages that do not support any type of reference can still create links by replacing pointers with array indices. The approach is to keep an array of records, where each record has integer fields indicating the index of the next (and possibly previous) node in the array. Not all nodes in the array need be used. If records are also not supported, parallel arrays can often be used instead.

As an example, consider the following linked list record that uses arrays instead of pointers:

```
record Entry {

    integer next; // index of next entry in array

    integer prev; // previous entry (if double-linked)

    string name;

    real balance;

}
```

A linked list can be built by creating an array of these structures, and an integer variable to store the index of the first element.

```
integer listHead

Entry Records[1000]
```

Links between elements are formed by placing the array index of the next (or previous) cell into the Next or Prev field within a given element. For example:

Index	Next	Prev	Name	Balance
0	1	4	Jones, John	123.45
1	−1	0	Smith, Joseph	234.56
2 (listHead)	4	−1	Adams, Adam	0.00
3			Ignore, Ignatius	999.99
4	0	2	Another, Anita	876.54
5				
6				
7				

In the above example, ListHead would be set to 2, the location of the first entry in the list. Notice that entry 3 and 5 through 7 are not part of the list. These cells are available for any additions to the list. By creating a ListFree integer variable, a free list could be created to keep track of what cells are available. If all entries are in use, the size of the array would have to be increased or some elements would have to be deleted before new entries could be stored in the list.

The following code would traverse the list and display names and account balance:

```
i := listHead

while i ≥ 0 // loop through the list

    print i, Records[i].name, Records[i].balance // print entry

    i := Records[i].next
```

When faced with a choice, the advantages of this approach include:

- The linked list is relocatable, meaning it can be moved about in memory at will, and it can also be quickly and directly serialized for storage on disk or transfer over a network.

- Especially for a small list, array indexes can occupy significantly less space than a full pointer on many architectures.

- Locality of reference can be improved by keeping the nodes together in memory and by periodically rearranging them, although this can also be done in a general store.

- Naïve dynamic memory allocators can produce an excessive amount of overhead storage for each node allocated; almost no allocation overhead is incurred per node in this approach.

- Seizing an entry from a pre-allocated array is faster than using dynamic memory allocation for each node, since dynamic memory allocation typically requires a search for a free memory block of the desired size.

This approach has one main disadvantage, however: it creates and manages a private memory space for its nodes. This leads to the following issues:

- It increases complexity of the implementation.

- Growing a large array when it is full may be difficult or impossible, whereas finding space for a new linked list node in a large, general memory pool may be easier.

- Adding elements to a dynamic array will occasionally (when it is full) unexpectedly take linear (O(n)) instead of constant time (although it's still an amortized constant).

- Using a general memory pool leaves more memory for other data if the list is smaller than expected or if many nodes are freed.

For these reasons, this approach is mainly used for languages that do not support dynamic memory allocation. These disadvantages are also mitigated if the maximum size of the list is known at the time the array is created.

Language Support

Many programming languages such as Lisp and Scheme have singly linked lists built in. In many functional languages, these lists are constructed from nodes, each called a *cons* or *cons cell*. The cons has two fields: the *car*, a reference to the data for that node, and the *cdr*, a reference to the next node. Although cons cells can be used to build other data structures, this is their primary purpose.

In languages that support abstract data types or templates, linked list ADTs or templates are available for building linked lists. In other languages, linked lists are typically built using references together with records.

Internal and External Storage

When constructing a linked list, one is faced with the choice of whether to store the data of the list directly in the linked list nodes, called *internal storage*, or merely to store a reference to the data, called *external storage*. Internal storage has the advantage of making access to the data more efficient, requiring less storage overall, having better locality of reference, and simplifying memory management for the list (its data is allocated and deallocated at the same time as the list nodes).

External storage, on the other hand, has the advantage of being more generic, in that the same data structure and machine code can be used for a linked list no matter what the size of the data is. It also makes it easy to place the same data in multiple linked lists. Although with internal storage the same data can be placed in multiple lists by including multiple *next* references in the node data structure, it would then be necessary to create separate routines to add or delete cells based on each field. It is possible to create additional linked lists of elements that use internal storage by using external storage, and having the cells of the additional linked lists store references to the nodes of the linked list containing the data.

In general, if a set of data structures needs to be included in linked lists, external storage is the best approach. If a set of data structures need to be included in only one linked list, then internal storage is slightly better, unless a generic linked list package using external storage is available. Likewise, if different sets of data that can be stored in the same data structure are to be included in a single linked list, then internal storage would be fine.

Another approach that can be used with some languages involves having different data structures, but all have the initial fields, including the *next* (and *prev* if double linked list) references in the same location. After defining separate structures for each type of data, a generic structure can be defined that contains the minimum amount of data shared by all the other structures and contained at the top (beginning) of the structures. Then generic routines can be created that use the minimal structure to perform linked list type operations, but separate routines can then handle the specific data. This approach is often used in message parsing routines, where several types of messages are received, but all start with the same set of fields, usually including a field for message type. The generic routines are used to add new messages to a queue when they are received, and remove them from the queue in order to process the message. The message type field is then used to call the correct routine to process the specific type of message.

Example of Internal and External Storage

Suppose you wanted to create a linked list of families and their members. Using internal storage, the structure might look like the following:

```
record member { // member of a family

    member next;

    string firstName;

    integer age;

}

record family { // the family itself

    family next;

    string lastName;

    string address;

    member members // head of list of members of this family

}
```

To print a complete list of families and their members using internal storage, we could write:

```
 aFamily := Families // start at head of families list

 while aFamily ≠ null // loop through list of families

     print information about family

     aMember := aFamily.members // get head of list of this family's members

     while aMember ≠ null // loop through list of members

         print information about member

         aMember := aMember.next

     aFamily := aFamily.next
```

Using external storage, we would create the following structures:

```
 record node { // generic link structure

     node next;

     pointer data // generic pointer for data at node

}

record member { // structure for family member

     string firstName;

     integer age

}

record family { // structure for family

     string lastName;

     string address;

     node members // head of list of members of this family
```

To print a complete list of families and their members using external storage, we could write:

```
 famNode := Families // start at head of families list

while famNode ≠ null // loop through list of families

     aFamily := (family) famNode.data // extract family from node

     print information about family

     memNode := aFamily.members // get list of family members

     while memNode ≠ null // loop through list of members

         aMember := (member)memNode.data // extract member from node

         print information about member

         memNode := memNode.next

     famNode := famNode.next
```

Notice that when using external storage, an extra step is needed to extract the record from the node and cast it into the proper data type. This is because both the list of families and the list of members within the family are stored in two linked lists using the same data structure (*node*), and this language does not have parametric types.

As long as the number of families that a member can belong to is known at compile time, internal storage works fine. If, however, a member needed to be included in an arbitrary number of families, with the specific number known only at run time, external storage would be necessary.

Speeding up Search

Finding a specific element in a linked list, even if it is sorted, normally requires O(n) time (linear search). This is one of the primary disadvantages of linked lists over other data structures. In addition to the variants discussed above, below are two simple ways to improve search time.

In an unordered list, one simple heuristic for decreasing average search time is the *move-to-front heuristic*, which simply moves an element to the beginning of the list once it is found. This scheme, handy for creating simple caches, ensures that the most recently used items are also the quickest to find again.

Another common approach is to "index" a linked list using a more efficient external data structure. For example, one can build a red-black tree or hash table whose elements are references to the linked list nodes. Multiple such indexes can be built on a single list. The disadvantage is that these indexes may need to be updated each time a node is added or removed (or at least, before that index is used again).

Random Access Lists

A random access list is a list with support for fast random access to read or modify any element in the list. One possible implementation is a skew binary random access list using the skew binary number system, which involves a list of trees with special properties; this allows worst-case constant time head/cons operations, and worst-case logarithmic time random access to an element by index. Random access lists can be implemented as persistent data structures.

Random access lists can be viewed as immutable linked lists in that they likewise support the same O(1) head and tail operations.

A simple extension to random access lists is the min-list, which provides an additional operation that yields the minimum element in the entire list in constant time (without mutation complexities).

Related Data Structures

Both stacks and queues are often implemented using linked lists, and simply restrict the type of operations which are supported.

The skip list is a linked list augmented with layers of pointers for quickly jumping over large numbers of elements, and then descending to the next layer. This process continues down to the bottom layer, which is the actual list.

A binary tree can be seen as a type of linked list where the elements are themselves linked lists of the same nature. The result is that each node may include a reference to the first node of one or two other linked lists, which, together with their contents, form the subtrees below that node.

An unrolled linked list is a linked list in which each node contains an array of data values. This leads to improved cache performance, since more list elements are contiguous in memory, and reduced memory overhead, because less metadata needs to be stored for each element of the list.

A hash table may use linked lists to store the chains of items that hash to the same position in the hash table.

A heap shares some of the ordering properties of a linked list, but is almost always implemented using an array. Instead of references from node to node, the next and previous data indexes are calculated using the current data's index.

A self-organizing list rearranges its nodes based on some heuristic which reduces search times for data retrieval by keeping commonly accessed nodes at the head of the list.

Linked Data Structure

In computer science, a linked data structure is a data structure which consists of a set of data records (*nodes*) linked together and organized by references (*links* or *pointers*). The link between data can also be called a connector.

In linked data structures, the links are usually treated as special data types that can only be dereferenced or compared for equality. Linked data structures are thus contrasted with arrays and other data structures that require performing arithmetic operations on pointers. This distinction holds even when the nodes are actually implemented as elements of a single array, and the references are actually array indices: as long as no arithmetic is done on those indices, the data structure is essentially a linked one.

Linking can be done in two ways – using dynamic allocation and using array index linking.

Linked data structures include linked lists, search trees, expression trees, and many other widely used data structures. They are also key building blocks for many efficient algorithms, such as topological sort and set union-find.

Common Types of Linked Data Structures

Linked Lists

A linked list is a collection of structures ordered not by their physical placement in memory but by logical links that are stored as part of the data in the structure itself. It is not necessary that it should be stored in the adjacent memory locations. Every structure has a data field and an address field. The Address field contains the address of its successor.

Linked list can be singly, doubly or multiply linked and can either be linear or circular.

Basic properties

- Objects, called nodes, are linked in a linear sequence.

- A reference to the first node of the list is always kept. This is called the 'head' or 'front'.

A linked list with three nodes contain two fields each: an integer value and a link to the next node

A linked list with a single node.

Example in Java

This is an example of the node class used to store integers in a Java implementation of a linked list:

```
public class IntNode {

    public int value;

    public IntNode link;

    public IntNode(int v) { value = v; }

}
```

Example in C

This is an example of the node structure used for implementation of linked list in C:

```
struct node

{

    int val;

    struct node *next;

};
```

This is an example using typedefs:

```
typedef struct node node;

struct node

{

    int val;

    node *next;

};
```

Note: A structure like this which contains a member that points to the same structure is called a self-referential structure.

Example in C++

This is an example of the node class structure used for implementation of linked list in C++:

```
class Node

{

    int val;
```

```
    Node *next;

};
```

Search Trees

A search tree is a tree data structure in whose nodes data values can be stored from some ordered set, which is such that in an in-order traversal of the tree the nodes are visited in ascending order of the stored values.

Basic properties

- Objects, called nodes, are stored in an ordered set.

- In-order traversal provides an ascending readout of the data in the tree.

Advantages and Disadvantages

Linked List Versus Arrays

Compared to arrays, linked data structures allow more flexibility in organizing the data and in allocating space for it. In arrays, the size of the array must be specified precisely at the beginning, which can be a potential waste of memory. A linked data structure is built dynamically and never needs to be bigger than the programmer requires. It also requires no guessing in terms of how much space must be allocated when using a linked data structure. This is a feature that is key in saving wasted memory.

In an array, the array elements have to be in a contiguous (connected and sequential) portion of memory. But in a linked data structure, the reference to each node gives users the information needed to find the next one. The nodes of a linked data structure can also be moved individually to different locations without affecting the logical connections between them, unlike arrays. With due care, a process can add or delete nodes to one part of a data structure even while other processes are working on other parts.

On the other hand, access to any particular node in a linked data structure requires following a chain of references that stored in it. If the structure has n nodes, and each node contains at most b links, there will be some nodes that cannot be reached in less than $\log_b n$ steps. For many structures, some nodes may require worst case up to $n-1$ steps. In contrast, many array data structures allow access to any element with a constant number of operations, independent of the number of entries.

Broadly the implementation of these linked data structure is through dynamic data structures. It gives us the chance to use particular space again. Memory can be utilized more efficiently by using this data structures. Memory is allocated as per the need and when memory is not further needed, deallocation is done.

General Disadvantages

Linked data structures may also incur in substantial memory allocation overhead (if nodes are allocated individually) and frustrate memory paging and processor caching algorithms (since they generally have poor locality of reference). In some cases, linked data structures may also use more memory (for the link fields) than competing array structures. This is because linked data structures are not contiguous. Instances of data can be found all over in memory, unlike arrays.

In arrays, nth element can be accessed immediately, while in a linked data structure we have to follow multiple pointers so element access time varies according to where in the structure the element is.

In some theoretical models of computation that enforce the constraints of linked structures, such as the pointer machine, many problems require more steps than in the unconstrained random access machine model.

References

- Antonakos, James L.; Mansfield, Kenneth C., Jr. (1999). Practical Data Structures Using C/C++. Prentice-Hall. pp. 165–190. ISBN 0-13-280843-9

- Black, Paul E. (13 November 2008). "array". Dictionary of Algorithms and Data Structures. National Institute of Standards and Technology. Retrieved 22 August 2010

- Garcia, Ronald; Lumsdaine, Andrew (2005). "MultiArray: a C++ library for generic programming with arrays". Software: Practice and Experience. 35 (2): 159–188. ISSN 0038-0644. doi:10.1002/spe.630

- Collins, William J. (2005) [2002]. Data Structures and the Java Collections Framework. New York: McGraw Hill. pp. 239–303. ISBN 0-07-282379-8

- "Array Code Examples - PHP Array Functions - PHP code". http://www.configure-all.com/: Computer Programming Web programming Tips. Retrieved 8 April 2011

- Chris Okasaki (1995). "Purely Functional Random-Access Lists". Proceedings of the Seventh International Conference on Functional Programming Languages and Computer Architecture: 86–95. doi:10.1145/224164.224187

- Cormen, Thomas H.; Leiserson, Charles E.; Rivest, Ronald L.; Stein, Clifford (2003). Introduction to Algorithms. MIT Press. pp. 205–213, 501–505. ISBN 0-262-03293-7

- "Chapter 6 - Arrays, Types, and Constants". Modula-2 Tutorial. http://www.modula2.org/tutor/index.php. Retrieved 8 April 2011

- Green, Bert F., Jr. (1961). "Computer Languages for Symbol Manipulation". IRE Transactions on Human Factors in Electronics (2): 3–8. doi:10.1109/THFE2.1961.4503292

- Cormen, Thomas H.; Leiserson, Charles E.; Rivest, Ronald L.; Stein, Clifford (2001). "10.2: Linked lists". Introduction to Algorithms (2nd ed.). MIT Press. pp. 204–209. ISBN 0-262-03293-7

- Black, Paul E. (2004-08-16). Pieterse, Vreda; Black, Paul E., eds. "linked list". Dictionary of Algorithms and Data Structures. National Institute of Standards and Technology. Retrieved 2004-12-14

- McCarthy, John (1960). "Recursive Functions of Symbolic Expressions and Their Computation by Machine, Part I". Communications of the ACM. 3 (4): 184. doi:10.1145/367177.367199

- Shaffer, Clifford A. (1998). A Practical Introduction to Data Structures and Algorithm Analysis. New Jersey: Prentice Hall. pp. 77–102. ISBN 0-13-660911-2

2

Understanding Algorithms

A calculating method that takes in data or inputs and produces outputs is referred to as algorithm. It contains specifications, body of algorithm, pre-conditions, and post-conditions. The chapter also delves deep into the concept of sorting algorithm that organizes a list of elements in an order. This section has been carefully written to provide an easy understanding of the varied facets of algorithms.

Algorithms

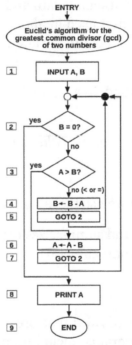

Flow chart of an algorithm (Euclid's algorithm) for calculating the greatest common divisor (g.c.d.) of two numbers *a* and *b* in locations named A and B. The algorithm proceeds by successive subtractions in two loops: IF the test B ≥ A yields "yes" (or true) (more accurately the *number b* in location B is greater than or equal to the *number a* in location A) THEN, the algorithm specifies B ← B − A (meaning the number *b* − *a* replaces the old *b*). Similarly, IF A > B, THEN A ← A − B. The process terminates when (the contents of) B is 0, yielding the g.c.d. in A. (Algorithm derived from Scott 2009:13; symbols and drawing style from Tausworthe 1977).

In mathematics and computer science, an algorithm is a self-contained sequence of actions to be performed. Algorithms can perform calculation, data processing and automated reasoning tasks.

An algorithm is an effective method that can be expressed within a finite amount of space and time and in a well-defined formal language for calculating a function. Starting from an initial state and initial input (perhaps empty), the instructions describe a computation that, when executed, proceeds through a finite number of well-defined successive states, eventually producing "output" and terminating at a final ending state. The transition from one state to the next is not necessarily deterministic; some algorithms, known as randomized algorithms, incorporate random input.

The concept of *algorithm* has existed for centuries; however, a partial formalization of what would become the modern *algorithm* began with attempts to solve the Entscheidungsproblem (the "decision problem") posed by David Hilbert in 1928. Subsequent formalizations were framed as attempts to define "effective calculability" or "effective method"; those formalizations included the Gödel–Herbrand–Kleene recursive functions of 1930, 1934 and 1935, Alonzo Church's lambda calculus of 1936, Emil Post's "Formulation 1" of 1936, and Alan Turing's Turing machines of 1936–7 and 1939. Giving a formal definition of algorithms, corresponding to the intuitive notion, remains a challenging problem.

Historical Background

Etymologically, the word 'algorithm' is a combination of the Latin word *algorismus*, named after Al-Khwarizmi, a 9th-century Persian mathematician, and the Greek word *arithmos*, i.e. αριθμός, meaning "number". In English, it was first used in about 1230 and then by Chaucer in 1391. English adopted the French term, but it wasn't until the late 19th century that "algorithm" took on the meaning that it has in modern English.

Another early use of the word is from 1240, in a manual titled *Carmen de Algorismo* composed by Alexandre de Villedieu. It begins thus:

Haec algorismus ars praesens dicitur, in qua / Talibus Indorum fruimur bis quinque figuris.

which translates as:

Algorism is the art by which at present we use those Indian figures, which number two times five.

The poem is a few hundred lines long and summarizes the art of calculating with the new style of Indian dice, or Talibus Indorum, or Hindu numerals.

Informal Definition

An informal definition could be "a set of rules that precisely defines a sequence of operations." which would include all computer programs, including programs that do not perform numeric calculations. Generally, a program is only an algorithm if it stops eventually.

A prototypical example of an algorithm is the Euclidean algorithm to determine the maximum common divisor of two integers; an example (there are others) is described by the flow chart above.

Boolos & Jeffrey (1974, 1999) offer an informal meaning of the word in the following quotation:

> No human being can write fast enough, or long enough, or small enough† (†"smaller and smaller without limit …you'd be trying to write on molecules, on atoms, on electrons") to list all members of an enumerably infinite set by writing out their names, one after another, in some notation. But humans can do something equally useful, in the case of certain enumerably infinite sets: They can give *explicit instructions for determining the nth member*

of the set, for arbitrary finite n. Such instructions are to be given quite explicitly, in a form in which *they could be followed by a computing machine*, or by a *human who is capable of carrying out only very elementary operations on symbols.*

An "enumerably infinite set" is one whose elements can be put into one-to-one correspondence with the integers. Thus, Boolos and Jeffrey are saying that an algorithm implies instructions for a process that "creates" output integers from an *arbitrary* "input" integer or integers that, in theory, can be arbitrarily large. Thus an algorithm can be an algebraic equation such as $y = m + n$ — two arbitrary "input variables" m and n that produce an output y. But various authors' attempts to define the notion indicate that the word implies much more than this, something on the order of (for the addition example):

> Precise instructions (in language understood by "the computer") for a fast, efficient, "good" process that specifies the "moves" of "the computer" (machine or human, equipped with the necessary internally contained information and capabilities) to find, decode, and then process arbitrary input integers/symbols m and n, symbols + and = ... and "effectively" produce, in a "reasonable" time, output-integer y at a specified place and in a specified format.

The concept of *algorithm* is also used to define the notion of decidability. That notion is central for explaining how formal systems come into being starting from a small set of axioms and rules. In logic, the time that an algorithm requires to complete cannot be measured, as it is not apparently related with our customary physical dimension. From such uncertainties, that characterize ongoing work, stems the unavailability of a definition of *algorithm* that suits both concrete (in some sense) and abstract usage of the term.

Formalization

Algorithms are essential to the way computers process data. Many computer programs contain algorithms that detail the specific instructions a computer should perform (in a specific order) to carry out a specified task, such as calculating employees' paychecks or printing students' report cards. Thus, an algorithm can be considered to be any sequence of operations that can be simulated by a Turing-complete system. Authors who assert this thesis include Minsky (1967), Savage (1987) and Gurevich (2000):

Minsky: "But we will also maintain, with Turing . . . that any procedure which could "naturally" be called effective, can in fact be realized by a (simple) machine. Although this may seem extreme, the arguments . . . in its favor are hard to refute".

Gurevich: "...Turing's informal argument in favor of his thesis justifies a stronger thesis: every algorithm can be simulated by a Turing machine ... according to Savage [1987], an algorithm is a computational process defined by a Turing machine".

Typically, when an algorithm is associated with processing information, data can be read from an input source, written to an output device and stored for further processing. Stored data are regarded as part of the internal state of the entity performing the algorithm. In practice, the state is stored in one or more data structures.

For some such computational process, the algorithm must be rigorously defined: specified in the way it applies in all possible circumstances that could arise. That is, any conditional steps must be systematically dealt with, case-by-case; the criteria for each case must be clear (and computable).

Because an algorithm is a precise list of precise steps, the order of computation is always crucial to the functioning of the algorithm. Instructions are usually assumed to be listed explicitly, and are described as starting "from the top" and going "down to the bottom", an idea that is described more formally by *flow of control*.

So far, this discussion of the formalization of an algorithm has assumed the premises of imperative programming. This is the most common conception, and it attempts to describe a task in discrete, "mechanical" means. Unique to this conception of formalized algorithms is the assignment operation, setting the value of a variable. It derives from the intuition of "memory" as a scratchpad. There is an example below of such an assignment.

Expressing Algorithms

Algorithms can be expressed in many kinds of notation, including natural languages, pseudocode, flowcharts, drakon-charts, programming languages or control tables (processed by interpreters). Natural language expressions of algorithms tend to be verbose and ambiguous, and are rarely used for complex or technical algorithms. Pseudocode, flowcharts, drakon-charts and control tables are structured ways to express algorithms that avoid many of the ambiguities common in natural language statements. Programming languages are primarily intended for expressing algorithms in a form that can be executed by a computer, but are often used as a way to define or document algorithms.

There is a wide variety of representations possible and one can express a given Turing machine program as a sequence of machine tables, as flowcharts and drakon-charts, or as a form of rudimentary machine code or assembly code called "sets of quadruples".

Representations of algorithms can be classed into three accepted levels of Turing machine description:

1 High-level description

> "...prose to describe an algorithm, ignoring the implementation details. At this level we do not need to mention how the machine manages its tape or head."

2 Implementation description

> "...prose used to define the way the Turing machine uses its head and the way that it stores data on its tape. At this level we do not give details of states or transition function."

3 Formal description

> Most detailed, "lowest level", gives the Turing machine's "state table".

For an example of the simple algorithm "Add m+n" described in all three levels.

Implementation

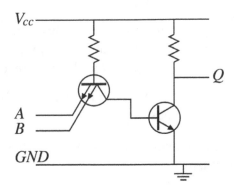

Logical NAND algorithm implemented electronically in 7400 chip.

Most algorithms are intended to be implemented as computer programs. However, algorithms are also implemented by other means, such as in a biological neural network (for example, the human brain implementing arithmetic or an insect looking for food), in an electrical circuit, or in a mechanical device.

Computer Algorithms

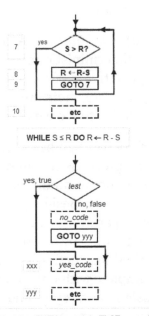

Flowchart examples of the canonical Böhm-Jacopini structures: the SEQUENCE (rectangles descending the page), the WHILE-DO and the IF-THEN-ELSE. The three structures are made of the primitive conditional GOTO (IF *test*=true THEN GOTO step xxx) (a diamond), the unconditional GOTO (rectangle), various assignment operators (rectangle), and HALT (rectangle).

In computer systems, an algorithm is basically an instance of logic written in software by software developers to be effective for the intended "target" computer(s) to produce *output* from given (perhaps null) *input*. An optimal algorithm, even running in old hardware, would produce faster results than a non-optimal (higher time complexity) algorithm for the same purpose, running in more efficient hardware; that is why algorithms, like computer hardware, are considered technology.

"Elegant" (compact) programs, "good" (fast) programs : The notion of "simplicity and elegance" appears informally in Knuth and precisely in Chaitin:

> Knuth: ". . .we want *good* algorithms in some loosely defined aesthetic sense. One criterion . . . is the length of time taken to perform the algorithm . . .. Other criteria are adaptability of the algorithm to computers, its simplicity and elegance, etc"

> Chaitin: " . . . a program is 'elegant,' by which I mean that it's the smallest possible program for producing the output that it does"

Chaitin prefaces his definition with: "I'll show you can't prove that a program is 'elegant'"—such a proof would solve the Halting problem.

Algorithm versus function computable by an algorithm: For a given function multiple algorithms may exist. This is true, even without expanding the available instruction set available to the programmer. Rogers observes that "It is . . . important to distinguish between the notion of *algorithm*, i.e. procedure and the notion of *function computable by algorithm*, i.e. mapping yielded by procedure. The same function may have several different algorithms".

Unfortunately there may be a tradeoff between goodness (speed) and elegance (compactness)—an elegant program may take more steps to complete a computation than one less elegant. An example that uses Euclid's algorithm appears below.

Computers (and computors), models of computation: A computer (or human "computor") is a restricted type of machine, a "discrete deterministic mechanical device" that blindly follows its instructions. Melzak's and Lambek's primitive models reduced this notion to four elements: (i) discrete, distinguishable *locations*, (ii) discrete, indistinguishable *counters* (iii) an agent, and (iv) a list of instructions that are *effective* relative to the capability of the agent.

Minsky describes a more congenial variation of Lambek's "abacus" model in his "Very Simple Bases for Computability". Minsky's machine proceeds sequentially through its five (or six, depending on how one counts) instructions, unless either a conditional IF–THEN GOTO or an unconditional GOTO changes program flow out of sequence. Besides HALT, Minsky's machine includes three *assignment* (replacement, substitution) operations: ZERO (e.g. the contents of location replaced by 0: $L \leftarrow 0$), SUCCESSOR (e.g. $L \leftarrow L+1$), and DECREMENT (e.g. $L \leftarrow L - 1$). Rarely must a programmer write "code" with such a limited instruction set. But Minsky shows (as do Melzak and Lambek) that his machine is Turing complete with only four general *types* of instructions: conditional GOTO, unconditional GOTO, assignment/replacement/substitution, and HALT.

Simulation of an algorithm: computer (computor) language: Knuth advises the reader that "the best way to learn an algorithm is to try it . . . immediately take pen and paper and work through an example". But what about a simulation or execution of the real thing? The programmer must translate the algorithm into a language that the simulator/computer/computor can *effectively* execute. Stone gives an example of this: when computing the roots of a quadratic equation the computor must know how to take a square root. If they don't, then the algorithm, to be effective, must provide a set of rules for extracting a square root.

This means that the programmer must know a "language" that is effective relative to the target computing agent (computer/computor).

But what model should be used for the simulation? Van Emde Boas observes "even if we base complexity theory on abstract instead of concrete machines, arbitrariness of the choice of a model remains. It is at this point that the notion of *simulation* enters". When speed is being measured, the instruction set matters. For example, the subprogram in Euclid's algorithm to compute the remainder would execute much faster if the programmer had a "modulus" instruction available rather than just subtraction (or worse: just Minsky's "decrement").

Structured programming, canonical structures: Per the Church–Turing thesis, any algorithm can be computed by a model known to be Turing complete, and per Minsky's demonstrations, Turing completeness requires only four instruction types—conditional GOTO, unconditional GOTO, assignment, HALT. Kemeny and Kurtz observe that, while "undisciplined" use of unconditional GOTOs and conditional IF-THEN GOTOs can result in "spaghetti code", a programmer can write structured programs using only these instructions; on the other hand "it is also possible, and not too hard, to write badly structured programs in a structured language". Tausworthe augments the three Böhm-Jacopini canonical structures: SEQUENCE, IF-THEN-ELSE, and WHILE-DO, with two more: DO-WHILE and CASE. An additional benefit of a structured program is that it lends itself to proofs of correctness using mathematical induction.

Canonical flowchart symbols: The graphical aide called a flowchart offers a way to describe and document an algorithm (and a computer program of one). Like program flow of a Minsky machine, a flowchart always starts at the top of a page and proceeds down. Its primary symbols are only four: the directed arrow showing program flow, the rectangle (SEQUENCE, GOTO), the diamond (IF-THEN-ELSE), and the dot (OR-tie). The Böhm–Jacopini canonical structures are made of these primitive shapes. Sub-structures can "nest" in rectangles, but only if a single exit occurs from the superstructure. The symbols, and their use to build the canonical structures, are shown in the diagram.

Examples

Algorithm Example

One of the simplest algorithms is to find the largest number in a list of numbers of random order. Finding the solution requires looking at every number in the list. From this follows a simple algorithm, which can be stated in a high-level description English prose, as:

High-level description:

1. If there are no numbers in the set then there is no highest number.

2. Assume the first number in the set is the largest number in the set.

3. For each remaining number in the set: if this number is larger than the current largest number, consider this number to be the largest number in the set.

4. When there are no numbers left in the set to iterate over, consider the current largest number to be the largest number of the set.

(Quasi-)formal description: Written in prose but much closer to the high-level language of a computer program, the following is the more formal coding of the algorithm in pseudocode or pidgin code:

```
Algorithm LargestNumber

 Input: A list of numbers L.

 Output: The largest number in the list L.

 if L.size = 0 return null

 largest ← L

 for each item in L, do

  if item > largest, then

    largest ← item

 return largest
```

- "←" is a shorthand for "changes to". For instance, "*largest ← item*" means that the value of *largest* changes to the value of *item*.

- "return" terminates the algorithm and outputs the value that follows.

Euclid's Algorithm

Euclid's algorithm to compute the greatest common divisor (GCD) to two numbers appears as Proposition II in Book VII ("Elementary Number Theory") of his *Elements*. Euclid poses the problem thus: "Given two numbers not prime to one another, to find their greatest common measure". He defines "A number [to be] a multitude composed of units": a counting number, a positive integer not including zero. To "measure" is to place a shorter measuring length s successively (q times) along longer length l until the remaining portion r is less than the shorter length s. In modern words, remainder $r = l - q \times s$, q being the quotient, or remainder r is the "modulus", the integer-fractional part left over after the division.

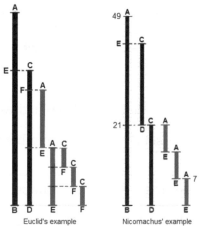

Euclid's example   Nicomachus' example

The example-diagram of Euclid's algorithm from T.L. Heath (1908), with more detail added. Euclid does not go beyond a third measuring, and gives no numerical examples. Nicomachus gives the example of 49 and 21: "I subtract the less from the greater; 28 is left; then again I subtract from this the same 21 (for this is possible); 7 is left; I subtract this from 21, 14 is left; from which I again subtract 7 (for this is possible); 7 is left, but 7 cannot be subtracted from 7." Heath comments that, "The last phrase is curious, but the meaning of it is obvious enough, as also the meaning of the phrase about ending 'at one and the same number'."(Heath 1908:300).

For Euclid's method to succeed, the starting lengths must satisfy two requirements: (i) the lengths must not be zero, AND (ii) the subtraction must be "proper"; i.e., a test must guarantee that the smaller of the two numbers is subtracted from the larger (alternately, the two can be equal so their subtraction yields zero).

Euclid's original proof adds a third requirement: the two lengths must not be prime to one another. Euclid stipulated this so that he could construct a reductio ad absurdum proof that the two numbers' common measure is in fact the *greatest*. While Nicomachus' algorithm is the same as Euclid's, when the numbers are prime to one another, it yields the number "1" for their common measure. So, to be precise, the following is really Nicomachus' algorithm.

Computer Language for Euclid's Algorithm

Only a few instruction *types* are required to execute Euclid's algorithm—some logical tests (conditional GOTO), unconditional GOTO, assignment (replacement), and subtraction.

- A *location* is symbolized by upper case letter(s), e.g. S, A, etc.

- The varying quantity (number) in a location is written in lower case letter(s) and (usually) associated with the location's name. For example, location L at the start might contain the number $l = 3009$.

An Inelegant Program for Euclid's Algorithm

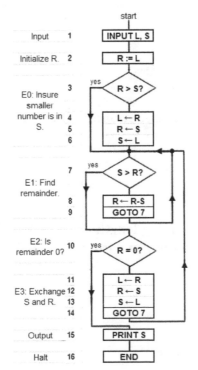

"Inelegant"

"Inelegant" is a translation of Knuth's version of the algorithm with a subtraction-based remainder-loop replacing his use of division (or a "modulus" instruction). Derived from Knuth 1973:2–4. Depending on the two numbers "Inelegant" may compute the g.c.d. in fewer steps than "Elegant".

The following algorithm is framed as Knuth's four-step version of Euclid's and Nicomachus', but, rather than using division to find the remainder, it uses successive subtractions of the shorter length *s* from the remaining length *r* until *r* is less than *s*. The high-level description, shown in boldface, is adapted from Knuth 1973:

Input:

1 [Into two locations L and S put the numbers *l* and *s* that represent the two lengths]:

  INPUT L, S

2 [Initialize R: make the remaining length *r* equal to the starting/initial/input length *l*]:

  R ← L

E0: [Ensure *r* ≥ *s*.]

3 [Ensure the smaller of the two numbers is in S and the larger in R]:

  IF R > S THEN

   the contents of L is the larger number so skip over the exchange-steps 4, 5 and 6:

   GOTO step 6

  ELSE

   swap the contents of R and S.

4 L ← R (this first step is redundant, but is useful for later discussion).

5 R ← S

6 S ← L

E1: [Find remainder]: Until the remaining length *r* in R is less than the shorter length *s* in S, repeatedly subtract the measuring number *s* in S from the remaining length *r* in R.

7 IF S > R THEN

  done measuring so

  GOTO 10

  ELSE

  measure again,

8 R ← R - S

```
9  [Remainder-loop]:

   GOTO 7.
```

E2: [Is the remainder zero?]: EITHER (i) the last measure was exact, the remainder in R is zero, and the program can halt, OR (ii) the algorithm must continue: the last measure left a remainder in R less than measuring number in S.

```
10 IF R = 0 THEN

   done so

   GOTO step 15

     ELSE

   CONTINUE TO step 11,
```

E3: [Interchange *s* and *r*]: The nut of Euclid's algorithm. Use remainder *r* to measure what was previously smaller number *s*; L serves as a temporary location.

```
11 L ← R

12 R ← S

13 S ← L

14 [Repeat the measuring process]:

   GOTO 7
```

Output:

```
15 [Done. S contains the greatest common divisor]:

   PRINT S
```

Done:

```
16 HALT, END, STOP.
```

An Elegant Program for Euclid's Algorithm

The following version of Euclid's algorithm requires only six core instructions to do what thirteen are required to do by "Inelegant"; worse, "Inelegant" requires more *types* of instructions. The flow-chart of "Elegant" can be found at the top of this article. In the (unstructured) Basic language, the steps are numbered, and the instruction LET [] = [] is the assignment instruction symbolized by ←.

```
5 REM Euclid's algorithm for greatest common divisor

6 PRINT "Type two integers greater than 0"
```

```
10 INPUT A,B

20 IF B=0 THEN GOTO 80

30 IF A > B THEN GOTO 60

40 LET B=B-A

50 GOTO 20

60 LET A=A-B

70 GOTO 20

80 PRINT A

90 END
```

The following version can be used with Object Oriented languages:

```
// Euclid's algorithm for greatest common divisor

integer euclidAlgorithm (int A, int B){

 A=Math.abs(A);

 B=Math.abs(B);

 while (B!=0){

   if (A>B) A=A-B;

   else B=B-A;

}

 return A;

{
```

How "Elegant" works: In place of an outer "Euclid loop", "Elegant" shifts back and forth between two "co-loops", an A > B loop that computes A ← A − B, and a B ≤ A loop that computes B ← B − A. This works because, when at last the minuend M is less than or equal to the subtrahend S (Difference = Minuend − Subtrahend), the minuend can become *s* (the new measuring length) and the subtrahend can become the new *r* (the length to be measured); in other words the "sense" of the subtraction reverses.

Testing the Euclid Algorithms

Does an algorithm do what its author wants it to do? A few test cases usually suffice to confirm core functionality. One source uses 3009 and 884. Knuth suggested 40902, 24140. Another interesting case is the two relatively prime numbers 14157 and 5950.

But exceptional cases must be identified and tested. Will "Inelegant" perform properly when R > S,

S > R, R = S? Ditto for "Elegant": B > A, A > B, A = B? (Yes to all). What happens when one number is zero, both numbers are zero? ("Inelegant" computes forever in all cases; "Elegant" computes forever when A = 0.) What happens if *negative* numbers are entered? Fractional numbers? If the input numbers, i.e. the domain of the function computed by the algorithm/program, is to include only positive integers including zero, then the failures at zero indicate that the algorithm (and the program that instantiates it) is a partial function rather than a total function. A notable failure due to exceptions is the Ariane 5 Flight 501 rocket failure (4 June 1996).

Proof of program correctness by use of mathematical induction: Knuth demonstrates the application of mathematical induction to an "extended" version of Euclid's algorithm, and he proposes "a general method applicable to proving the validity of any algorithm". Tausworthe proposes that a measure of the complexity of a program be the length of its correctness proof.

Measuring and Improving the Euclid Algorithms

Elegance (compactness) versus goodness (speed): With only six core instructions, "Elegant" is the clear winner, compared to "Inelegant" at thirteen instructions. However, "Inelegant" is *faster* (it arrives at HALT in fewer steps). Algorithm analysis indicates why this is the case: "Elegant" does *two* conditional tests in every subtraction loop, whereas "Inelegant" only does one. As the algorithm (usually) requires many loop-throughs, *on average* much time is wasted doing a "B = 0?" test that is needed only after the remainder is computed.

Can the algorithms be improved?: Once the programmer judges a program "fit" and "effective"—that is, it computes the function intended by its author—then the question becomes, can it be improved?

The compactness of "Inelegant" can be improved by the elimination of five steps. But Chaitin proved that compacting an algorithm cannot be automated by a generalized algorithm; rather, it can only be done heuristically; i.e., by exhaustive search (examples to be found at Busy beaver), trial and error, cleverness, insight, application of inductive reasoning, etc. Observe that steps 4, 5 and 6 are repeated in steps 11, 12 and 13. Comparison with "Elegant" provides a hint that these steps, together with steps 2 and 3, can be eliminated. This reduces the number of core instructions from thirteen to eight, which makes it "more elegant" than "Elegant", at nine steps.

The speed of "Elegant" can be improved by moving the "B=0?" test outside of the two subtraction loops. This change calls for the addition of three instructions (B = 0?, A = 0?, GOTO). Now "Elegant" computes the example-numbers faster; whether this is always the case for any given A, B and R, S would require a detailed analysis.

Algorithmic Analysis

It is frequently important to know how much of a particular resource (such as time or storage) is theoretically required for a given algorithm. Methods have been developed for the analysis of algorithms to obtain such quantitative answers (estimates); for example, the sorting algorithm above has a time requirement of $O(n)$, using the big O notation with n as the length of the list. At all times the algorithm only needs to remember two values: the largest number found so far, and its current position in the input list. Therefore, it is said to have a space requirement of *O(1)*, if the space required to store the input numbers is not counted, or O(n) if it is counted.

Different algorithms may complete the same task with a different set of instructions in less or more time, space, or 'effort' than others. For example, a binary search algorithm (with cost O(log n)) outperforms a sequential search (cost O(n)) when used for table lookups on sorted lists or arrays.

Formal Versus Empirical

The analysis and study of algorithms is a discipline of computer science, and is often practiced abstractly without the use of a specific programming language or implementation. In this sense, algorithm analysis resembles other mathematical disciplines in that it focuses on the underlying properties of the algorithm and not on the specifics of any particular implementation. Usually pseudocode is used for analysis as it is the simplest and most general representation. However, ultimately, most algorithms are usually implemented on particular hardware / software platforms and their algorithmic efficiency is eventually put to the test using real code. For the solution of a "one off" problem, the efficiency of a particular algorithm may not have significant consequences (unless n is extremely large) but for algorithms designed for fast interactive, commercial or long life scientific usage it may be critical. Scaling from small n to large n frequently exposes inefficient algorithms that are otherwise benign.

Empirical testing is useful because it may uncover unexpected interactions that affect performance. Benchmarks may be used to compare before/after potential improvements to an algorithm after program optimization.

Execution Efficiency

To illustrate the potential improvements possible even in well established algorithms, a recent significant innovation, relating to FFT algorithms (used heavily in the field of image processing), can decrease processing time up to 1,000 times for applications like medical imaging. In general, speed improvements depend on special properties of the problem, which are very common in practical applications. Speedups of this magnitude enable computing devices that make extensive use of image processing (like digital cameras and medical equipment) to consume less power.

Classification

There are various ways to classify algorithms, each with its own merits.

By Implementation

One way to classify algorithms is by implementation means.

Recursion

A recursive algorithm is one that invokes (makes reference to) itself repeatedly until a certain condition (also known as termination condition) matches, which is a method common to functional programming. Iterative algorithms use repetitive constructs like loops and sometimes additional data structures like stacks to solve the given problems. Some problems are naturally suited for one implementation or the other. For example, towers of

Hanoi is well understood using recursive implementation. Every recursive version has an equivalent (but possibly more or less complex) iterative version, and vice versa.

Logical

An algorithm may be viewed as controlled logical deduction. This notion may be expressed as: *Algorithm = logic + control*. The logic component expresses the axioms that may be used in the computation and the control component determines the way in which deduction is applied to the axioms. This is the basis for the logic programming paradigm. In pure logic programming languages the control component is fixed and algorithms are specified by supplying only the logic component. The appeal of this approach is the elegant semantics: a change in the axioms has a well-defined change in the algorithm.

Serial, parallel or distributed

Algorithms are usually discussed with the assumption that computers execute one instruction of an algorithm at a time. Those computers are sometimes called serial computers. An algorithm designed for such an environment is called a serial algorithm, as opposed to parallel algorithms or distributed algorithms. Parallel algorithms take advantage of computer architectures where several processors can work on a problem at the same time, whereas distributed algorithms utilize multiple machines connected with a network. Parallel or distributed algorithms divide the problem into more symmetrical or asymmetrical subproblems and collect the results back together. The resource consumption in such algorithms is not only processor cycles on each processor but also the communication overhead between the processors. Some sorting algorithms can be parallelized efficiently, but their communication overhead is expensive. Iterative algorithms are generally parallelizable. Some problems have no parallel algorithms, and are called inherently serial problems.

Deterministic or non-deterministic

Deterministic algorithms solve the problem with exact decision at every step of the algorithm whereas non-deterministic algorithms solve problems via guessing although typical guesses are made more accurate through the use of heuristics.

Exact or approximate

While many algorithms reach an exact solution, approximation algorithms seek an approximation that is close to the true solution. Approximation may use either a deterministic or a random strategy. Such algorithms have practical value for many hard problems.

Quantum algorithm

They run on a realistic model of quantum computation. The term is usually used for those algorithms which seem inherently quantum, or use some essential feature of quantum computation such as quantum superposition or quantum entanglement.

By Design Paradigm

Another way of classifying algorithms is by their design methodology or paradigm. There is a certain number of paradigms, each different from the other. Furthermore, each of these categories include many different types of algorithms. Some common paradigms are:

Brute-force or exhaustive search

> This is the naive method of trying every possible solution to see which is best.

Divide and conquer

> A divide and conquer algorithm repeatedly reduces an instance of a problem to one or more smaller instances of the same problem (usually recursively) until the instances are small enough to solve easily. One such example of divide and conquer is merge sorting. Sorting can be done on each segment of data after dividing data into segments and sorting of entire data can be obtained in the conquer phase by merging the segments. A simpler variant of divide and conquer is called a *decrease and conquer algorithm*, that solves an identical subproblem and uses the solution of this subproblem to solve the bigger problem. Divide and conquer divides the problem into multiple subproblems and so the conquer stage is more complex than decrease and conquer algorithms. An example of decrease and conquer algorithm is the binary search algorithm.

Search and enumeration

> Many problems (such as playing chess) can be modeled as problems on graphs. A graph exploration algorithm specifies rules for moving around a graph and is useful for such problems. This category also includes search algorithms, branch and bound enumeration and backtracking.

Randomized algorithm

> Such algorithms make some choices randomly (or pseudo-randomly). They can be very useful in finding approximate solutions for problems where finding exact solutions can be impractical. For some of these problems, it is known that the fastest approximations must involve some randomness. Whether randomized algorithms with polynomial time complexity can be the fastest algorithms for some problems is an open question known as the P versus NP problem. There are two large classes of such algorithms:

1. Monte Carlo algorithms return a correct answer with high-probability. E.g. RP is the subclass of these that run in polynomial time.

2. Las Vegas algorithms always return the correct answer, but their running time is only probabilistically bound, e.g. ZPP.

Reduction of complexity

> This technique involves solving a difficult problem by transforming it into a better known problem for which we have (hopefully) asymptotically optimal algorithms. The goal is to find a reducing algorithm whose complexity is not dominated by the resulting reduced algorithm's. For example, one selection algorithm for finding the median in an unsorted list involves first sorting the list (the expensive portion) and then pulling out the middle element in the sorted list (the cheap portion). This technique is also known as *transform and conquer.*

Optimization Problems

For optimization problems there is a more specific classification of algorithms; an algorithm for such problems may fall into one or more of the general categories described above as well as into one of the following:

Linear programming

When searching for optimal solutions to a linear function bound to linear equality and inequality constraints, the constraints of the problem can be used directly in producing the optimal solutions. There are algorithms that can solve any problem in this category, such as the popular simplex algorithm. Problems that can be solved with linear programming include the maximum flow problem for directed graphs. If a problem additionally requires that one or more of the unknowns must be an integer then it is classified in integer programming. A linear programming algorithm can solve such a problem if it can be proved that all restrictions for integer values are superficial, i.e., the solutions satisfy these restrictions anyway. In the general case, a specialized algorithm or an algorithm that finds approximate solutions is used, depending on the difficulty of the problem.

Dynamic programming

When a problem shows optimal substructures — meaning the optimal solution to a problem can be constructed from optimal solutions to subproblems — and overlapping subproblems, meaning the same subproblems are used to solve many different problem instances, a quicker approach called *dynamic programming* avoids recomputing solutions that have already been computed. For example, Floyd–Warshall algorithm, the shortest path to a goal from a vertex in a weighted graph can be found by using the shortest path to the goal from all adjacent vertices. Dynamic programming and memoization go together. The main difference between dynamic programming and divide and conquer is that subproblems are more or less independent in divide and conquer, whereas subproblems overlap in dynamic programming. The difference between dynamic programming and straightforward recursion is in caching or memoization of recursive calls. When subproblems are independent and there is no repetition, memoization does not help; hence dynamic programming is not a solution for all complex problems. By using memoization or maintaining a table of subproblems already solved, dynamic programming reduces the exponential nature of many problems to polynomial complexity.

The greedy method

A greedy algorithm is similar to a dynamic programming algorithm in that it works by examining substructures, in this case not of the problem but of a given solution. Such algorithms start with some solution, which may be given or have been constructed in some way, and improve it by making small modifications. For some problems they can find the optimal solution while for others they stop at local optima, that is, at solutions that cannot be improved by the algorithm but are not optimum. The most popular use of greedy algorithms is for finding the minimal spanning tree where finding the optimal solution is possible with this method. Huffman Tree, Kruskal, Prim, Sollin are greedy algorithms that can solve this optimization problem.

The heuristic method

In optimization problems, heuristic algorithms can be used to find a solution close to the optimal solution in cases where finding the optimal solution is impractical. These algorithms work by getting closer and closer to the optimal solution as they progress. In principle, if run for an infinite amount of time, they will find the optimal solution. Their merit is that they can find a solution very close to the optimal solution in a relatively short time. Such algorithms include local search, tabu search, simulated annealing, and genetic algorithms. Some of them, like simulated annealing, are non-deterministic algorithms while others, like tabu search, are deterministic. When a bound on the error of the non-optimal solution is known, the algorithm is further categorized as an approximation algorithm.

By Field of Study

Every field of science has its own problems and needs efficient algorithms. Related problems in one field are often studied together. Some example classes are search algorithms, sorting algorithms, merge algorithms, numerical algorithms, graph algorithms, string algorithms, computational geometric algorithms, combinatorial algorithms, medical algorithms, machine learning, cryptography, data compression algorithms and parsing techniques.

Fields tend to overlap with each other, and algorithm advances in one field may improve those of other, sometimes completely unrelated, fields. For example, dynamic programming was invented for optimization of resource consumption in industry, but is now used in solving a broad range of problems in many fields.

By Complexity

Algorithms can be classified by the amount of time they need to complete compared to their input size:

- Constant time: if the time needed by the algorithm is the same, regardless of the input size. E.g. an access to an array element.

- Linear time: if the time is proportional to the input size. E.g. the traverse of a list.

- Logarithmic time: if the time is a logarithmic function of the input size. E.g. binary search algorithm.

- Polynomial time: if the time is a power of the input size. E.g. the bubble sort algorithm has quadratic time complexity.

- Exponential time: if the time is an exponential function of the input size. E.g. Brute-force search.

Some problems may have multiple algorithms of differing complexity, while other problems might have no algorithms or no known efficient algorithms. There are also mappings from some problems to other problems. Owing to this, it was found to be more suitable to classify the problems themselves instead of the algorithms into equivalence classes based on the complexity of the best possible algorithms for them.

Continuous Algorithms

The adjective "continuous" when applied to the word "algorithm" can mean:

- An algorithm operating on data that represents continuous quantities, even though this data is represented by discrete approximations—such algorithms are studied in numerical analysis; or

- An algorithm in the form of a differential equation that operates continuously on the data, running on an analog computer.

Legal Issues

Algorithms, by themselves, are not usually patentable. In the United States, a claim consisting solely of simple manipulations of abstract concepts, numbers, or signals does not constitute "processes" (USPTO 2006), and hence algorithms are not patentable (as in Gottschalk v. Benson). However, practical applications of algorithms are sometimes patentable. For example, in Diamond v. Diehr, the application of a simple feedback algorithm to aid in the curing of synthetic rubber was deemed patentable. The patenting of software is highly controversial, and there are highly criticized patents involving algorithms, especially data compression algorithms, such as Unisys' LZW patent.

Etymology

The words 'algorithm' and 'algorism' come from the name al-Khwārizmī. Al-Khwārizmī was a Persian mathematician, astronomer, geographer, and scholar in the House of Wisdom in Baghdad, whose name means 'the native of Khwarezm', a region that was part of Greater Iran and is now in Uzbekistan. About 825, he wrote a treatise in the Arabic language, which was translated into Latin in the 12th century under the title *Algoritmi de numero Indorum*. This title means "Algoritmi on the numbers of the Indians", where "Algoritmi" was the translator's Latinization of Al-Khwarizmi's name. Al-Khwarizmi was the most widely read mathematician in Europe in the late Middle Ages, primarily through his other book, the Algebra. In late medieval Latin, *algorismus*, English 'algorism', the corruption of his name, simply meant the "decimal number system". In the 15th century, under the influence of the Greek word 'number' (*cf.* 'arithmetic'), the Latin word was altered to *algorithmus*, and the corresponding English term 'algorithm' is first attested in the 17th century; the modern sense was introduced in the 19th century.

History: Development of the Notion of "Algorithm"

Ancient Near East

Algorithms were used in ancient Greece. Two examples are the Sieve of Eratosthenes, which was described in Introduction to Arithmetic by Nicomachus, and the Euclidean algorithm, which was first described in Euclid's Elements (c. 300 BC). Babylonian clay tablets describe and employ algorithmic procedures to compute the time and place of significant astronomical events.

Discrete and Distinguishable Symbols

Tally-marks: To keep track of their flocks, their sacks of grain and their money the ancients used tallying: accumulating stones or marks scratched on sticks, or making discrete symbols in clay. Through the Babylonian and Egyptian use of marks and symbols, eventually Roman numerals and the abacus evolved (Dilson, p. 16–41). Tally marks appear prominently in unary numeral system arithmetic used in Turing machine and Post–Turing machine computations.

Manipulation of Symbols as "place holders" for Numbers: Algebra

The work of the ancient Greek geometers (Euclidean algorithm), the Indian mathematician Brahmagupta, and the Islamic mathematics Al-Khwarizmi (from whose name the terms "algorism" and "algorithm" are derived), and Western European mathematicians culminated in Leibniz's notion of the calculus ratiocinator (ca 1680):

A good century and a half ahead of his time, Leibniz proposed an algebra of logic, an algebra that would specify the rules for manipulating logical concepts in the manner that ordinary algebra specifies the rules for manipulating numbers.

Mechanical Contrivances with Discrete States

The clock: Bolter credits the invention of the weight-driven clock as "The key invention [of Europe in the Middle Ages]", in particular the verge escapement that provides us with the tick and tock of a mechanical clock. "The accurate automatic machine" led immediately to "mechanical automata" beginning in the 13th century and finally to "computational machines"—the difference engine and analytical engines of Charles Babbage and Countess Ada Lovelace, mid-19th century. Lovelace is credited with the first creation of an algorithm intended for processing on a computer – Babbage's analytical engine, the first device considered a real Turing-complete computer instead of just a calculator – and is sometimes called "history's first programmer" as a result, though a full implementation of Babbage's second device would not be realized until decades after her lifetime.

Logical machines 1870—Stanley Jevons' "logical abacus" and "logical machine": The technical problem was to reduce Boolean equations when presented in a form similar to what are now known as Karnaugh maps. Jevons (1880) describes first a simple "abacus" of "slips of wood furnished with pins, contrived so that any part or class of the [logical] combinations can be picked out mechanically ... More recently however I have reduced the system to a completely mechanical form, and have thus embodied the whole of the indirect process of inference in what may be called a *Logical Machine*" His machine came equipped with "certain moveable wooden rods" and "at the foot are 21 keys like those of a piano [etc] . . .". With this machine he could analyze a "syllogism or any other simple logical argument".

This machine he displayed in 1870 before the Fellows of the Royal Society. Another logician John Venn, however, in his 1881 *Symbolic Logic*, turned a jaundiced eye to this effort: "I have no high estimate myself of the interest or importance of what are sometimes called logical machines ... it does not seem to me that any contrivances at present known or likely to be discovered really deserve the name of logical machines". But not to be outdone he too presented "a plan somewhat analogous, I apprehend, to Prof. Jevon's *abacus* ... [And] [a]gain, corresponding to Prof. Jevons's logical machine, the following contrivance may be described. I prefer to call it merely a logical-diagram machine ... but I suppose that it could do very completely all that can be rationally expected of any logical machine".

Jacquard loom, Hollerith punch cards, telegraphy and telephony—the electromechanical relay: Bell and Newell (1971) indicate that the Jacquard loom (1801), precursor to Hollerith cards (punch cards, 1887), and "telephone switching technologies" were the roots of a tree leading to the development of the first computers. By the mid-19th century the telegraph, the precursor of the telephone, was in use throughout the world, its discrete and distinguishable encoding of letters as "dots and dashes" a common sound. By the late 19th century the ticker tape (ca 1870s) was in use, as was the use of Hollerith cards in the 1890 U.S. census. Then came the teleprinter (ca. 1910) with its punched-paper use of Baudot code on tape.

Telephone-switching networks of electromechanical relays (invented 1835) was behind the work of George Stibitz (1937), the inventor of the digital adding device. As he worked in Bell Laboratories, he observed the "burdensome' use of mechanical calculators with gears. "He went home one evening in 1937 intending to test his idea... When the tinkering was over, Stibitz had constructed a binary adding device".

Davis (2000) observes the particular importance of the electromechanical relay (with its two "binary states" *open* and *closed*):

> It was only with the development, beginning in the 1930s, of electromechanical calculators using electrical relays, that machines were built having the scope Babbage had envisioned."

Mathematics During the 19th Century up to the Mid-20th Century

Symbols and rules: In rapid succession the mathematics of George Boole (1847, 1854), Gottlob Frege (1879), and Giuseppe Peano (1888–1889) reduced arithmetic to a sequence of symbols manipulated by rules. Peano's *The principles of arithmetic, presented by a new method* (1888) was "the first attempt at an axiomatization of mathematics in a symbolic language".

But Heijenoort gives Frege (1879) this kudos: Frege's is "perhaps the most important single work ever written in logic. ... in which we see a " 'formula language', that is a *lingua characterica*, a language written with special symbols, "for pure thought", that is, free from rhetorical embellishments ... constructed from specific symbols that are manipulated according to definite rules". The work of Frege was further simplified and amplified by Alfred North Whitehead and Bertrand Russell in their Principia Mathematica (1910–1913).

The paradoxes: At the same time a number of disturbing paradoxes appeared in the literature, in particular the Burali-Forti paradox (1897), the Russell paradox (1902–03), and the Richard Paradox. The resultant considerations led to Kurt Gödel's paper (1931)—he specifically cites the paradox of the liar—that completely reduces rules of recursion to numbers.

Effective calculability: In an effort to solve the Entscheidungsproblem defined precisely by Hilbert in 1928, mathematicians first set about to define what was meant by an "effective method" or "effective calculation" or "effective calculability" (i.e., a calculation that would succeed). In rapid succession the following appeared: Alonzo Church, Stephen Kleene and J.B. Rosser's λ-calculus a finely honed definition of "general recursion" from the work of Gödel acting on suggestions of Jacques Herbrand (cf. Gödel's Princeton lectures of 1934) and subsequent simplifications by Kleene. Church's proof that the Entscheidungsproblem was unsolvable, Emil Post's definition of effective calculability as a worker mindlessly following a list of instructions to move left or right through a sequence of rooms and while there either mark or erase a paper or observe the paper and make a yes-no decision about the next instruction. Alan Turing's proof of that the Entscheidungsproblem was unsolvable by use of his "a- [automatic-] machine"—in effect almost identical to Post's "formulation", J. Barkley Rosser's definition of "effective method" in terms of "a machine". S. C. Kleene's proposal of a precursor to "Church thesis" that he called "Thesis I", and a few years later Kleene's renaming his Thesis "Church's Thesis" and proposing "Turing's Thesis".

Emil Post (1936) and Alan Turing (1936–37, 1939)

Here is a remarkable coincidence of two men not knowing each other but describing a process of men-as-computers working on computations—and they yield virtually identical definitions.

Emil Post (1936) described the actions of a "computer" (human being) as follows:

> "...two concepts are involved: that of a *symbol space* in which the work leading from problem to answer is to be carried out, and a fixed unalterable *set of directions*.

His symbol space would be

> "a two way infinite sequence of spaces or boxes... The problem solver or worker is to move and work in this symbol space, being capable of being in, and operating in but one box at a time.... a box is to admit of but two possible conditions, i.e., being empty or unmarked, and having a single mark in it, say a vertical stroke.

> "One box is to be singled out and called the starting point. ...a specific problem is to be given in symbolic form by a finite number of boxes [i.e., INPUT] being marked with a stroke. Likewise the answer [i.e., OUTPUT] is to be given in symbolic form by such a configuration of marked boxes.

> "A set of directions applicable to a general problem sets up a deterministic process when applied to each specific problem. This process terminates only when it comes to the direction of type (C) [i.e., STOP]".

Alan Turing's statue at Bletchley Park.

Alan Turing's work preceded that of Stibitz (1937); it is unknown whether Stibitz knew of the work of Turing. Turing's biographer believed that Turing's use of a typewriter-like model derived from a youthful interest: "Alan had dreamt of inventing typewriters as a boy; Mrs. Turing had a typewriter; and he could well have begun by asking himself what was meant by calling a typewriter 'mechanical'". Given the prevalence of Morse code and telegraphy, ticker tape machines, and teletypewriters we might conjecture that all were influences.

Turing—his model of computation is now called a Turing machine—begins, as did Post, with an analysis of a human computer that he whittles down to a simple set of basic motions and "states of mind". But he continues a step further and creates a machine as a model of computation of numbers.

> "Computing is normally done by writing certain symbols on paper. We may suppose this paper is divided into squares like a child's arithmetic book....I assume then that the computation is carried out on one-dimensional paper, i.e., on a tape divided into squares. I shall also suppose that the number of symbols which may be printed is finite....

> "The behaviour of the computer at any moment is determined by the symbols which he is observing, and his "state of mind" at that moment. We may suppose that there is a bound B to the number of symbols or squares which the computer can observe at one moment. If he wishes to observe more, he must use successive observations. We will also suppose that the number of states of mind which need be taken into account is finite...

> "Let us imagine that the operations performed by the computer to be split up into 'simple operations' which are so elementary that it is not easy to imagine them further divided."

Turing's reduction yields the following:

> "The simple operations must therefore include:

> "(a) Changes of the symbol on one of the observed squares

> "(b) Changes of one of the squares observed to another square within L squares of one of the previously observed squares.

"It may be that some of these change necessarily invoke a change of state of mind. The most general single operation must therefore be taken to be one of the following:

> "(A) A possible change (a) of symbol together with a possible change of state of mind.

> "(B) A possible change (b) of observed squares, together with a possible change of state of mind"

> "We may now construct a machine to do the work of this computer."

A few years later, Turing expanded his analysis (thesis, definition) with this forceful expression of it:

> "A function is said to be "effectively calculable" if its values can be found by some purely mechanical process. Though it is fairly easy to get an intuitive grasp of this idea, it is nevertheless desirable to have some more definite, mathematical expressible definition . . . [he discusses the history of the definition pretty much as presented above with respect to Gödel, Herbrand, Kleene, Church, Turing and Post] . . . We may take this statement literally, understanding by a purely mechanical process one which could be carried out by a machine. It is possible

to give a mathematical description, in a certain normal form, of the structures of these machines. The development of these ideas leads to the author's definition of a computable function, and to an identification of computability † with effective calculability . . . .

"† We shall use the expression "computable function" to mean a function calculable by a machine, and we let "effectively calculable" refer to the intuitive idea without particular identification with any one of these definitions".

J. B. Rosser (1939) and S. C. Kleene (1943)

J. Barkley Rosser defined an 'effective [mathematical] method' in the following manner (italicization added):

"'Effective method' is used here in the rather special sense of a method each step of which is precisely determined and which is certain to produce the answer in a finite number of steps. With this special meaning, three different precise definitions have been given to date. The simplest of these to state (due to Post and Turing) says essentially that *an effective method of solving certain sets of problems exists if one can build a machine which will then solve any problem of the set with no human intervention beyond inserting the question and (later) reading the answer.* All three definitions are equivalent, so it doesn't matter which one is used. Moreover, the fact that all three are equivalent is a very strong argument for the correctness of any one." (Rosser 1939:225–6)

Rosser's footnote #5 references the work of (1) Church and Kleene and their definition of λ-definability, in particular Church's use of it in his *An Unsolvable Problem of Elementary Number Theory* (1936); (2) Herbrand and Gödel and their use of recursion in particular Gödel's use in his famous paper *On Formally Undecidable Propositions of Principia Mathematica and Related Systems I* (1931); and (3) Post (1936) and Turing (1936–7) in their mechanism-models of computation.

Stephen C. Kleene defined as his now-famous "Thesis I" known as the Church–Turing thesis. But he did this in the following context (boldface in original):

"12. *Algorithmic theories*... In setting up a complete algorithmic theory, what we do is to describe a procedure, performable for each set of values of the independent variables, which procedure necessarily terminates and in such manner that from the outcome we can read a definite answer, "yes" or "no," to the question, "is the predicate value true?"" (Kleene 1943:273)

History After 1950

A number of efforts have been directed toward further refinement of the definition of "algorithm", and activity is on-going because of issues surrounding, in particular, foundations of mathematics (especially the Church–Turing thesis) and philosophy of mind (especially arguments about artificial intelligence).

Algorithms in Today's Society

Algorithms are complex codes which are instructions for solving a problem or completing a task. They are often considered as an automated process in which mathematical equations compute data to achieve an end result. Algorithms have been shaped by many technological advances which help extend their use and functionality in society. The internet today relies on algorithms and all online searching tools are accomplished through them. Our electronic devices, such as phones, cameras, and laptops, rely on algorithmic codes to help process numbers and calculations.

The Use of Algorithms in Popular Technology

Google's Search Engine

Google's goals as a search engine tool is to "organize the world's information and make it universally accessible and useful". Its search engine relies on the use of algorithms to help deliver its search results while collecting information from its visitors to help improve its search results. When a user inputs a keyword, the algorithmic code works by searching through millions of online web pages that match the keywords used to search. Its search engine also assigns a rank to each page, including how many times the keywords appear within a web page. Web pages that are categorized as having a high rank typically appear on the top, showing only the links closely relating to the keyword search.

Facebook'S News Feed

Facebook is a social networking site that makes it easy for people to connect and keep in touch online. In 2006, Facebook introduced the "News Feed" tool which shows a personalized list of news stories which are influenced by your connections and activity on Facebook. The company relies on a system of metrics which monitors user engagement with content, which users provide unintentionally through online metrics. This information is then used to better serve the Facebook user with the help of algorithms embedded into its online platform, which are continuously developed and modified by engineers at Facebook.

Controversy Surrounding the use of Algorithms

Facebook

In 2014, Facebook was criticized for experimenting on its users. A paper in the "Proceedings of the National Academy of Sciences" revealed that Facebook manipulated the newsfeeds of 689,000 users in order to study their emotions through social networks. The academic paper, titled "Experimental evidence of massive-scale emotional contagion through social network's" concluded that the emotions experienced by users online were influenced by the posts they read, which may have also lead to a behavioral change in their real life.

A spokeswoman from Facebook responded that the study was carried out "to improve our services and to make the content people see on Facebook as relevant and engaging as possible" and that "a big part of this is understanding how people respond to different types of content, whether it's positive or negative in tone, news from friends, or information from pages they follow."

In 2016, a former journalist who worked at Facebook revealed that the employees who were responsible on curating news suppressed conservative news stories. According to Gizmodo, the employees were tasked to promote different news stories on the trending news section, even though the conservative news was highly trending.

Google

In 2016, Google faced public criticism after receiving a number of complaints over the autocomplete suggestions in its search engine which suggested anti-semitic and other hateful recommendations in the search. Google has since then altered its algorithm to deter any hateful suggestions from appearing.

2016 U.S. Election Period

During the 2016 U.S. presidential election, the promulgation of fake news stories gained much attention in headlines by news outlets. Issues in the automated process of algorithms helped spread fake news across various online websites such as Google news and Facebook. Researchers from news outlets criticized that misleading headlines, news content, and pictures deceived people into believing these stories were substantially true. The issue at hand was not just with fake news, it seemed that algorithms played an important role in delivering fake news to people's newsfeed. It seemed like that the algorithms had a flaw when detecting the truthfulness between real news and fake news. Companies such as Facebook and Google were criticized for being at forefront of the problem, and began to address that their algorithms required revision, and publicly admitted to the fault in their algorithms.

Legal Concerns

Researcher, Andrew Tutt, argues that algorithms should be FDA regulated. His academic work emphasizes that the rise of increasingly complex algorithms calls for the need to think about the effects of algorithms today. Due to the nature and complexity of algorithms, it will prove to be difficult to hold algorithms accountable under criminal law. Tutt recognizes that while some algorithms will be beneficial to help meet technological demand, others should not be used or sold if they fail to meet safety requirements. Thus, for Tutt, algorithms will require "closer forms of federal uniformity, expert judgment, political independence, and pre-market review to prevent the introduction of unacceptably dangerous algorithms into the market."

Sorting Algorithm

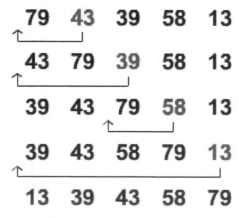

An Applet Demonstrating Insertion Sort.

- Now, we take a more complex problem called sorting.

- Problem Definition: Sort given n numbers by non-descending order.

- There are many sorting algorithm. Insertion sort is a simple algorithm.

- Insertion Sort: We can assume up to first number is sorted. Then sort up to two numbers. Next, sort up to three numbers. This process continue till we sort all n numbers.

- Consider the following example of five integer:

  79 43 39 58 13 : Up to first number, 79, is sorted.

  43 79 39 58 13 : Sorted up to two numbers.

  39 43 79 58 13 : Sorted up to three numbers.

  39 43 58 79 13 : Sorted up to four numbers.

  13 39 43 58 79 : Sorted all numbers.

- That is, if first (i-1) numbers are sorted then insert i^{th} number into its correct position. This can be done by shifting numbers right one number at a time till a position for i^{th} number is found.

- That is, shift number at $(i-1)^{th}$ position to i^{th} position, number in $(i-2)^{th}$ position to $(i-1)^{th}$ position, and so on, till we find a correct position for the number in i^{th} position. This method is depicted in the figure.

- The algorithmic description of insertion sort is given below.

```
Algorithm Insertion_Sort (a[n])

Step 1:        for i = 2 to n do

Step 2:        current_num = a[i]

Step 3:        j = i

Step 4:        while (( j >1) and (a[j-1] > current_num)) do

Step 5:                a[j] = a[j-1]

Step 6:                j = j-1

Step 7:        a[j] = current_num
```

In computer science a sorting algorithm is an algorithm that puts elements of a list in a certain order. The most-used orders are numerical order and lexicographical order. Efficient sorting is important for optimizing the use of other algorithms (such as search and merge algorithms) which require input data to be in sorted lists; it is also often useful for canonicalizing data and for producing human-readable output. More formally, the output must satisfy two conditions:

1. The output is in nondecreasing order (each element is no smaller than the previous element according to the desired total order);

2. The output is a permutation (reordering) of the input.

Further, the data is often taken to be in an array, which allows random access, rather than a list, which only allows sequential access, though often algorithms can be applied with suitable modification to either type of data.

History

From the beginning of computing, the sorting problem has attracted a great deal of research, perhaps due to the complexity of solving it efficiently despite its simple, familiar statement. Among the authors of early sorting algorithms around 1951 was Betty Holberton (née Snyder), who worked on ENIAC and UNIVAC. Bubble sort was analyzed as early as 1956. Comparison sorting algorithms have a fundamental requirement of $O(n \log n)$ comparisons (some input sequences will require a multiple of $n \log n$ comparisons); algorithms not based on comparisons, such as counting sort, can have better performance. Although many consider sorting a solved problem—asymptotically optimal algorithms have been known since the mid-20th century—useful new algorithms are still being invented, with the now widely used Timsort dating to 2002, and the library sort being first published in 2006.

Sorting algorithms are prevalent in introductory computer science classes, where the abundance of algorithms for the problem provides a gentle introduction to a variety of core algorithm concepts, such as big O notation, divide and conquer algorithms, data structures such as heaps and binary trees, randomized algorithms, best, worst and average case analysis, time-space tradeoffs, and upper and lower bounds.

Classification

Sorting algorithms are often classified by:

- Computational complexity (worst, average and best behavior) in terms of the size of the list (n). For typical serial sorting algorithms good behavior is $O(n \log n)$, with parallel sort in $O(\log^2 n)$, and bad behavior is $O(n^2)$. Ideal behavior for a serial sort is $O(n)$, but this is not possible in the average case. Optimal parallel sorting is $O(\log n)$. Comparison-based sorting algorithms need at least $O(n \log n)$ comparisons for most inputs.

- Computational complexity of swaps (for "in-place" algorithms).

- Memory usage (and use of other computer resources). In particular, some sorting algorithms are "in-place". Strictly, an in-place sort needs only $O(1)$ memory beyond the items being sorted; sometimes $O(\log(n))$ additional memory is considered "in-place".

- Recursion. Some algorithms are either recursive or non-recursive, while others may be both (e.g., merge sort).

- Stability: stable sorting algorithms maintain the relative order of records with equal keys (i.e., values).

- Whether or not they are a comparison sort. A comparison sort examines the data only by comparing two elements with a comparison operator.

- General method: insertion, exchange, selection, merging, *etc.* Exchange sorts include bubble sort and quicksort. Selection sorts include shaker sort and heapsort. Also whether the algorithm is serial or parallel. The remainder of this discussion almost exclusively concentrates upon serial algorithms and assumes serial operation.

- Adaptability: Whether or not the presortedness of the input affects the running time. Algorithms that take this into account are known to be adaptive.

Stability

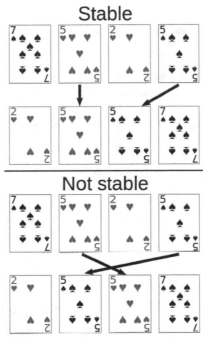

An example of stable sort on playing cards. When the cards are sorted by rank with a stable sort, the two 5s must remain in the same order in the sorted output that they were originally in. When they are sorted with a non-stable sort, the 5s may end up in the opposite order in the sorted output.

When sorting some kinds of data, only part of the data is examined when determining the sort order. For example, in the card sorting example to the right, the cards are being sorted by their rank, and their suit is being ignored. This allows the possibility of multiple different correctly sorted versions of the original list. Stable sorting algorithms choose one of these, according to the following rule: if two items compare as equal, like the two 5 cards, then their relative order will be preserved, so that if one came before the other in the input, it will also come before the other in the output.

More formally, the data being sorted can be represented as a record or tuple of values, and the part of the data that is used for sorting is called the *key*. In the card example, cards are represented as a record (rank, suit), and the key is the rank. A sorting algorithm is stable if whenever there are two records R and S with the same key, and R appears before S in the original list, then R will always appear before S in the sorted list.

When equal elements are indistinguishable, such as with integers, or more generally, any data where the entire element is the key, stability is not an issue. Stability is also not an issue if all keys are different.

Unstable sorting algorithms can be specially implemented to be stable. One way of doing this is to artificially extend the key comparison, so that comparisons between two objects with otherwise equal keys are decided using the order of the entries in the original input list as a tie-breaker. Remembering this order, however, may require additional time and space.

One application for stable sorting algorithms is sorting a list using a primary and secondary key. For example, suppose we wish to sort a hand of cards such that the suits are in the order clubs (♣), diamonds (♦), hearts (♥), spades (♠), and within each suit, the cards are sorted by rank. This can be done by first sorting the cards by rank (using any sort), and then doing a stable sort by suit:

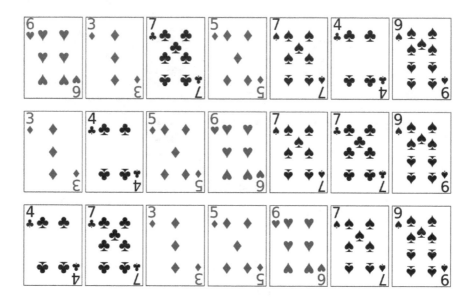

Within each suit, the stable sort preserves the ordering by rank that was already done. This idea can be extended to any number of keys, and is leveraged by radix sort. The same effect can be achieved with an unstable sort by using a lexicographic key comparison, which, e.g., compares first by suit, and then compares by rank if the suits are the same.

Popular Sorting Algorithms

While there are a large number of sorting algorithms, in practical implementations a few algorithms predominate. Insertion sort is widely used for small data sets, while for large data sets an asymptotically efficient sort is used, primarily heap sort, merge sort, or quicksort. Efficient implementations generally use a hybrid algorithm, combining an asymptotically efficient algorithm for the overall sort with insertion sort for small lists at the bottom of a recursion. Highly tuned implementations use more sophisticated variants, such as Timsort (merge sort, insertion sort, and additional logic), used in Android, Java, and Python, and introsort (quicksort and heap sort), used (in variant forms) in some C++ sort implementations and in .NET.

For more restricted data, such as numbers in a fixed interval, distribution sorts such as counting sort or radix sort are widely used. Bubble sort and variants are rarely used in practice, but are commonly found in teaching and theoretical discussions.

When physically sorting objects, such as alphabetizing papers (such as tests or books), people intuitively generally use insertion sorts for small sets. For larger sets, people often first bucket, such as by initial letter, and multiple bucketing allows practical sorting of very large sets. Often space is relatively cheap, such as by spreading objects out on the floor or over a large area, but operations are expensive, particularly moving an object a large distance – locality of reference is important. Merge sorts are also practical for physical objects, particularly as two hands can be used, one for each list to merge, while other algorithms, such as heap sort or quick sort, are poorly suited for human use. Other algorithms, such as library sort, a variant of insertion sort that leaves spaces, are also practical for physical use.

Simple Sorts

Two of the simplest sorts are insertion sort and selection sort, both of which are efficient on small data, due to low overhead, but not efficient on large data. Insertion sort is generally faster than selection sort in practice, due to fewer comparisons and good performance on almost-sorted data, and thus is preferred in practice, but selection sort uses fewer writes, and thus is used when write performance is a limiting factor.

Insertion Sort

Insertion sort is a simple sorting algorithm that is relatively efficient for small lists and mostly sorted lists, and is often used as part of more sophisticated algorithms. It works by taking elements from the list one by one and inserting them in their correct position into a new sorted list. In arrays, the new list and the remaining elements can share the array's space, but insertion is expensive, requiring shifting all following elements over by one. Shellsort is a variant of insertion sort that is more efficient for larger lists.

Selection Sort

Selection sort is an in-place comparison sort. It has $O(n^2)$ complexity, making it inefficient on large lists, and generally performs worse than the similar insertion sort. Selection sort is noted for its simplicity, and also has performance advantages over more complicated algorithms in certain situations.

The algorithm finds the minimum value, swaps it with the value in the first position, and repeats these steps for the remainder of the list. It does no more than n swaps, and thus is useful where swapping is very expensive.

Efficient Sorts

Practical general sorting algorithms are almost always based on an algorithm with average time complexity (and generally worst-case complexity) $O(n \log n)$, of which the most common are heap sort, merge sort, and quicksort. Each has advantages and drawbacks, with the most significant being that simple implementation of merge sort uses $O(n)$ additional space, and simple implementation of quicksort has $O(n^2)$ worst-case complexity. These problems can be solved or ameliorated at the cost of a more complex algorithm.

While these algorithms are asymptotically efficient on random data, for practical efficiency on real-world data various modifications are used. First, the overhead of these algorithms becomes significant on smaller data, so often a hybrid algorithm is used, commonly switching to insertion sort once the data is small enough. Second, the algorithms often perform poorly on already sorted data or almost sorted data – these are common in real-world data, and can be sorted in $O(n)$ time by appropriate algorithms. Finally, they may also be unstable, and stability is often a desirable property in a sort. Thus more sophisticated algorithms are often employed, such as Timsort (based on merge sort) or introsort (based on quicksort, falling back to heap sort).

Merge Sort

Merge sort takes advantage of the ease of merging already sorted lists into a new sorted list. It starts by comparing every two elements (i.e., 1 with 2, then 3 with 4...) and swapping them if the first should come after the second. It then merges each of the resulting lists of two into lists of four, then merges those lists of four, and so on; until at last two lists are merged into the final sorted list. Of the algorithms described here, this is the first that scales well to very large lists, because its worst-case running time is $O(n \log n)$. It is also easily applied to lists, not only arrays, as it only requires sequential access, not random access. However, it has additional $O(n)$ space complexity, and involves a large number of copies in simple implementations.

Merge sort has seen a relatively recent surge in popularity for practical implementations, due to its use in the sophisticated algorithm Timsort, which is used for the standard sort routine in the programming languages Python and Java (as of JDK7). Merge sort itself is the standard routine in Perl, among others, and has been used in Java at least since 2000 in JDK1.3.

Heapsort

Heapsort is a much more efficient version of selection sort. It also works by determining the largest (or smallest) element of the list, placing that at the end (or beginning) of the list, then continuing with the rest of the list, but accomplishes this task efficiently by using a data structure called a heap, a special type of binary tree. Once the data list has been made into a heap, the root node is guaranteed to be the largest (or smallest) element. When it is removed and placed at the end of the list, the heap is rearranged so the largest element remaining moves to the root. Using the heap, finding the next largest element takes $O(\log n)$ time, instead of $O(n)$ for a linear scan as in simple selection sort. This allows Heapsort to run in $O(n \log n)$ time, and this is also the worst case complexity.

Quicksort

Quicksort is a divide and conquer algorithm which relies on a *partition* operation: to partition an array an element called a *pivot* is selected. All elements smaller than the pivot are moved before it and all greater elements are moved after it. This can be done efficiently in linear time and in-place. The lesser and greater sublists are then recursively sorted. This yields average time complexity of $O(n \log n)$, with low overhead, and thus this is a popular algorithm. Efficient implementations of quicksort (with in-place partitioning) are typically unstable sorts and somewhat complex, but are among the fastest sorting algorithms in practice. Together with its modest $O(\log n)$ space usage, quicksort is one of the most popular sorting algorithms and is available in many standard programming libraries.

The important caveat about quicksort is that its worst-case performance is O(n^2); while this is rare, in naive implementations (choosing the first or last element as pivot) this occurs for sorted data, which is a common case. The most complex issue in quicksort is thus choosing a good pivot element, as consistently poor choices of pivots can result in drastically slower O(n^2) performance, but good choice of pivots yields O($n \log n$) performance, which is asymptotically optimal. For example, if at each step the median is chosen as the pivot then the algorithm works in O($n \log n$). Finding the median, such as by the median of medians selection algorithm is however an O(n) operation on unsorted lists and therefore exacts significant overhead with sorting. In practice choosing a random pivot almost certainly yields O($n \log n$) performance.

Bubble Sort and Variants

Bubble sort, and variants such as the cocktail sort, are simple but highly inefficient sorts. They are thus frequently seen in introductory texts, and are of some theoretical interest due to ease of analysis, but they are rarely used in practice, and primarily of recreational interest. Some variants, such as the Shell sort, have open questions about their behavior.

Bubble Sort

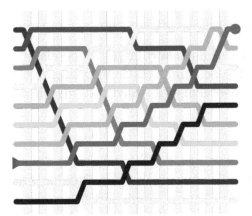

A bubble sort, a sorting algorithm that continuously steps through a list, swapping items until they appear in the correct order.

Bubble sort is a simple sorting algorithm. The algorithm starts at the beginning of the data set. It compares the first two elements, and if the first is greater than the second, it swaps them. It continues doing this for each pair of adjacent elements to the end of the data set. It then starts again with the first two elements, repeating until no swaps have occurred on the last pass. This algorithm's average time and worst-case performance is O(n^2), so it is rarely used to sort large, unordered data sets. Bubble sort can be used to sort a small number of items (where its asymptotic inefficiency is not a high penalty). Bubble sort can also be used efficiently on a list of any length that is nearly sorted (that is, the elements are not significantly out of place). For example, if any number of elements are out of place by only one position (e.g. 0123546789 and 1032547698), bubble sort's exchange will get them in order on the first pass, the second pass will find all elements in order, so the sort will take only 2n time.

Shellsort

Shellsort was invented by Donald Shell in 1959. It improves upon bubble sort and insertion sort by moving out of order elements more than one position at a time. The concept behind Shellsort is that both of these algorithms perform in O(kn) time, where k is the greatest distance between two out-of-place elements. This means that generally, they perform in O(n^2), but for data that is mostly sorted, with only a few elements out of place, they perform faster. So, by first sorting elements far away, and progressively shrinking the gap between the elements to sort, the final sort computes much faster. One implementation can be described as arranging the data sequence in a two-dimensional array and then sorting the columns of the array using insertion sort.

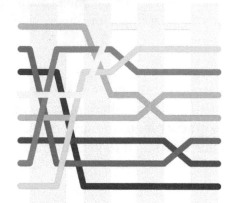

A Shell sort, different from bubble sort in that it moves elements to numerous swapping positions.

The worst-case time complexity of Shell sort largely depends on the gap sequence used, and can range from O(n^2) to O($n \log^2 n$). Also, unlike efficient sorting algorithms, Shellsort does not require use of the call stack, making it useful in embedded systems where memory is at a premium.

Comb Sort

Comb sort is a relatively simple sorting algorithm originally designed by Wlodzimierz Dobosiewicz in 1980. It was later rediscovered and popularized by Stephen Lacey and Richard Box with a *Byte* Magazine article published in April 1991. Comb sort improves on bubble sort. The basic idea is to eliminate *turtles*, or small values near the end of the list, since in a bubble sort these slow the sorting down tremendously. (*Rabbits*, large values around the beginning of the list, do not pose a problem in bubble sort)

Distribution Sort

Distribution sort refers to any sorting algorithm where data are distributed from their input to multiple intermediate structures which are then gathered and placed on the output. For example, both bucket sort and flashsort are distribution based sorting algorithms. Distribution sorting algorithms can be used on a single processor, or they can be a distributed algorithm, where individual subsets are separately sorted on different processors, then combined. This allows external sorting of data too large to fit into a single computer's memory.

Counting Sort

Counting sort is applicable when each input is known to belong to a particular set, S, of possibilities. The algorithm runs in O($|S| + n$) time and O($|S|$) memory where n is the length of the input.

It works by creating an integer array of size $|S|$ and using the ith bin to count the occurrences of the ith member of S in the input. Each input is then counted by incrementing the value of its corresponding bin. Afterward, the counting array is looped through to arrange all of the inputs in order. This sorting algorithm often cannot be used because S needs to be reasonably small for the algorithm to be efficient, but it is extremely fast and demonstrates great asymptotic behavior as n increases. It also can be modified to provide stable behavior.

Bucket Sort

Bucket sort is a divide and conquer sorting algorithm that generalizes counting sort by partitioning an array into a finite number of buckets. Each bucket is then sorted individually, either using a different sorting algorithm, or by recursively applying the bucket sorting algorithm.

A bucket sort works best when the elements of the data set are evenly distributed across all buckets.

Radix Sort

Radix sort is an algorithm that sorts numbers by processing individual digits. n numbers consisting of k digits each are sorted in $O(n \cdot k)$ time. Radix sort can process digits of each number either starting from the least significant digit (LSD) or starting from the most significant digit (MSD). The LSD algorithm first sorts the list by the least significant digit while preserving their relative order using a stable sort. Then it sorts them by the next digit, and so on from the least significant to the most significant, ending up with a sorted list. While the LSD radix sort requires the use of a stable sort, the MSD radix sort algorithm does not (unless stable sorting is desired). In-place MSD radix sort is not stable. It is common for the counting sort algorithm to be used internally by the radix sort. A hybrid sorting approach, such as using insertion sort for small bins improves performance of radix sort significantly.

Memory usage Patterns and Index Sorting

When the size of the array to be sorted approaches or exceeds the available primary memory, so that (much slower) disk or swap space must be employed, the memory usage pattern of a sorting algorithm becomes important, and an algorithm that might have been fairly efficient when the array fit easily in RAM may become impractical. In this scenario, the total number of comparisons becomes (relatively) less important, and the number of times sections of memory must be copied or swapped to and from the disk can dominate the performance characteristics of an algorithm. Thus, the number of passes and the localization of comparisons can be more important than the raw number of comparisons, since comparisons of nearby elements to one another happen at system bus speed (or, with caching, even at CPU speed), which, compared to disk speed, is virtually instantaneous.

For example, the popular recursive quicksort algorithm provides quite reasonable performance with adequate RAM, but due to the recursive way that it copies portions of the array it becomes much less practical when the array does not fit in RAM, because it may cause a number of slow copy or move operations to and from disk. In that scenario, another algorithm may be preferable even if it requires more total comparisons.

One way to work around this problem, which works well when complex records (such as in a relational database) are being sorted by a relatively small key field, is to create an index into the array and then sort the index, rather than the entire array. (A sorted version of the entire array can then be produced with one pass, reading from the index, but often even that is unnecessary, as having the sorted index is adequate.) Because the index is much smaller than the entire array, it may fit easily in memory where the entire array would not, effectively eliminating the disk-swapping problem. This procedure is sometimes called "tag sort".

Another technique for overcoming the memory-size problem is using external sorting, for example one of the ways is to combine two algorithms in a way that takes advantage of the strength of each to improve overall performance. For instance, the array might be subdivided into chunks of a size that will fit in RAM, the contents of each chunk sorted using an efficient algorithm (such as quicksort), and the results merged using a k-way merge similar to that used in mergesort. This is faster than performing either mergesort or quicksort over the entire list.

Techniques can also be combined. For sorting very large sets of data that vastly exceed system memory, even the index may need to be sorted using an algorithm or combination of algorithms designed to perform reasonably with virtual memory, i.e., to reduce the amount of swapping required.

Related Algorithms

Related problems include partial sorting (sorting only the k smallest elements of a list, or alternatively computing the k smallest elements, but unordered) and selection (computing the kth smallest element). These can be solved inefficiently by a total sort, but more efficient algorithms exist, often derived by generalizing a sorting algorithm. The most notable example is quickselect, which is related to quicksort. Conversely, some sorting algorithms can be derived by repeated application of a selection algorithm; quicksort and quickselect can be seen as the same pivoting move, differing only in whether one recurses on both sides (quicksort, divide and conquer) or one side (quickselect, decrease and conquer).

A kind of opposite of a sorting algorithm is a shuffling algorithm. These are fundamentally different because they require a source of random numbers. Interestingly, shuffling can also be implemented by a sorting algorithm, namely by a random sort: assigning a random number to each element of the list and then sorting based on the random numbers. This is generally not done in practice, however, and there is a well-known simple and efficient algorithm for shuffling: the Fisher–Yates shuffle.

Sorting algorithms are also given for parallel computers. These algorithms can all be run on a single instruction stream multiple data stream computer. Habermann's parallel neighbor-sort (or the glory of the induction principle) sorts k elements using k processors in k steps. This article introduces Optimal Algorithms for Paraller Computers where rk elements can be sorted using k processors in k steps.

Dspace

In computational complexity theory, DSPACE or SPACE is the computational resource describing the resource of memory space for a deterministic Turing machine. It represents the total amount of memory space that a "normal" physical computer would need to solve a given computational problem with a given algorithm. It is one of the most well-studied complexity measures, because it corresponds so closely to an important real-world resource: the amount of physical computer memory needed to run a given program.

Complexity Classes

The measure DSPACE is used to define complexity classes, sets of all of the decision problems that can be solved using a certain amount of memory space. For each function $f(n)$, there is a complexity class SPACE($f(n)$), the set of decision problems that can be solved by a deterministic Turing machine using space $O(f(n))$. There is no restriction on the amount of computation time that can be used, though there may be restrictions on some other complexity measures (like alternation).

Several important complexity classes are defined in terms of DSPACE. These include:

- REG = DSPACE($O(1)$), where REG is the class of regular languages. In fact, REG = DSPACE($o(\log \log n)$) (that is, $\Omega(\log \log n)$ space is required to recognize any non-regular language).

Proof: Suppose that there exists a non-regular language $L \in$ DSPACE($s(n)$), for $s(n) = o(\log \log n)$. Let M be a Turing machine deciding L in space $s(n)$. By our assumption $L \notin$ DSPACE($O(1)$); thus, for any arbitrary $k \in \mathbb{N}$, there exists an input of M requiring more space than k.

Let x be an input of smallest size, denoted by n, that requires more space than k, and $\mathcal{C}$ be the set of all configurations of M on input x. Because $M \in$ DSPACE($s(n)$), then $|\mathcal{C}| \leq 2^{c.s(n)} = o(\log n)$, where c is a constant depending on M.

Let S denote the set of all possible crossing sequences of M on x. Note that the length of a crossing sequence of M on x is at most $|\mathcal{C}|$: if it is longer than that, then some configuration will repeat, and M will go into an infinite loop. There are also at most $|\mathcal{C}|$ possibilities for every element of a crossing sequence, so the number of different crossing sequences of M on x is

$$|S| \leq |\mathcal{C}|^{|\mathcal{C}|} \leq (2^{c.s(n)})^{2^{c.s(n)}} = 2^{c.s(n).2^{c.s(n)}} < 2^{2^{2c.s(n)}} = 2^{2^{o(\log \log n)}} = o(n)$$

According to pigeonhole principle, there exist indexes $i < j$ such that $C_i(x) = C_j(x)$, where $C_i(x)$ and $C_j(x)$ are the crossing sequences at boundary i and j, respectively.

Let x' be the string obtained from x by removing all cells from $i + 1$ to j. The machine M still behaves exactly the same way on input x' as on input x, so it needs the same space to compute x' as to compute x. However, $|x'| < |x|$, contradicting the definition of x. Hence, there does not exist such a language L as assumed.

The above theorem implies the necessity of the space-constructible function assumption in the space hierarchy theorem.

- L = DSPACE($O(\log n)$)

- PSPACE = $\bigcup_{k \in \mathbb{N}}$ DSPACE(n^k),

- EXPSPACE = $\bigcup_{k \in \mathbb{N}}$ DSPACE(2^{n^k})

Machine Models

DSPACE is traditionally measured on a deterministic Turing machine. Several important space complexity classes are sublinear, that is, smaller than the size of the input. Thus, "charging" the algorithm for the size of the input, or for the size of the output, would not truly capture the memory space used. This is solved by defining the multi-string Turing machine with input and output, which is a standard multi-tape Turing machine, except that the input tape may never be written-to, and the output tape may never be read from. This allows smaller space classes, such as L (logarithmic space), to be defined in terms of the amount of space used by all of the work tapes (excluding the special input and output tapes).

Since many symbols might be packed into one by taking a suitable power of the alphabet, for all $c \geq 1$ and f such that $f(n) \geq 1$, the class of languages recognizable in $c\,f(n)$ space is the same as the class of languages recognizable in $f(n)$ space. This justifies usage of big O notation in the definition.

Hierarchy Theorem

The space hierarchy theorem shows that, for every space-constructible function $f : \mathbb{N} \to \mathbb{N}$, there exists some language L which is decidable in space $O(f(n))$ but not in space $o(f(n))$.

Relation with other Complexity Classes

DSPACE is the deterministic counterpart of NSPACE, the class of memory space on a nondeterministic Turing machine. By Savitch's theorem, we have that

$$\text{DSPACE}[s(n)] \subseteq \text{NSPACE}[s(n)] \subseteq \text{DSPACE}[(s(n))^2].$$

NTIME is related to DSPACE in the following way. For any time constructible function $t(n)$, we have

$$\text{NTIME}(t(n)) \subseteq \text{DSPACE}(t(n)).$$

Time Complexity

In computer science, the time complexity of an algorithm quantifies the amount of time taken by an algorithm to run as a function of the length of the string representing the input.[226] The time complexity of an algorithm is commonly expressed using big O notation, which excludes coefficients and lower order terms. When expressed this way, the time complexity is said to be described *asymptotically*, i.e., as the input size goes to infinity. For example, if the time required by an algorithm on all inputs of size n is at most $5n^3 + 3n$ for any n (bigger than some n_o), the asymptotic time complexity is $O(n^3)$.

Time complexity is commonly estimated by counting the number of elementary operations performed by the algorithm, where an elementary operation takes a fixed amount of time to perform. Thus, the amount of time taken and the number of elementary operations performed by the algorithm differ by at most a constant factor.

Since an algorithm's performance time may vary with different inputs of the same size, one commonly uses the worst-case time complexity of an algorithm, denoted as $T(n)$, which is defined as the maximum amount of time taken on any input of size n. Less common, and usually specified explicitly, is the measure of average-case complexity. Time complexities are classified by the nature of the function $T(n)$. For instance, an algorithm with $T(n) = O(n)$ is called a *linear time algorithm*, and an algorithm with $\log T(n) = \Omega(n^\alpha)$ for some constant $\alpha \geq 1$ 1is said to be an *exponential time algorithm*.

Table of Common Time Complexities

The following table summarizes some classes of commonly encountered time complexities. In the table, $\text{poly}(x) = x^{O(1)}$, i.e., polynomial in x.

Name	Complexity class	Running time ($T(n)$)	Examples of running times	Example algorithms
constant time		$O(1)$	10	Determining if an integer (represented in binary) is even or odd
inverse Ackermann time		$O(\alpha(n))$		Amortized time per operation using a disjoint set
iterated logarithmic time		$O(\log^* n)$		Distributed coloring of cycles
log-logarithmic		$O(\log \log n)$		Amortized time per operation using a bounded priority queue
logarithmic time	DLOGTIME	$O(\log n)$	$\log n, \log(n^2)$	Binary search
polylogarithmic time		$\text{poly}(\log n)$	$(\log n)^2$	
fractional power		$O(n^c)$ where $0 < c < 1$	$n^{1/2}, n^{2/3}$	Searching in a kd-tree
linear time		$O(n)$	n	Finding the smallest or largest item in an unsorted array
"n log star n" time		$O(n \log^* n)$		Seidel's polygon triangulation algorithm.
quasilinear time		$O(n \log n)$	$n \log n, \log n!$	Fastest possible comparison sort; Fast Fourier transform.
quadratic time		$O(n^2)$	n^2	Bubble sort; Insertion sort; Direct convolution
cubic time		$O(n^3)$	n^3	Naive multiplication of two $n \times n$ matrices. Calculating partial correlation.
polynomial time	P	$2^{O(\log n)} = \text{poly}(n)$	$n, n \log n, n^{10}$	Karmarkar's algorithm for linear programming; AKS primality test
quasi-polynomial time	QP	$2^{\text{poly}(\log n)}$	$n^{\log \log n}, n^{\log n}$	Best-known $O(\log^2 n)$-approximation algorithm for the directed Steiner tree problem.
sub-exponential time (first definition)	SUBEXP	$O(2^{n\varepsilon})$ for all $\varepsilon > 0$	$O(2^{\log n \log \log n})$	Assuming complexity theoretic conjectures, BPP is contained in SUBEXP.
sub-exponential time (second definition)		$2^{o(n)}$	$2^{n1/3}$	Best-known algorithm for integer factorization and graph isomorphism

exponential time (with linear exponent)	E	$2^{O(n)}$	1.1^n, 10^n	Solving the traveling salesman problem using dynamic programming
exponential time	EXPTIME	$2^{\text{poly}(n)}$	2^n, 2^{n^2}	Solving matrix chain multiplication via brute-force search
factorial time		$O(n!)$	$n!$	Solving the traveling salesman problem via brute-force search
double exponential time	2-EXPTIME	$2^{2^{\text{poly}(n)}}$	2^{2^n}	Deciding the truth of a given statement in Presburger arithmetic

Constant Time

An algorithm is said to be constant time (also written as O(1) time) if the value of $T(n)$ is bounded by a value that does not depend on the size of the input. For example, accessing any single element in an array takes constant time as only one operation has to be performed to locate it. However, finding the minimal value in an unordered array is not a constant time operation as a scan over each element in the array is needed in order to determine the minimal value. Hence it is a linear time operation, taking O(n) time. If the number of elements is known in advance and does not change, however, such an algorithm can still be said to run in constant time.

Despite the name "constant time", the running time does not have to be independent of the problem size, but an upper bound for the running time has to be bounded independently of the problem size. For example, the task "exchange the values of a and b if necessary so that $a \leq b$" is called constant time even though the time may depend on whether or not it is already true that $a \leq b$. However, there is some constant t such that the time required is always *at most t*.

Here are some examples of code fragments that run in constant time:

```
int index = 5;

int item = list[index];

if (condition true) then

  perform some operation that runs in constant time

else

  perform some other operation that runs in constant time

for i = 1 to 100

  for j = 1 to 200

    perform some operation that runs in constant time
```

If $T(n)$ is O(*any constant value*), this is equivalent to and stated in standard notation as $T(n)$ being O(1).

Logarithmic Time

An algorithm is said to take logarithmic time if $T(n) = O(\log n)$. Due to the use of the binary numeral system by computers, the logarithm is frequently base 2 (that is, $\log_2 n$, sometimes written lg

n). However, by the change of base for logarithms, $\log_a n$ and $\log_b n$ differ only by a constant multiplier, which in big-O notation is discarded; thus O(log n) is the standard notation for logarithmic time algorithms regardless of the base of the logarithm.

Algorithms taking logarithmic time are commonly found in operations on binary trees or when using binary search.

An O(log n) algorithm is considered highly efficient, as the operations per instance required to complete decrease with each instance.

A very simple example of this type is an algorithm that cuts a string in half, then cuts the right half in half, and so on. It will take O(log n) time (n being the length of the string) since we chop the string in half before each print (we make the assumption that *console.log* and *str.substring* run in constant time). This means, in order to increase the number of prints, we have to double the length of the string.

```
// Function to recursively print the right half of a string

var right = function(str){

  var length = str.length;

  // Helper function

  var help = function(index){

     // Recursive Case: Print right half

     if(index < length){

        // Prints characters from index until the end of the array

        console.log(str.substring(index, length));

        // Recursive Call: call help on right half

        help(Math.ceil((length + index)/2));

   }
  // Base Case: Do Nothing

  }
 help(0);

}
```

Polylogarithmic Time

An algorithm is said to run in polylogarithmic time if $T(n) = O((\log n)^k)$, for some constant k. For example, matrix chain ordering can be solved in polylogarithmic time on a Parallel Random Access Machine.

Sub-linear Time

An algorithm is said to run in sub-linear time (often spelled sublinear time) if $T(n) = o(n)$. In particular this includes algorithms with the time complexities defined above, as well as others such as the $O(n^{1/2})$ Grover's search algorithm.

Typical algorithms that are exact and yet run in sub-linear time use parallel processing (as the NC_1 matrix determinant calculation does), non-classical processing (as Grover's search does), or alternatively have guaranteed assumptions on the input structure (as the logarithmic time binary search and many tree maintenance algorithms do). However, formal languages such as the set of all strings that have a 1-bit in the position indicated by the first log(n) bits of the string may depend on every bit of the input and yet be computable in sub-linear time.

The specific term *sublinear time algorithm* is usually reserved to algorithms that are unlike the above in that they are run over classical serial machine models and are not allowed prior assumptions on the input. They are however allowed to be randomized, and indeed must be randomized for all but the most trivial of tasks.

As such an algorithm must provide an answer without reading the entire input, its particulars heavily depend on the access allowed to the input. Usually for an input that is represented as a binary string $b_1,...,b_k$ it is assumed that the algorithm can in time $O(1)$ request and obtain the value of b_i for any i.

Sub-linear time algorithms are typically randomized, and provide only approximate solutions. In fact, the property of a binary string having only zeros (and no ones) can be easily proved not to be decidable by a (non-approximate) sub-linear time algorithm. Sub-linear time algorithms arise naturally in the investigation of property testing.

Linear Time

An algorithm is said to take linear time, or $O(n)$ time, if its time complexity is $O(n)$. Informally, this means that for large enough input sizes the running time increases linearly with the size of the input. For example, a procedure that adds up all elements of a list requires time proportional to the length of the list. This description is slightly inaccurate, since the running time can significantly deviate from a precise proportionality, especially for small values of n.

Linear time is the best possible time complexity in situations where the algorithm has to sequentially read its entire input. Therefore, much research has been invested into discovering algorithms exhibiting linear time or, at least, nearly linear time. This research includes both software and hardware methods. In the case of hardware, some algorithms which, mathematically speaking, can never achieve linear time with standard computation models are able to run in linear time. There are several hardware technologies which exploit parallelism to provide this. An example is content-addressable memory. This concept of linear time is used in string matching algorithms such as the Boyer-Moore Algorithm and Ukkonen's Algorithm.

Quasilinear Time

An algorithm is said to run in quasilinear time if $T(n) = O(n \log^k n)$ for some positive constant k; linearithmic time is the case $k = 1$. Using soft-O notation these algorithms are $\tilde{O}(n)$. Quasilinear time algorithms are also $O(n^{1+\varepsilon})$ for every $\varepsilon > 0$, and thus run faster than any polynomial in n with exponent strictly greater than 1.

Algorithms which run in quasilinear time include:

- In-place merge sort, O($n \log^2 n$).

- Quicksort, O($n \log n$), in its randomized version, has a running time that is O($n \log n$) linearithmic in expectation on the worst-case input. Its non-randomized version has a O($n \log n$) linearithmic running time only when considering average case complexity.

- Heapsort, O($n \log n$), merge sort, introsort, binary tree sort, smoothsort, patience sorting, etc. in the worst case.

- Fast Fourier transforms, O($n \log n$).

- Monge array calculation, O($n \log n$).

Linearithmic Time

Linearithmic time is a special case of quasilinear time where the exponent k equals one on the logarithmic term.

A linearithmic function is a function of the form $n \cdot \log n$ (i.e., a product of a linear and a logarithmic term). An algorithm is said to run in linearithmic time if $T(n) = O(n \log n)$. Thus, a linearithmic term grows faster than a linear term but slower than any polynomial in n with degree greater than 1.

In many cases, the $n \cdot \log n$ running time is simply the result of performing a $\Theta(\log n)$ operation n times. For example, binary tree sort creates a binary tree by inserting each element of the n-sized array one by one. Since the insert operation on a self-balancing binary search tree takes $O(\log n)$ time, the entire algorithm takes linearithmic time.

Comparison sorts require at least linearithmic number of comparisons in the worst case because $\log(n!) = \Theta(n \log n)$, by Stirling's approximation. They also frequently arise from the recurrence relation $T(n) = 2T(n/2) + O(n)$.

Sub-quadratic Time

An algorithm is said to be subquadratic time if $T(n) = o(n^2)$.

For example, simple, comparison-based sorting algorithms are quadratic (e.g. insertion sort), but more advanced algorithms can be found that are subquadratic (e.g. Shell sort). No general-purpose sorts run in linear time, but the change from quadratic to sub-quadratic is of great practical importance.

Polynomial Time

An algorithm is said to be of polynomial time if its running time is upper bounded by a polynomial expression in the size of the input for the algorithm, i.e., $T(n) = O(n^k)$ for some constant k. Problems for which a deterministic polynomial time algorithm exists belong to the complexity class P, which is central in the field of computational complexity theory. Cobham's thesis states that polynomial time is a synonym for "tractable", "feasible", "efficient", or "fast".

Some examples of polynomial time algorithms:

- The selection sort sorting algorithm on n integers performs An^2 operations for some constant A. Thus it runs in time $O(n^2)$ and is a polynomial time algorithm.

- All the basic arithmetic operations (addition, subtraction, multiplication, division, and comparison) can be done in polynomial time.

- Maximum matchings in graphs can be found in polynomial time.

Strongly and Weakly Polynomial Time

In some contexts, especially in optimization, one differentiates between strongly polynomial time and weakly polynomial time algorithms. These two concepts are only relevant if the inputs to the algorithms consist of integers.

Strongly polynomial time is defined in the arithmetic model of computation. In this model of computation the basic arithmetic operations (addition, subtraction, multiplication, division, and comparison) take a unit time step to perform, regardless of the sizes of the operands. The algorithm runs in strongly polynomial time if

1. the number of operations in the arithmetic model of computation is bounded by a polynomial in the number of integers in the input instance; and

2. the space used by the algorithm is bounded by a polynomial in the size of the input.

Any algorithm with these two properties can be converted to a polynomial time algorithm by replacing the arithmetic operations by suitable algorithms for performing the arithmetic operations on a Turing machine. If the second of the above requirement is not met, then this is not true anymore. Given the integer 2^n (which takes up space proportional to n in the Turing machine model), it is possible to compute 2^{2^n} with n multiplications using repeated squaring. However, the space used to represent 2^{2^n} is proportional to 2^n, and thus exponential rather than polynomial in the space used to represent the input. Hence, it is not possible to carry out this computation in polynomial time on a Turing machine, but it is possible to compute it by polynomially many arithmetic operations.

Conversely, there are algorithms which run in a number of Turing machine steps bounded by a polynomial in the length of binary-encoded input, but do not take a number of arithmetic operations bounded by a polynomial in the number of input numbers. The Euclidean algorithm for computing the greatest common divisor of two integers is one example. Given two integers a and b the running time of the algorithm is bounded by $O((\log a + \log b)^2)$ Turing machine steps. This is polynomial in the size of a binary representation of a and b as the size of such a representation is roughly $\log a + \log b$. At the same time, the number of arithmetic operations cannot be bound by the number of integers in the input (which is constant in this case, there are always only two integers in the input). Due to the latter observation, the algorithm does not run in strongly polynomial time. Its real running time depends on the magnitudes of a and b and not only on the number of integers in the input.

An algorithm which runs in polynomial time but which is not strongly polynomial is said to run in weakly polynomial time. A well-known example of a problem for which a weakly polynomial-time algorithm is known, but is not known to admit a strongly polynomial-time algorithm, is linear programming. Weakly polynomial-time should not be confused with pseudo-polynomial time.

Complexity Classes

The concept of polynomial time leads to several complexity classes in computational complexity theory. Some important classes defined using polynomial time are the following.

- P: The complexity class of decision problems that can be solved on a deterministic Turing machine in polynomial time.

- NP: The complexity class of decision problems that can be solved on a non-deterministic Turing machine in polynomial time.

- ZPP: The complexity class of decision problems that can be solved with zero error on a probabilistic Turing machine in polynomial time.

- RP: The complexity class of decision problems that can be solved with 1-sided error on a probabilistic Turing machine in polynomial time.

- BPP: The complexity class of decision problems that can be solved with 2-sided error on a probabilistic Turing machine in polynomial time.

- BQP: The complexity class of decision problems that can be solved with 2-sided error on a quantum Turing machine in polynomial time.

P is the smallest time-complexity class on a deterministic machine which is robust in terms of machine model changes. (For example, a change from a single-tape Turing machine to a multi-tape machine can lead to a quadratic speedup, but any algorithm that runs in polynomial time under one model also does so on the other.) Any given abstract machine will have a complexity class corresponding to the problems which can be solved in polynomial time on that machine.

Superpolynomial Time

An algorithm is said to take superpolynomial time if $T(n)$ is not bounded above by any polynomial. It is $\omega(n^c)$ time for all constants c, where n is the input parameter, typically the number of bits in the input.

For example, an algorithm that runs for 2^n steps on an input of size n requires superpolynomial time (more specifically, exponential time).

An algorithm that uses exponential resources is clearly superpolynomial, but some algorithms are only very weakly superpolynomial. For example, the Adleman–Pomerance–Rumely primality test runs for $n^{O(\log \log n)}$ time on n-bit inputs; this grows faster than any polynomial for large enough n, but the input size must become impractically large before it cannot be dominated by a polynomial with small degree.

An algorithm that requires superpolynomial time lies outside the complexity class P. Cobham's thesis posits that these algorithms are impractical, and in many cases they are. Since the P versus NP problem is unresolved, no algorithm for an NP-complete problem is currently known to run in polynomial time.

Quasi-polynomial Time

Quasi-polynomial time algorithms are algorithms that run slower than polynomial time, yet not so slow as to be exponential time. The worst case running time of a quasi-polynomial time algorithm is $2^{O((\log n)^c)}$ for some fixed $c > 0$. If the constant "c" in the definition of quasi-polynomial time algorithms is equal to 1, we get a polynomial time algorithm, and if it is less than 1, we get a sub-linear time algorithm.

Quasi-polynomial time algorithms typically arise in reductions from an NP-hard problem to another problem. For example, one can take an instance of an NP hard problem, say 3SAT, and convert it to an instance of another problem B, but the size of the instance becomes $2^{O((\log n)^c)}$. In that case, this reduction does not prove that problem B is NP-hard; this reduction only shows that there is no polynomial time algorithm for B unless there is a quasi-polynomial time algorithm for 3SAT (and thus all of NP). Similarly, there are some problems for which we know quasi-polynomial time algorithms, but no polynomial time algorithm is known. Such problems arise in approximation algorithms; a famous example is the directed Steiner tree problem, for which there is a quasi-polynomial time approximation algorithm achieving an approximation factor of $O(\log^3 n)$ (n being the number of vertices), but showing the existence of such a polynomial time algorithm is an open problem.

Other computational problems with quasi-polynomial time solutions but no known polynomial time solution include the planted clique problem in which the goal is to find a large clique in the union of a clique and a random graph. Although quasi-polynomially solvable, it has been conjectured that the planted clique problem has no polynomial time solution; this planted clique conjecture has been used as a computational hardness assumption to prove the difficulty of several other problems in computational game theory, property testing, and machine learning.

The complexity class QP consists of all problems that have quasi-polynomial time algorithms. It can be defined in terms of DTIME as follows.

$$QP = \bigcup_{c \in \mathbb{N}} DTIME(2^{(\log n)^c})$$

Relation to NP-complete Problems

In complexity theory, the unsolved P versus NP problem asks if all problems in NP have polynomial-time algorithms. All the best-known algorithms for NP-complete problems like 3SAT etc. take exponential time. Indeed, it is conjectured for many natural NP-complete problems that they do not have sub-exponential time algorithms. Here "sub-exponential time" is taken to mean the second definition presented below. (On the other hand, many graph problems represented in the natural way by adjacency matrices are solvable in subexponential time simply because the size of the input is square of the number of vertices.) This conjecture (for the k-SAT problem) is known as the exponential time hypothesis. Since it is conjectured that NP-complete problems do not have quasi-polynomial time algorithms, some inapproximability results in the field of approximation algorithms make the assumption that NP-complete problems do not have quasi-polynomial time algorithms.

Sub-exponential Time

The term sub-exponential time is used to express that the running time of some algorithm may grow faster than any polynomial but is still significantly smaller than an exponential. In this sense, problems that have sub-exponential time algorithms are somewhat more tractable than those that only have exponential algorithms. The precise definition of "sub-exponential" is not generally agreed upon, and we list the two most widely used ones below.

First Definition

A problem is said to be sub-exponential time solvable if it can be solved in running times whose logarithms grow smaller than any given polynomial. More precisely, a problem is in sub-exponential time if for every $\varepsilon > 0$ there exists an algorithm which solves the problem in time $O(2^{n^{\varepsilon}})$. The set of all such problems is the complexity class SUBEXP which can be defined in terms of DTIME as follows.

$$SUBEXP = \bigcap_{\varepsilon > 0} DTIME\left(2^{n^{\varepsilon}}\right)$$

Note that this notion of sub-exponential is non-uniform in terms of ε in the sense that ε is not part of the input and each ε may have its own algorithm for the problem.

Second Definition

Some authors define sub-exponential time as running times in $2^{o(n)}$. This definition allows larger running times than the first definition of sub-exponential time. An example of such a sub-exponential time algorithm is the best-known classical algorithm for integer factorization, the general number field sieve, which runs in time about $2^{\tilde{O}(n^{1/3})}$, where the length of the input is n. Another example is the best-known algorithm for the graph isomorphism problem, which runs in time $2^{O(\sqrt{n \log n})}$.

Note that it makes a difference whether the algorithm is allowed to be sub-exponential in the size of the instance, the number of vertices, or the number of edges. In parameterized complexity, this difference is made explicit by considering pairs (L, k) of decision problems and parameters k. SUBEPT is the class of all parameterized problems that run in time sub-exponential in k and polynomial in the input size n:

$$SUBEPT = DTIME\left(2^{o(k)} \cdot poly(n)\right).$$

More precisely, SUBEPT is the class of all parameterized problems (L, k) for which there is a computable function $f : \mathbb{N} \to \mathbb{N}$ with $f \in o(k)$ and an algorithm that decides L in time .

Exponential Time Hypothesis

The exponential time hypothesis (ETH) is that 3SAT, the satisfiability problem of Boolean formulas in conjunctive normal form with at most three literals per clause and with n variables, cannot be solved in time $2^{o(n)}$. More precisely, the hypothesis is that there is some absolute constant $c>0$ such that 3SAT cannot be decided in time 2^{cn} by any deterministic Turing machine. With m denoting the number of clauses, ETH is equivalent to the hypothesis that kSAT cannot be solved in time $2^{o(m)}$ for any integer $k \geq 3$. The exponential time hypothesis implies P $\neq$ NP.

Exponential Time

An algorithm is said to be exponential time, if $T(n)$ is upper bounded by $2^{\text{poly}(n)}$, where poly(n) is some polynomial in n. More formally, an algorithm is exponential time if $T(n)$ is bounded by $O(2^{n^k})$ for some constant k. Problems which admit exponential time algorithms on a deterministic Turing machine form the complexity class known as EXP.

$$\text{EXP} = \bigcup_{c\in\mathbb{N}} \text{DTIME}\left(2^{n^c}\right)$$

Sometimes, exponential time is used to refer to algorithms that have $T(n) = 2^{O(n)}$, where the exponent is at most a linear function of n. This gives rise to the complexity class E.

$$\text{E} = \bigcup_{c\in\mathbb{N}} \text{DTIME}\left(2^{cn}\right)$$

Double Exponential Time

An algorithm is said to be double exponential time if $T(n)$ is upper bounded by $2^{2^{\text{poly}(n)}}$, where poly(n) is some polynomial in n. Such algorithms belong to the complexity class 2-EXPTIME.

$$\text{2-EXPTIME} = \bigcup_{c\in\mathbb{N}} \text{DTIME}\left(2^{2^{n^c}}\right)$$

Well-known double exponential time algorithms include:

- Decision procedures for Presburger arithmetic

- Computing a Gröbner basis (in the worst case)

- Quantifier elimination on real closed fields takes at least double exponential time, and can be done in this time.

- Execution time of an algorithm depends on numbers of instruction executed.

- Consider the following algorithm fragment:

```
for i = 1 to n do

sum = sum + i ;
```

- The for loop executed n+1 times for i values 1,2,……. n, n+1. Each instruction in the body of the loop is executed once for each value of i = 1,2,……, n. So number of steps executed is

2n+1.

- Consider another algorithm fragment:

```
for i = 1 to n do
for j = 1 to n do
k = k +1
```

- From prevoius example, number of instruction executed in the inner loop is $2n+1$ which is the body of outer loop.

- Total number of instruction executed is

$$= n+1+n(2n+1)$$
$$= 2n^2 + 2n + 1$$

- To measure the time complexity in absolute time unit has the following problems

    1. The time required for an algorithm depends on number of instructions executed, which is a complex polynomial.

    2. The execution time of an instruction depends on computer's power. Since, different computers take different amount of time for the same instruction.

    3. Different types of instructions take different amount of time on same computer.

- Complexity analysis technique abstracts away these machine dependent factors . In this approach, we assume all instruction takes constant amount of time for execution.

- Asymptotic bounds as polynomials are used as a measure of the estimation of the number of instructions to be executed by the algorithm . Three main types of asymptotic order notations are used in practice:

1. Θ - notation : For a given function g(n), $\theta(g(n))$ is defined as

$$\theta(g(n)) = \left\{ \begin{array}{l} f(n) : there\ exist\ c_1 > 0, c_2 > 0\ and\ n_0 \in N \\ such\ that\ 0 \le c_1 g(n) \le f(n) \le c_2 g(n), for\ all\ n \ge n_0 \end{array} \right\}$$

2. O - notation : For a given function g(n), O(g(n)) is defined as

$$O(g(n)) = \left\{ \begin{array}{l} f(n) : there\ exist\ c > 0, n_0 \in N \\ such\ that\ 0 \le f(n) \le cg(n), for\ all\ n \ge n_0 \end{array} \right\}$$

3. Ω - notation: This notation provides asymptotic lower bound. For a given g(n) , $\Omega(g(n))$ is defined as

$$\Omega(g(n)) = \left\{ \begin{array}{l} f(n) : there\ exist\ c > 0, n_0 \in N \\ such\ that\ 0 \le cg(n) \le f(n), for\ all\ n \ge n_0 \end{array} \right\}$$

Recurrence Relation

In mathematics, a recurrence relation is an equation that recursively defines a sequence or multidimensional array of values, once one or more initial terms are given: each further term of the sequence or array is defined as a function of the preceding terms.

The term difference equation sometimes refers to a specific type of recurrence relation. However, "difference equation" is frequently used to refer to *any* recurrence relation.

Examples

Logistic Map

An example of a recurrence relation is the logistic map:

$$x_{n+1} = rx_n(1-x_n),$$

with a given constant r; given the initial term x_0 each subsequent term is determined by this relation.

Some simply defined recurrence relations can have very complex (chaotic) behaviours, and they are a part of the field of mathematics known as nonlinear analysis.

Solving a recurrence relation means obtaining a closed-form solution: a non-recursive function of n.

Fibonacci Numbers

The recurrence satisfied by the Fibonacci numbers is the archetype of a homogeneous linear recurrence relation with constant coefficients. The Fibonacci sequence is defined using the recurrence

$$F_n = F_{n-1} + F_{n-2}$$

with seed values

$$F_0 = 0$$
$$F_1 = 1.$$

Explicitly, the recurrence yields the equations

$$F_2 = F_1 + F_0$$
$$F_3 = F_2 + F_1$$
$$F_4 = F_3 + F_2$$

etc.

We obtain the sequence of Fibonacci numbers, which begins

0, 1, 1, 2, 3, 5, 8, 13, 21, 34, 55, 89, ...

The recurrence can be solved by methods described below yielding Binet's formula, which involves powers of the two roots of the characteristic polynomial $t^2 = t + 1$; the generating function of the sequence is the rational function

$$\frac{t}{1-t-t^2}.$$

Binomial Coefficients

A simple example of a multidimensional recurrence relation is given by the binomial coefficients $\binom{n}{k}$, which count the number of ways of selecting k elements out of a set of n elements. They can be computed by the recurrence relation

$$\binom{n}{k} = \binom{n-1}{k-1} + \binom{n-1}{k},$$

with the base cases $\binom{n}{0} = \binom{n}{n} = 1$. Using this formula to compute the values of all binomial coefficients generates an infinite array called Pascal's triangle. The same values can also be computed directly by a different formula that is not a recurrence, but that requires multiplication and not just addition to compute: $\binom{n}{k} = \frac{n!}{k!(n-k)!}.$

Relationship to difference Equations Narrowly Defined

Given an ordered sequence $\{a_n\}_{n=1}^{\infty}$ of real numbers: the first difference $\Delta(a_n)$ is defined as

$$\Delta(a_n) = a_{n+1} - a_n$$

The second difference $\Delta^2(a_n)$ is defined as

$$\Delta^2(a_n) = \Delta(a_{n+1}) - \Delta(a_n),$$

which can be simplified to

$$\Delta^2(a_n) = a_{n+2} - 2a_{n+1} + a_n$$

More generally: the kth difference of the sequence a_n written as $\Delta^k(a_n)$ is defined recursively as

$$\Delta^k(a_n) = \Delta^{k-1}(a_{n+1}) - \Delta^{k-1}(a_n) = \sum_{t=0}^{k}\binom{k}{t}(-1)^t a_{n+k-t}$$

(The sequence and its differences are related by a binomial transform.) The more restrictive definition of difference equation is an equation composed of a_n and its kth differences. (A widely used broader definition treats "difference equation" as synonymous with "recurrence relation".

Actually, it is easily seen that,

$$a_{n+k} = \binom{k}{0}a_n + \binom{k}{1}\Delta(a_n) + \cdots + \binom{k}{k}\Delta^k(a_n)$$

Thus, a difference equation can be defined as an equation that involves a_n, a_{n-1}, a_{n-2} etc. (or equivalently a_n, a_{n+1}, a_{n+2} etc.)

Since difference equations are a very common form of recurrence, some authors use the two terms interchangeably. For example, the difference equation

$$3\Delta^2(a_n) + 2\Delta(a_n) + 7a_n = 0$$

is equivalent to the recurrence relation

$$3a_{n+2} = 4a_{n+1} - 8a_n$$

Thus one can solve many recurrence relations by rephrasing them as difference equations, and then solving the difference equation, analogously to how one solves ordinary differential equations. However, the Ackermann numbers are an example of a recurrence relation that do not map to a difference equation, much less points on the solution to a differential equation.

Summation equations relate to difference equations as integral equations relate to differential equations.

From Sequences to Grids

Single-variable or one-dimensional recurrence relations are about sequences (i.e. functions defined on one-dimensional grids). Multi-variable or n-dimensional recurrence relations are about n-dimensional grids. Functions defined on n-grids can also be studied with partial difference equations.

Solving Homogeneous Linear Recurrence Relations with Constant Coefficients

Roots of the Characteristic Polynomial

An order-d homogeneous linear recurrence with constant coefficients is an equation of the form

$$a_n = c_1 a_{n-1} + c_2 a_{n-2} + \cdots + c_d a_{n-d},$$

where the d coefficients c_i (for all i) are constants.

A constant-recursive sequence is a sequence satisfying a recurrence of this form. There are d degrees of freedom for solutions to this recurrence, i.e., the initial values $a_0, \ldots, a_{d-1}$ can be taken to be any values but then the recurrence determines the sequence uniquely.

The same coefficients yield the characteristic polynomial (also "auxiliary polynomial")

$$p(t) = t^d - c_1 t^{d-1} - c_2 t^{d-2} - \cdots - c_d$$

whose d roots play a crucial role in finding and understanding the sequences satisfying the recurrence. If the roots r_1, r_2, ... are all distinct, then each solution to the recurrence takes the form

$$a_n = k_1 r_1^n + k_2 r_2^n + \cdots + k_d r_d^n,$$

where the coefficients k_i are determined in order to fit the initial conditions of the recurrence. When the same roots occur multiple times, the terms in this formula corresponding to the second and later occurrences of the same root are multiplied by increasing powers of n. For instance, if the characteristic polynomial can be factored as $(x-r)^3$, with the same root r occurring three times, then the solution would take the form

$$a_n = k_1 r^n + k_2 n r^n + k_3 n^2 r^n.$$

As well as the Fibonacci numbers, other constant-recursive sequences include the Lucas numbers and Lucas sequences, the Jacobsthal numbers, the Pell numbers and more generally the solutions to Pell's equation.

For order 1, the recurrence

$$a_n = r a_{n-1}$$

has the solution $a_n = r^n$ with $a_0 = 1$ and the most general solution is $a_n = k r^n$ with $a_0 = k$. The characteristic polynomial equated to zero (the characteristic equation) is simply $t - r = 0$.

Solutions to such recurrence relations of higher order are found by systematic means, often using the fact that $a_n = r^n$ is a solution for the recurrence exactly when $t = r$ is a root of the characteristic polynomial. This can be approached directly or using generating functions (formal power series) or matrices.

Consider, for example, a recurrence relation of the form

$$a_n = A a_{n-1} + B a_{n-2}.$$

When does it have a solution of the same general form as $a_n = r^n$? Substituting this guess (ansatz) in the recurrence relation, we find that

$$r^n = A r^{n-1} + B r^{n-2}$$

must be true for all $n > 1$.

Dividing through by r^{n-2}, we get that all these equations reduce to the same thing:

$$r^2 = Ar + B,$$

$$r^2 - Ar - B = 0,$$

which is the characteristic equation of the recurrence relation. Solve for r to obtain the two roots λ_1, λ_2: these roots are known as the characteristic roots or eigenvalues of the characteristic equation. Different solutions are obtained depending on the nature of the roots: If these roots are distinct, we have the general solution

$$a_n = C \lambda_1^n + D \lambda_2^n$$

while if they are identical (when $A^2 + 4B = 0$), we have

$$a_n = C\lambda^n + Dn\lambda^n$$

This is the most general solution; the two constants C and D can be chosen based on two given initial conditions a_0 and a_1 to produce a specific solution.

In the case of complex eigenvalues (which also gives rise to complex values for the solution parameters C and D), the use of complex numbers can be eliminated by rewriting the solution in trigonometric form. In this case we can write the eigenvalues as $\lambda_1, \lambda_2 = \alpha \pm \beta i$. Then it can be shown that

$$a_n = C\lambda_1^n + D\lambda_2^n$$

can be rewritten as

$$a_n = 2M^n \left(E\cos(\theta n) + F\sin(\theta n) \right) = 2GM^n \cos(\theta n - \delta),$$

where

$$M = \sqrt{\alpha^2 + \beta^2} \quad \cos(\theta) = \frac{\alpha}{M} \quad \sin(\theta) = \frac{\beta}{M}$$

$$C, D = E \mp Fi$$

$$G = \sqrt{E^2 + F^2} \quad \cos(\delta) = \frac{E}{G} \quad \sin(\delta) = \frac{F}{G}$$

Here E and F (or equivalently, G and δ) are real constants which depend on the initial conditions. Using

$$\lambda_1 + \lambda_2 = 2\alpha = A,$$

$$\lambda_1 \cdot \lambda_2 = \alpha^2 + \beta^2 = -B,$$

one may simplify the solution given above as

$$a_n = (-B)^{\frac{n}{2}} \left(E\cos(\theta n) + F\sin(\theta n) \right),$$

where a_1 and a_2 are the initial conditions and

$$E = \frac{-Aa_1 + a_2}{B}$$

$$F = -i\frac{A^2 a_1 - Aa_2 + 2a_1 B}{B\sqrt{A^2 + 4B}}$$

$$\theta = \arccos\left(\frac{A}{2\sqrt{-B}}\right)$$

In this way there is no need to solve for λ_1 and λ_2.

In all cases—real distinct eigenvalues, real duplicated eigenvalues, and complex conjugate eigen-values—the equation is stable (that is, the variable a converges to a fixed value [specifically, zero]) if and only if *both* eigenvalues are smaller than one in absolute value. In this second-order case, this condition on the eigenvalues can be shown to be equivalent to $|A| < 1 - B < 2$, which is equivalent to $|B| < 1$ and $|A| < 1 - B$.

The equation in the above example was homogeneous, in that there was no constant term. If one starts with the non-homogeneous recurrence

$$b_n = Ab_{n-1} + Bb_{n-2} + K$$

with constant term K, this can be converted into homogeneous form as follows: The steady state is found by setting $b_n = b_{n-1} = b_{n-2} = b^*$ to obtain

$$b^* = \frac{K}{1 - A - B}.$$

Then the non-homogeneous recurrence can be rewritten in homogeneous form as

$$[b_n - b^*] = A[b_{n-1} - b^*] + B[b_{n-2} - b^*],$$

which can be solved as above.

The stability condition stated above in terms of eigenvalues for the second-order case remains valid for the general n^{th}-order case: the equation is stable if and only if all eigenvalues of the characteristic equation are less than one in absolute value.

Given a homogeneous linear recurrence relation with constant coefficients of order d, let $p(t)$ be the characteristic polynomial (also "auxiliary polynomial")

$$t^d - c_1 t^{d-1} - c_2 t^{d-2} - \cdots - c_d = 0$$

such that each c_i corresponds to each c_i in the original recurrence relation. Suppose λ is a root of $p(t)$ having multiplicity r. This is to say that $(t-\lambda)^r$ divides $p(t)$. The following two properties hold:

1. Each of the r sequences $\lambda^n, n\lambda^n, n^2\lambda^n, \ldots, n^{r-1}\lambda^n$ satisfies the recurrence relation.

2. Any sequence satisfying the recurrence relation can be written uniquely as a linear combination of solutions constructed in part 1 as λ varies over all distinct roots of $p(t)$.

As a result of this theorem a homogeneous linear recurrence relation with constant coefficients can be solved in the following manner:

1. Find the characteristic polynomial $p(t)$.

2. Find the roots of $p(t)$ counting multiplicity.

3. Write a_n as a linear combination of all the roots (counting multiplicity as shown in the theorem above) with unknown coefficients b_i.

$$a_n = \left(b_1\lambda_1^n + b_2 n\lambda_1^n + b_3 n^2\lambda_1^n + \cdots + b_r n^{r-1}\lambda_1^n\right) + \cdots + \left(b_{d-q+1}\lambda_*^n + \cdots + b_d n^{q-1}\lambda_*^n\right)$$

This is the general solution to the original recurrence relation. (q is the multiplicity of λ_*.)

4. Equate each $a_0, a_1, \ldots, a_d$ from part 3 (plugging in $n = 0, \ldots, d$ into the general solution of the recurrence relation) with the known values $a_0, a_1, \ldots, a_d$ from the original recurrence relation. However, the values a_n from the original recurrence relation used do not usually have to be contiguous: excluding exceptional cases, just d of them are needed (i.e., for an original homogeneous linear recurrence relation of order 3 one could use the values a_0, a_1, a_4). This process will produce a linear system of d equations with d unknowns. Solving these equations for the unknown coefficients $b_1, b_2, \ldots, b_d$ of the general solution and plugging these values back into the general solution will produce the particular solution to the original recurrence relation that fits the original recurrence relation's initial conditions (as well as all subsequent values $a_0, a_1, a_2, \ldots$ of the original recurrence relation).

The method for solving linear differential equations is similar to the method above—the "intelligent guess" (ansatz) for linear differential equations with constant coefficients is $e^{\lambda x}$ where λ is a complex number that is determined by substituting the guess into the differential equation.

This is not a coincidence. Considering the Taylor series of the solution to a linear differential equation:

$$\sum_{n=0}^{\infty} \frac{f^{(n)}(a)}{n!}(x-a)^n$$

it can be seen that the coefficients of the series are given by the nth derivative of $f(x)$ evaluated at the point a. The differential equation provides a linear difference equation relating these coefficients.

This equivalence can be used to quickly solve for the recurrence relationship for the coefficients in the power series solution of a linear differential equation.

The rule of thumb (for equations in which the polynomial multiplying the first term is non-zero at zero) is that:

$$y^{[k]} \to f[n+k]$$

and more generally

$$x^m * y^{[k]} \to n(n-1)\ldots(n-m+1)f[n+k-m]$$

Example: The recurrence relationship for the Taylor series coefficients of the equation:

$$(x^2+3x-4)y^{[3]} - (3x+1)y^{[2]} + 2y = 0$$

is given by

$$n(n-1)f[n+1]+3nf[n+2]-4f[n+3]-3nf[n+1]-f[n+2]+2f[n]=0$$

or

$$-4f[n+3]+2nf[n+2]+n(n-4)f[n+1]+2f[n]=0.$$

This example shows how problems generally solved using the power series solution method taught in normal differential equation classes can be solved in a much easier way.

Example: The differential equation

$$ay''+by'+cy=0$$

has solution

$$y=e^{ax}.$$

The conversion of the differential equation to a difference equation of the Taylor coefficients is

$$af[n+2]+bf[n+1]+cf[n]=0.$$

It is easy to see that the nth derivative of e^{ax} evaluated at 0 is a^n

Solving Via Linear Algebra

A linearly recursive sequence y of order n

$$y_{n+k}-c_{n-1}y_{n-1+k}-c_{n-2}y_{n-2+k}+\cdots-c_0y_k=0$$

is identical to

$$y_n=c_{n-1}y_{n-1}+c_{n-2}y_{n-2}+\cdots+c_0y_0.$$

Expanded with n-1 identities of kind $y_{n-k}=y_{n-k}$, this n-th order equation is translated into a matrix difference equation system of n first-order linear equations,

$$\vec{y}_n=\begin{bmatrix} y_n \\ y_{n-1} \\ \vdots \\ \vdots \\ y_1 \end{bmatrix}=\begin{bmatrix} c_{n-1} & c_{n-2} & \cdots & \cdots & c_0 \\ 1 & 0 & \cdots & \cdots & 0 \\ 0 & \ddots & \ddots & & \vdots \\ \vdots & \ddots & \ddots & \ddots & \vdots \\ 0 & \cdots & 0 & 1 & 0 \end{bmatrix}\begin{bmatrix} y_{n-1} \\ y_{n-2} \\ \vdots \\ \vdots \\ y_0 \end{bmatrix}=C\,\vec{y}_{n-1}=C^n\vec{y}_0.$$

Observe that the vector $\vec{y}_n$ can be computed by n applications of the companion matrix, C, to the initial state vector, y_0. Thereby, n-th entry of the sought sequence y, is the top component of $\vec{y}_n$, $y_n=\vec{y}_n[n]$.

Eigendecomposition, $\vec{y}_n=C^n\vec{y}_0=c_1\lambda_1^n\vec{e}_1+c_2\lambda_2^n\vec{e}_2+\cdots+c_n\lambda_n^n\vec{e}_n$ into eigenvalues, $\lambda_1,\lambda_2,\ldots,\lambda_n$, and eigenvectors, $\vec{e}_1,\vec{e}_2,\ldots,\vec{e}_n$, is used to compute $\vec{y}_n$. Thanks to the crucial fact that system C time-shifts every eigenvector, e, by simply scaling its components λ times,

$$C\vec{e}_i = \lambda_i \vec{e}_i = C \begin{bmatrix} e_{i,n} \\ e_{i,n-1} \\ \vdots \\ e_{i,1} \end{bmatrix} = \begin{bmatrix} \lambda_i e_{i,n} \\ \lambda_i e_{i,n-1} \\ \vdots \\ \lambda_i e_{i,1} \end{bmatrix}$$

that is, time-shifted version of eigenvector, e, has components λ times larger, the eigenvector components are powers of λ, $\vec{e}_i = \begin{bmatrix} \lambda_i^{n-1} & \cdots & \lambda_i^2 & \lambda_i & 1 \end{bmatrix}^T$ and, thus, recurrent homogeneous linear equation solution is a combination of exponential functions, $\vec{y}_n = \sum_1^n c_i \lambda_i^n \vec{e}_i$. The components c_i can be determined out of initial conditions:

$$\vec{y}_0 = \begin{bmatrix} y_0 \\ y_{-1} \\ \vdots \\ y_{-n+1} \end{bmatrix} = \sum_{i=1}^n c_i \lambda_i^0 \vec{e}_i = \begin{bmatrix} \vec{e}_1 & \vec{e}_2 & \cdots & \vec{e}_n \end{bmatrix} \begin{bmatrix} c_1 \\ c_2 \\ \cdots \\ c_n \end{bmatrix} = E \begin{bmatrix} c_1 \\ c_2 \\ \cdots \\ c_n \end{bmatrix}$$

Solving for coefficients,

$$\begin{bmatrix} c_1 \\ c_2 \\ \cdots \\ c_n \end{bmatrix} = E^{-1} \vec{y}_0 = \begin{bmatrix} \lambda_1^{n-1} & \lambda_2^{n-1} & \cdots & \lambda_n^{n-1} \\ \vdots & \vdots & \ddots & \vdots \\ \lambda_1 & \lambda_2 & \cdots & \lambda_n \\ 1 & 1 & \cdots & 1 \end{bmatrix}^{-1} \begin{bmatrix} y_0 \\ y_{-1} \\ \vdots \\ y_{-n+1} \end{bmatrix}.$$

This also works with arbitrary boundary conditions $\underbrace{y_a, y_b, \cdots}$, not necessary the initial ones,

$$\begin{bmatrix} y_a \\ y_b \\ \vdots \end{bmatrix} = \begin{bmatrix} \vec{y}_a[n] \\ \vec{y}_b[n] \\ \vdots \end{bmatrix} = \begin{bmatrix} \sum_{i=1}^n c_i \lambda_i^a \vec{e}_i[n] \\ \sum_{i=1}^n c_i \lambda_i^b \vec{e}_i[n] \\ \vdots \end{bmatrix}^n \begin{bmatrix} \sum_{i=1}^n c_i \lambda_i^a \lambda_i^{n-1} \\ \sum_{i=1}^n c_i \lambda_i^b \lambda_i^{n-1} \\ \vdots \end{bmatrix}$$

$$= \begin{bmatrix} \sum c_i \lambda_i^{a+n-1} \\ \sum c_i \lambda_i^{b+n-1} \\ \vdots \end{bmatrix} = \begin{bmatrix} \lambda_1^{a+n-1} & \lambda_2^{a+n-1} & \cdots & \lambda_n^{a+n-1} \\ \lambda_1^{b+n-1} & \lambda_2^{b+n-1} & \cdots & \lambda_n^{b+n-1} \\ \vdots & \vdots & & \ddots & \vdots \end{bmatrix} \begin{bmatrix} c_1 \\ c_2 \\ \vdots \\ c_n \end{bmatrix}.$$

This description is really no different from general method above, however it is more succinct. It also works nicely for situations like.

$$\begin{cases} a_n = a_{n-1} - b_{n-1} \\ b_n = 2a_{n-1} + b_{n-1} \end{cases}.$$

where there are several linked recurrences.

Solving with z-transforms

Certain difference equations - in particular, linear constant coefficient difference equations - can be solved using z-transforms. The z-transforms are a class of integral transforms that lead to more convenient algebraic manipulations and more straightforward solutions. There are cases in which obtaining a direct solution would be all but impossible, yet solving the problem via a thoughtfully chosen integral transform is straightforward.

Solving non-homogeneous Linear Recurrence Relations with Constant Coefficients

If the recurrence is non-homogeneous, a particular solution can be found by the method of undetermined coefficients and the solution is the sum of the solution of the homogeneous and the particular solutions. Another method to solve an non-homogeneous recurrence is the method of *symbolic differentiation*. For example, consider the following recurrence:

$$a_{n+1} = a_n + 1$$

This is an non-homogeneous recurrence. If we substitute $n \mapsto n+1$, we obtain the recurrence

$$a_{n+2} = a_{n+1} + 1$$

Subtracting the original recurrence from this equation yields

$$a_{n+2} - a_{n+1} = a_{n+1} - a_n$$

or equivalently

$$a_{n+2} = 2a_{n+1} - a_n$$

This is a homogeneous recurrence, which can be solved by the methods explained above. In general, if a linear recurrence has the form

$$a_{n+k} = \lambda_{k-1}a_{n+k-1} + \lambda_{k-2}a_{n+k-2} + \cdots + \lambda_1 a_{n+1} + \lambda_0 a_n + p(n)$$

where $\lambda_0, \lambda_1, \ldots, \lambda_{k-1}$ are constant coefficients and $p(n)$ is the inhomogeneity, then if $p(n)$ is a polynomial with degree r, then this non-homogeneous recurrence can be reduced to a homogeneous recurrence by applying the method of symbolic differencing r times.

If

$$P(x) = \sum_{n=0}^{\infty} p_n x^n$$

is the generating function of the inhomogeneity, the generat   ing function

$$A(x) = \sum_{n=0}^{\infty} a(n) x^n$$

of the non-homogeneous recurrence

$$a_n = \sum_{i=1}^{s} c_i a_{n-i} + p_n, \quad n \ge n_r,$$

with constant coefficients c_i is derived from

$$\left(1 - \sum_{i=1}^{s} c_i x^i\right) A(x) = P(x) + \sum_{n=0}^{n_r-1} [a_n - p_n] x^n - \sum_{i=1}^{s} c_i x^i \sum_{n=0}^{n_r-i-1} a_n x^n.$$

If $P(x)$ is a rational generating function, $A(x)$ is also one. The case discussed above, where $p_n = K$ is a constant, emerges as one example of this formula, with $P(x) = K/(1-x)$. Another example, the recurrence $a_n = 10a_{n-1} + n$ with linear inhomogeneity, arises in the definition of the schizophrenic numbers. The solution of homogeneous recurrences is incorporated as $p = P = 0$.

Solving First-order Non-homogeneous Recurrence Relations with Variable Coefficients

Moreover, for the general first-order non-homogeneous linear recurrence relation with variable coefficients:

$$a_{n+1} = f_n a_n + g_n, \qquad f_n \ne 0,$$

there is also a nice method to solve it:

$$a_{n+1} - f_n a_n = g_n$$

$$\frac{a_{n+1}}{\displaystyle\prod_{k=0}^{n} f_k} - \frac{f_n a_n}{\displaystyle\prod_{k=0}^{n} f_k} = \frac{g_n}{\displaystyle\prod_{k=0}^{n} f_k}$$

$$\frac{a_{n+1}}{\displaystyle\prod_{k=0}^{n} f_k} - \frac{a_n}{\displaystyle\prod_{k=0}^{n-1} f_k} = \frac{g_n}{\displaystyle\prod_{k=0}^{n} f_k}$$

Let

$$A_n = \frac{a_n}{\displaystyle\prod_{k=0}^{n-1} f_k},$$

Then

$$A_{n+1} - A_n = \frac{g_n}{\displaystyle\prod_{k=0}^{n} f_k}$$

$$\sum_{m=0}^{n-1}(A_{m+1}-A_m)=A_n-A_0=\sum_{m=0}^{n-1}\frac{g_m}{\prod_{k=0}^{m}f_k}$$

$$\frac{a_n}{\prod_{k=0}^{n-1}f_k}=A_0+\sum_{m=0}^{n-1}\frac{g_m}{\prod_{k=0}^{m}f_k}$$

$$a_n=\left(\prod_{k=0}^{n-1}f_k\right)\left(A_0+\sum_{m=0}^{n-1}\frac{g_m}{\prod_{k=0}^{m}f_k}\right)$$

If we apply the formula to $a_{n+1}=(1+hf_{nh})a_n+hg_{nh}$ and take the limit $h\to0$, we get the formula for first order linear differential equations with variable coefficients; the sum becomes an integral, and the product becomes the exponent of an integral.

Solving General Homogeneous Linear Recurrence Relations

Many homogeneous linear recurrence relations may be solved by means of the generalized hypergeometric series. Special cases of these lead to recurrence relations for the orthogonal polynomials, and many special functions. For example, the solution to

$$J_{n+1}=\frac{2n}{z}J_n-J_{n-1}$$

is given by

$$J_n=J_n(z),$$

the Bessel function, while

$$(b-n)M_{n-1}+(2n-b-z)M_n-nM_{n+1}=0$$

is solved by

$$M_n=M(n,b;z)$$

the confluent hypergeometric series.

Solving First-order Rational Difference Equations

A first order rational difference equation has the form $w_{t+1}=\frac{aw_t+b}{cw_t+d}$. Such an equation can be solved by writing w_t as a nonlinear transformation of another variable x_t which itself evolves linearly. Then standard methods can be used to solve the linear difference equation in x_t.

Stability

Stability of Linear Higher-order Recurrences

The linear recurrence of order d,

$$a_n = c_1 a_{n-1} + c_2 a_{n-2} + \cdots + c_d a_{n-d},$$

has the characteristic equation

$$\lambda^d - c_1 \lambda^{d-1} - c_2 \lambda^{d-2} - \cdots - c_d \lambda^0 = 0.$$

The recurrence is stable, meaning that the iterates converge asymptotically to a fixed value, if and only if the eigenvalues (i.e., the roots of the characteristic equation), whether real or complex, are all less than unity in absolute value.

Stability of Linear First-order Matrix Recurrences

In the first-order matrix difference equation

$$[x_t - x^*] = A[x_{t-1} - x^*]$$

with state vector x and transition matrix A, x converges asymptotically to the steady state vector x^* if and only if all eigenvalues of the transition matrix A (whether real or complex) have an absolute value which is less than 1.

Stability of Nonlinear First-order Recurrences

Consider the nonlinear first-order recurrence

$$x_n = f(x_{n-1}).$$

This recurrence is locally stable, meaning that it converges to a fixed point x^* from points sufficiently close to x^*, if the slope of f in the neighborhood of x^* is smaller than unity in absolute value: that is,

$$|f'(x^*)| < 1.$$

A nonlinear recurrence could have multiple fixed points, in which case some fixed points may be locally stable and others locally unstable; for continuous f two adjacent fixed points cannot both be locally stable.

A nonlinear recurrence relation could also have a cycle of period k for $k > 1$. Such a cycle is stable, meaning that it attracts a set of initial conditions of positive measure, if the composite function

$$g(x) := f \circ f \circ \cdots \circ f(x)$$

with f appearing k times is locally stable according to the same criterion:

$$|g'(x^*)| < 1,$$

where x^* is any point on the cycle.

In a chaotic recurrence relation, the variable x stays in a bounded region but never converges to a fixed point or an attracting cycle; any fixed points or cycles of the equation are unstable.

Relationship to Differential Equations

When solving an ordinary differential equation numerically, one typically encounters a recurrence relation. For example, when solving the initial value problem

$$y'(t) = f(t, y(t)), \quad y(t_0) = y_0,$$

with Euler's method and a step size h, one calculates the values

$$y_0 = y(t_0), \quad y_1 = y(t_0 + h), \quad y_2 = y(t_0 + 2h), \ldots$$

by the recurrence

$$y_{n+1} = y_n + hf(t_n, y_n).$$

Systems of linear first order differential equations can be discretized exactly analytically using the methods shown in the discretization article.

Applications

Biology

Some of the best-known difference equations have their origins in the attempt to model population dynamics. For example, the Fibonacci numbers were once used as a model for the growth of a rabbit population.

The logistic map is used either directly to model population growth, or as a starting point for more detailed models of population dynamics. In this context, coupled difference equations are often used to model the interaction of two or more populations. For example, the Nicholson-Bailey model for a host-parasite interaction is given by

$$N_{t+1} = \lambda N_t e^{-aP_t}$$

$$P_{t+1} = N_t (1 - e^{-aP_t}),$$

with N_t representing the hosts, and P_t the parasites, at time t.

Integrodifference equations are a form of recurrence relation important to spatial ecology. These and other difference equations are particularly suited to modeling univoltine populations.

Computer Science

Recurrence relations are also of fundamental importance in analysis of algorithms. If an algorithm is designed so that it will break a problem into smaller subproblems (divide and conquer), its running time is described by a recurrence relation.

A simple example is the time an algorithm takes to find an element in an ordered vector with n elements, in the worst case.

A naive algorithm will search from left to right, one element at a time. The worst possible scenario is when the required element is the last, so the number of comparisons is n.

A better algorithm is called binary search. However, it requires a sorted vector. It will first check if the element is at the middle of the vector. If not, then it will check if the middle element is greater or lesser than the sought element. At this point, half of the vector can be discarded, and the algorithm can be run again on the other half. The number of comparisons will be given by

$$c_1 = 1$$

$$c_n = 1 + c_{n/2}$$

which will be close to $\log_2(n)$.

Digital Signal Processing

In digital signal processing, recurrence relations can model feedback in a system, where outputs at one time become inputs for future time. They thus arise in infinite impulse response (IIR) digital filters.

For example, the equation for a "feedforward" IIR comb filter of delay T is:

$$y_t = (1 - \alpha)x_t + \alpha y_{t-T}$$

Where x_t is the input at time t, y_t is the output at time t, and α controls how much of the delayed signal is fed back into the output. From this we can see that

$$y_t = (1 - \alpha)x_t + \alpha((1 - \alpha)x_{t-T} + \alpha y_{t-2T})$$

$$y_t = (1 - \alpha)x_t + (\alpha - \alpha^2)x_{t-T} + \alpha^2 y_{t-2T})$$

etc.

Economics

Recurrence relations, especially linear recurrence relations, are used extensively in both theoretical and empirical economics. In particular, in macroeconomics one might develop a model of various broad sectors of the economy (the financial sector, the goods sector, the labor market, etc.) in which some agents' actions depend on lagged variables. The model would then be solved for current values of key variables (interest rate, real GDP, etc.) in terms of exogenous variables and lagged endogenous variables.

- Another way of finding number of instruction executed is by recursive equation. Let $T(n)$ be the time required to sort n numbers. $T(n)$ can be expressed as a sum of $T(n-1)$ and the time required to insert n^{th} element in the sorted array of n-1 element.

- The time required to insert an element in sorted array of n-1 elements takes cn steps, where c is a positive constant. This is because to insert n^{th} element, in worst case, we have to shift all n-1 elements one after other.

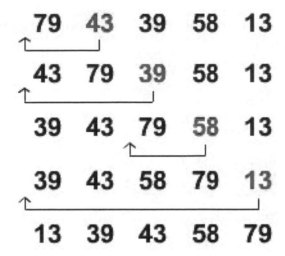

- Hence, the recurrence relation for Insertion sort is

```
T(n)= T(n-1) + cn, if n > 1

   = 1 if n = 1
```

- There are three main approach to solve recurrence relations. They are substitution, iterative and master theorem methods.

- Iterative Method:

$$= T(n-1) + cn$$

$T(n)$

$$= T(n-2) + c(n-1) + cn$$

$$= T(n-3) + c(n-2) + c(n-1) + cn$$

$$= T(1) + 2c + 3c + \ldots\ldots\ldots + c(n-2) + c(n-1) + cn$$

$$= 1 + 2c + 3c + \ldots\ldots\ldots + c(n-2) + c(n-1) + cn$$

$$< c(1 + 2 + 3 + \ldots\ldots\ldots + n-2 + n-1 + n)$$

$$= c (n (n+1)/2)$$

$$= c \; n^2/2 + c \; n/2$$

$$= O(n^2)$$

- Consider another recurrence:

$T(n)$

$$= O(1) \quad \text{if } n = 1$$

```
= 2T(n/2) + O(n)    if n > 1
```

- In the above recurrence relation O(1) means a constant. So we can replace with some constant c_1.

- Similarly, O(n) means a function of order n. So we can replace with $C_2 n$. Hence, the recurrence can be rewritten as

```
T(n) <= C  if n=1
        1
     <= 2T(n/2) + C n if n > 1
                   2
```

- Solution by Iterative method:

```
      T(n)  <= 2T(n/2) + C n
                          2

            <= 2( 2T(n/4) + C n/2) + C n
                             2        2

            <= T() + C n + C n
                      2     2

            <= (2 T() + C ) + C n + C n
                         2     2      2

            <= T() + C n + C n + C n
                      2     2     2

               .

               .

               .

            <= T() + C  n i
                      2
```

- Assume $n = 2^i$ for some value of i. That is, i = log n

```
T(n)
```

$$= nT(1) + C_2 n*log(n)$$

$$= C_1 n + C_2 n*log(n)$$

$$= O(n*log(n))$$

- If $n \neq 2^i$ for some i, consider

```
T(n)
```

$$< 2nT(1) + c_2 n*log(n)$$

$$= 2c_1 n + c_2 n*log(n)$$

$$= O(n*log(n))$$

Analysis of Algorithms

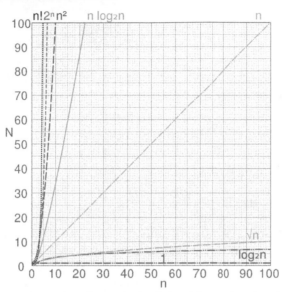

Graphs of functions commonly used in the analysis of algorithms, showing the number of operations N versus input size n for each function.

In computer science, the analysis of algorithms is the determination of the amount of time, storage and/or other resources necessary to execute them. Usually, this involves determining a function that relates the length of an algorithm's input to the number of steps it takes (its time complexity) or the number of storage locations it uses (its space complexity). An algorithm is said to be efficient when this function's values are small. Since different inputs of the same length may cause the algorithm to have different behavior, the function describing its performance is usually an upper bound on the actual performance, determined from the worst case inputs to the algorithm.

The term "analysis of algorithms" was coined by Donald Knuth. Algorithm analysis is an important part of a broader computational complexity theory, which provides theoretical estimates for the resources needed by any algorithm which solves a given computational problem. These estimates provide an insight into reasonable directions of search for efficient algorithms.

In theoretical analysis of algorithms it is common to estimate their complexity in the asymptotic sense, i.e., to estimate the complexity function for arbitrarily large input. Big O notation, Big-omega notation and Big-theta notation are used to this end. For instance, binary search is said to run in a number of steps proportional to the logarithm of the length of the sorted list being searched, or in O(log(n)), colloquially "in logarithmic time". Usually asymptotic estimates are used because different implementations of the same algorithm may differ in efficiency. However the efficiencies of any two "reasonable" implementations of a given algorithm are related by a constant multiplicative factor called a *hidden constant*.

Exact (not asymptotic) measures of efficiency can sometimes be computed but they usually require certain assumptions concerning the particular implementation of the algorithm, called model of computation. A model of computation may be defined in terms of an abstract computer, e.g., Turing machine, and/or by postulating that certain operations are executed in unit time. For example, if the sorted list to which we apply binary search has n elements, and we can guarantee that each lookup of an element in the list can be done in unit time, then at most $\log_2 n + 1$ time units are needed to return an answer.

Cost Models

Time efficiency estimates depend on what we define to be a step. For the analysis to correspond usefully to the actual execution time, the time required to perform a step must be guaranteed to be bounded above by a constant. One must be careful here; for instance, some analyses count an addition of two numbers as one step. This assumption may not be warranted in certain contexts. For example, if the numbers involved in a computation may be arbitrarily large, the time required by a single addition can no longer be assumed to be constant.

Two cost models are generally used:

- the uniform cost model, also called uniform-cost measurement (and similar variations), assigns a constant cost to every machine operation, regardless of the size of the numbers involved

- the logarithmic cost model, also called logarithmic-cost measurement (and similar variations), assigns a cost to every machine operation proportional to the number of bits involved

The latter is more cumbersome to use, so it's only employed when necessary, for example in the analysis of arbitrary-precision arithmetic algorithms, like those used in cryptography.

A key point which is often overlooked is that published lower bounds for problems are often given for a model of computation that is more restricted than the set of operations that you could use in practice and therefore there are algorithms that are faster than what would naively be thought possible.

Run-time Analysis

Run-time analysis is a theoretical classification that estimates and anticipates the increase in *running time* (or run-time) of an algorithm as its *input size* (usually denoted as n) increases. Run-time efficiency is a topic of great interest in computer science: A program can take seconds, hours, or even years to finish executing, depending on which algorithm it implements. While software profiling techniques can be used to measure an algorithm's run-time in practice, they cannot provide timing data for all infinitely many possible inputs; the latter can only be achieved by the theoretical methods of run-time analysis.

Shortcomings of Empirical Metrics

Since algorithms are platform-independent (i.e. a given algorithm can be implemented in an arbitrary programming language on an arbitrary computer running an arbitrary operating system), there are additional significant drawbacks to using an empirical approach to gauge the comparative performance of a given set of algorithms.

Take as an example a program that looks up a specific entry in a sorted list of size n. Suppose this program were implemented on Computer A, a state-of-the-art machine, using a linear search algorithm, and on Computer B, a much slower machine, using a binary search algorithm. Benchmark testing on the two computers running their respective programs might look something like the following:

n (list size)	Computer A run-time (in nanoseconds)	Computer B run-time (in nanoseconds)
16	8	100,000
63	32	150,000
250	125	200,000
1,000	500	250,000

Based on these metrics, it would be easy to jump to the conclusion that *Computer A* is running an algorithm that is far superior in efficiency to that of *Computer B*. However, if the size of the input-list is increased to a sufficient number, that conclusion is dramatically demonstrated to be in error:

n (list size)	Computer A run-time (in nanoseconds)	Computer B run-time (in nanoseconds)
16	8	100,000
63	32	150,000
250	125	200,000
1,000	500	250,000
...	...	...
1,000,000	500,000	500,000
4,000,000	2,000,000	550,000
16,000,000	8,000,000	600,000
...	...	...
$63,072 \times 10^{12}$	$31,536 \times 10^{12}$ ns, or 1 year	1,375,000 ns, or 1.375 milliseconds

Computer A, running the linear search program, exhibits a linear growth rate. The program's run-time is directly proportional to its input size. Doubling the input size doubles the run time, quadrupling the input size quadruples the run-time, and so forth. On the other hand, Computer B, running the binary search program, exhibits a logarithmic growth rate. Quadrupling the input size only increases the run time by a constant amount (in this example, 50,000 ns). Even though Computer A is ostensibly a faster machine, Computer B will inevitably surpass Computer A in run-time because it's running an algorithm with a much slower growth rate.

Orders of Growth

Informally, an algorithm can be said to exhibit a growth rate on the order of a mathematical function if beyond a certain input size n, the function $f(n)$ times a positive constant provides an upper bound or limit for the run-time of that algorithm. In other words, for a given input size n greater than some n_0 and a constant c, the running time of that algorithm will never be larger than $c \times f(n)$. This concept is frequently expressed using Big O notation. For example, since the run-time of insertion sort grows quadratically as its input size increases, insertion sort can be said to be of order $O(n^2)$.

Big O notation is a convenient way to express the worst-case scenario for a given algorithm, although it can also be used to express the average-case — for example, the worst-case scenario for quicksort is $O(n^2)$, but the average-case run-time is $O(n \log n)$.

Empirical Orders of Growth

Assuming the execution time follows power rule, $t \approx k\, n^a$, the coefficient a can be found by taking empirical measurements of run time $\{t_1, t_2\}$ at some problem-size points $\{n_1, n_2\}$, and calculating $t_2 / t_1 = (n_2 / n_1)^a$ so that $a = \log(t_2 / t_1) / \log(n_2 / n_1)$. In other words, this measures the slope of the empirical line on the log–log plot of execution time vs. problem size, at some size point. If the order of growth indeed follows the power rule (and so the line on log–log plot is indeed a straight line), the empirical value of a will stay constant at different ranges, and if not, it will change (and the line is a curved line) - but still could serve for comparison of any two given algorithms as to their *empirical local orders of growth* behaviour. Applied to the above table:

n (list size)	Computer A run-time (in nanoseconds)	Local order of growth (n^_)	Computer B run-time (in nanoseconds)	Local order of growth (n^_)
15	7		100,000	
65	32	1.04	150,000	0.28
250	125	1.01	200,000	0.21
1,000	500	1.00	250,000	0.16
...	...		...	
1,000,000	500,000	1.00	500,000	0.10
4,000,000	2,000,000	1.00	550,000	0.07
16,000,000	8,000,000	1.00	600,000	0.06
...	...		...	

It is clearly seen that the first algorithm exhibits a linear order of growth indeed following the power rule. The empirical values for the second one are diminishing rapidly, suggesting it follows another rule of growth and in any case has much lower local orders of growth (and improving further still), empirically, than the first one.

Evaluating Run-time Complexity

The run-time complexity for the worst-case scenario of a given algorithm can sometimes be evaluated by examining the structure of the algorithm and making some simplifying assumptions. Consider the following pseudocode:

```
1   get a positive integer from input

2   if n > 10

3   print "This might take a while..."

4   for i = 1 to n

5   for j = 1 to i

6   print i * j

7   print "Done!"
```

A given computer will take a discrete amount of time to execute each of the instructions involved with carrying out this algorithm. The specific amount of time to carry out a given instruction will vary depending on which instruction is being executed and which computer is executing it, but on a conventional computer, this amount will be deterministic. Say that the actions carried out in step 1 are considered to consume time T_1, step 2 uses time T_2, and so forth.

In the algorithm above, steps 1, 2 and 7 will only be run once. For a worst-case evaluation, it should be assumed that step 3 will be run as well. Thus the total amount of time to run steps 1-3 and step 7 is:

$$T_1 + T_2 + T_3 + T_7.$$

The loops in steps 4, 5 and 6 are trickier to evaluate. The outer loop test in step 4 will execute ($n + 1$) times (note that an extra step is required to terminate the for loop, hence n + 1 and not n executions), which will consume T_4 ($n + 1$) time. The inner loop, on the other hand, is governed by the value of i, which iterates from 1 to i. On the first pass through the outer loop, j iterates from 1 to 1: The inner loop makes one pass, so running the inner loop body (step 6) consumes T_6 time, and the inner loop test (step 5) consumes $2T_5$ time. During the next pass through the outer loop, j iterates from 1 to 2: the inner loop makes two passes, so running the inner loop body (step 6) consumes $2T_6$ time, and the inner loop test (step 5) consumes $3T_5$ time.

Altogether, the total time required to run the inner loop body can be expressed as an arithmetic progression:

$$T_6 + 2T_6 + 3T_6 + \cdots + (n-1)T_6 + nT_6$$

which can be factored as

$$T_6 \left[1 + 2 + 3 + \cdots + (n-1) + n \right] = T_6 \left[\frac{1}{2}(n^2 + n) \right]$$

The total time required to run the outer loop test can be evaluated similarly:

$$2T_5 + 3T_5 + 4T_5 + \cdots + (n-1)T_5 + nT_5 + (n+1)T_5$$
$$= \quad T_5 + 2T_5 + 3T_5 + 4T_5 + \cdots + (n-1)T_5 + nT_5 + (n+1)T_5 - T_5$$

which can be factored as

$$T_5\left[1+2+3+\cdots+(n-1)+n+(n+1)\right]-T_5$$

$$=\quad\left[\frac{1}{2}(n^2+n)\right]T_5+(n+1)T_5-T_5$$

$$=\quad T_5\left[\frac{1}{2}(n^2+n)\right]+nT_5$$

$$\left[\frac{1}{2}(n^2+3n)\right]T_5$$

Therefore, the total running time for this algorithm is:

$$f(n)=T_1+T_2+T_3+T_7+(n+1)T_4+\left[\frac{1}{2}(n^2+n)\right]T_6+\left[\frac{1}{2}(n^2+3n)\right]T_5$$

which reduces to

$$f(n)=\left[\frac{1}{2}(n^2+n)\right]T_6+\left[\frac{1}{2}(n^2+3n)\right]T_5+(n+1)T_4+T_1+T_2+T_3+T_7$$

As a rule-of-thumb, one can assume that the highest-order term in any given function dominates its rate of growth and thus defines its run-time order. In this example, n² is the highest-order term, so one can conclude that f(n) = O(n²). Formally this can be proven as follows:

Prove that $\left[\frac{1}{2}(n^2+n)\right]T_6+\left[\frac{1}{2}(n^2+3n)\right]T_5+(n+1)T_4+T_1+T_2+T_3+T_7\le cn^2,n\ge n_0$

$$\left[\frac{1}{2}(n^2+n)\right]T_6+\left[\frac{1}{2}(n^2+3n)\right]T_5+(n+1)T_4+T_1+T_2+T_3+T_7$$

$$\le\ (n^2+n)T_6+(n^2+3n)T_5+(n+1)T_4+T_1+T_2+T_3+T_7\ (\text{for }n\ge0)$$

Let k be a constant greater than or equal to $[T_1..T_7]$

$$T_6(n^2+n)+T_5(n^2+3n)+(n+1)T_4+T_1+T_2+T_3+T_7\le k(n^2+n)+k(n^2+3n)+kn+5k$$
$$=\ 2kn^2+5kn+5k\le2kn^2+5kn^2+5kn^2\ (\text{for }n\ge1)=12kn^2$$

Therefore

$$\left[\frac{1}{2}(n^2+n)\right]T_6+\left[\frac{1}{2}(n^2+3n)\right]T_5+(n+1)T_4+T_1+T_2+T_3+T_7\le cn^2,n\ge n_0\ \text{ for }c=12k,n_0=1$$

A more elegant approach to analyzing this algorithm would be to declare that $[T_1..T_7]$ are all equal to one unit of time, in a system of units chosen so that one unit is greater than or equal to the actual times for these steps. This would mean that the algorithm's running time breaks down as follows:

$$4 + \sum_{i=1}^{n} i \le 4 + \sum_{i=1}^{n} n = 4 + n^2 \le 5n^2 \ (\text{for } n \ge 1) = O(n^2).$$

Growth Rate Analysis of Other Resources

The methodology of run-time analysis can also be utilized for predicting other growth rates, such as consumption of memory space. As an example, consider the following pseudocode which manages and reallocates memory usage by a program based on the size of a file which that program manages:

```
while (file still open)

  let n = size of file

  for every 100,000 kilobytes of increase in file size

  double the amount of memory reserved
```

In this instance, as the file size n increases, memory will be consumed at an exponential growth rate, which is order $O(2^n)$. This is an extremely rapid and most likely unmanageable growth rate for consumption of memory resources.

Relevance

Algorithm analysis is important in practice because the accidental or unintentional use of an inefficient algorithm can significantly impact system performance. In time-sensitive applications, an algorithm taking too long to run can render its results outdated or useless. An inefficient algorithm can also end up requiring an uneconomical amount of computing power or storage in order to run, again rendering it practically useless.

Constant Factors

Analysis of algorithms typically focuses on the asymptotic performance, particularly at the elementary level, but in practical applications constant factors are important, and real-world data is in practice always limited in size. The limit is typically the size of addressable memory, so on 32-bit machines $2^{32} = 4$ GiB (greater if segmented memory is used) and on 64-bit machines $2^{64} = 16$ EiB. Thus given a limited size, an order of growth (time or space) can be replaced by a constant factor, and in this sense all practical algorithms are O(1) for a large enough constant, or for small enough data.

This interpretation is primarily useful for functions that grow extremely slowly: (binary) iterated logarithm ($\log^*$) is less than 5 for all practical data (2^{65536} bits); (binary) log-log ($\log \log n$) is less than 6 for virtually all practical data (2^{64} bits); and binary log ($\log n$) is less than 64 for virtually all practical data (2^{64} bits). An algorithm with non-constant complexity may nonetheless be more efficient than an algorithm with constant complexity on practical data if the overhead of the constant time algorithm results in a larger constant factor, e.g., one may have $K > k \log \log n$ so long as $K / k > 6$ and $n < 2^{2^6} = 2^{64}$.

For large data linear or quadratic factors cannot be ignored, but for small data an asymptotically inefficient algorithm may be more efficient. This is particularly used in hybrid algorithms, like Timsort, which use an asymptotically efficient algorithm (here merge sort, with time complexity $n \log n$), but switch to an asymptotically inefficient algorithm (here insertion sort, with time complexity n^2) for small data, as the simpler algorithm is faster on small data.

String Algorithms

A string is a sequence of characters. In computer science, strings are more often used than numbers. We have all used text editors for editing programs and documents. Some of the important operations which are used on strings are: searching for a word, find -and -replace operations, etc.

There are many functions which can be defined on strings. Some important functions are :

- String length : Determines length of a given string.

- String concatenation : Concatenation of two or more strings. coping.

- String copy : Creating another string which is a copy of the original or a copy of a part of the original.

- String matching : Searching for a query string in given string.

String Length

- Strings can have an arbitrary but finite length.

- There are two types of string data types:

  o Fixed length strings

  o Variable length strings

- Fixed length strings have a maximum length and all the strings uses same amount of space despite of their actual size.

- Variable length strings uses varying amount of memory depending on their actual size. Throughout of our discussion we assume that strings are of variable length type.

- Variable length string is an array of characters terminated by a special character.

- To find the length of a string we scan through the string from left to right until we find the special symbol and each time incrementing a counter to keep track of number of characters scanned so far.

Algorithm For String Length

We assume that the given string STR is terminated by special symbol '\o'.

1. length = 0, i=0;   //Indentity starts from 'o'.

2. while STR[i] != '\o'   //In C '\o' is used as end-of-string markes.

    i++;

    length=i;

3. return length

String Concatenation

- Appending one string to the end of another string is called string concatenation

    Example let STR1= "hello"

    STR2= "world"

- If we concatenate STR2 with STR1, then we get the string "helloworld"

Algorithm

1. i= 0, j=0;

2. while STR1[i] != '\o'

            i++;

3. while STR2[j] != '\o'

            STR1[i]= STR2[j];

            i =i+1

            j = j+1

4. STR1[i]= '\o';

5. Return STR1;

String Copy

- By string copy, we mean copying one string to another string character by character.

- The size of the destination string should be greater than equal to the size of the source string.

Algorithm

```
1. Set i=0

2. while STR[i] != '\o'

        {
```

```
        STR2[i]=STR1[i];
        i =i+1;
        }
```

3. Set STR2[i]='\o'

4. Return STR2

String Searching Algorithm

In computer science, string searching algorithms, sometimes called string matching algorithms, are an important class of string algorithms that try to find a place where one or several strings (also called patterns) are found within a larger string or text.

Let Σ be an alphabet (finite set). Formally, both the pattern and searched text are vectors of elements of Σ. The Σ may be a usual human alphabet (for example, the letters A through Z in the Latin alphabet). Other applications may use *binary alphabet* ($\Sigma = \{0,1\}$) or *DNA alphabet* ($\Sigma = \{A,C,G,T\}$) in bioinformatics.

In practice, how the string is encoded can affect the feasible string search algorithms. In particular if a variable width encoding is in use then it is slow (time proportional to N) to find the Nth character. This will significantly slow down many of the more advanced search algorithms. A possible solution is to search for the sequence of code units instead, but doing so may produce false matches unless the encoding is specifically designed to avoid it.

Basic Classification

The various algorithms can be classified by the number of patterns each uses.

Single Pattern Algorithms

Let m be the length of the pattern, n be the length of the searchable text and $k = |\Sigma|$ be the size of the alphabet.

Algorithm	Preprocessing time	Matching time
Naïve string search algorithm	0 (no preprocessing)	$\Theta(nm)$
Rabin–Karp string search algorithm	$\Theta(m)$	average $\Theta(n + m)$, worst $\Theta((n-m)m)$
Finite-state automaton based search	$\Theta(mk)$	$\Theta(n)$
Knuth–Morris–Pratt algorithm	$\Theta(m)$	$\Theta(n)$
Boyer–Moore string search algorithm	$\Theta(m + k)$	best $\Omega(n/m)$, worst $O(mn)$
Bitap algorithm (*shift-or, shift-and, Baeza–Yates–Gonnet*)	$\Theta(m + k)$	$O(mn)$
Two-way string-matching algorithm	$\Theta(m)$	$O(n+m)$

BNDM (Backward Non-Deterministic Dawg Matching)	O(m)	O(n)
BOM (Backward Oracle Matching)	O(m)	O(n)

Algorithms using a Finite Set of Patterns

- Aho–Corasick string matching algorithm (extension of Knuth-Morris-Pratt)

- Commentz-Walter algorithm (extension of Boyer-Moore)

- Set-BOM (extension of Backward Oracle Matching)

- Rabin–Karp string search algorithm

Algorithms using an Infinite Number of Patterns

Naturally, the patterns can not be enumerated finitely in this case. They are represented usually by a regular grammar or regular expression.

Other Classification

Other classification approaches are possible. One of the most common uses preprocessing as main criteria.

Classes of string searching algorithms		
	Text not preprocessed	Text preprocessed
Patterns not preprocessed	Elementary algorithms	Index methods
Patterns preprocessed	Constructed search engines	Signature methods

Another one classifies the algorithms by their matching strategy:

- Match the prefix first (Knuth-Morris-Pratt, Shift-And, Aho-Corasick)

- Match the suffix first (Boyer-Moore and variants, Commentz-Walter)

- Match the best factor first (BNDM, BOM, Set-BOM)

- Other strategy (Naive, Rabin-Karp)

Naïve String Search

A simple but inefficient way to see where one string occurs inside another is to check each place it could be, one by one, to see if it's there. So first we see if there's a copy of the needle in the first character of the haystack; if not, we look to see if there's a copy of the needle starting at the second character of the haystack; if not, we look starting at the third character, and so forth. In the normal case, we only have to look at one or two characters for each wrong position to see that it is a wrong position, so in the average case, this takes $O(n + m)$ steps, where n is the length of the haystack and

m is the length of the needle; but in the worst case, searching for a string like "aaaab" in a string like "aaaaaaaab", it takes O(nm)

Finite State Automaton Based Search

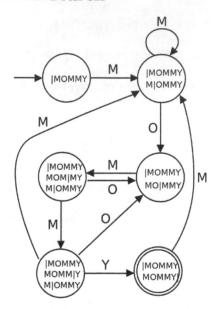

In this approach, we avoid backtracking by constructing a deterministic finite automaton (DFA) that recognizes stored search string. These are expensive to construct—they are usually created using the powerset construction—but are very quick to use. For example, the DFA shown to the right recognizes the word "MOMMY". This approach is frequently generalized in practice to search for arbitrary regular expressions.

Stubs

Knuth–Morris–Pratt computes a DFA that recognizes inputs with the string to search for as a suffix, Boyer–Moore starts searching from the end of the needle, so it can usually jump ahead a whole needle-length at each step. Baeza–Yates keeps track of whether the previous j characters were a prefix of the search string, and is therefore adaptable to fuzzy string searching. The bitap algorithm is an application of Baeza–Yates' approach.

Index Methods

Faster search algorithms are based on preprocessing of the text. After building a substring index, for example a suffix tree or suffix array, the occurrences of a pattern can be found quickly. As an example, a suffix tree can be built in $\Theta(n)$ time, and all z occurrences of a pattern can be found in O(m) time under the assumption that the alphabet has a constant size and all inner nodes in the suffix tree know what leaves are underneath them. The latter can be accomplished by running a DFS algorithm from the root of the suffix tree.

Other Variants

Some search methods, for instance trigram search, are intended to find a "closeness" score between the search string and the text rather than a "match/non-match". These are sometimes called "fuzzy" searches.

References

- Bell, C. Gordon and Newell, Allen (1971), Computer Structures: Readings and Examples, McGraw–Hill Book Company, New York. ISBN 0-07-004357-4

- Sedgewick, R. (1978). "Implementing Quicksort programs". Comm. ACM. 21 (10): 847–857. doi:10.1145/359619.359631

- Thorup, M. (February 2002). "Randomized Sorting in O(n log log n) Time and Linear Space Using Addition, Shift, and Bit-wise Boolean Operations". Journal of Algorithms. 42 (2): 205–230. doi:10.1006/jagm.2002.1211

- Kleene, Stephen C. (1991) [1952]. Introduction to Metamathematics (Tenth ed.). North-Holland Publishing Company. ISBN 0-7204-2103-9

- Lohr, Steve (Dec 17, 2001). "Frances E. Holberton, 84, Early Computer Programmer". NYTimes. Retrieved 16 December 2014

- Han, Y. (January 2004). "Deterministic sorting in O(n log log n) time and linear space". Journal of Algorithms. 50: 96–105. doi:10.1016/j.jalgor.2003.09.001

- Huang, B. C.; Langston, M. A. (December 1992). "Fast Stable Merging and Sorting in Constant Extra Space" (PDF). Comput. J. 35 (6): 643–650. CiteSeerX 10.1.1.54.8381. doi:10.1093/comjnl/35.6.643

- Impagliazzo, R.; Paturi, R. (2001). "On the complexity of k-SAT". Journal of Computer and System Sciences. Elsevier. 62 (2): 367–375. ISSN 1090-2724. doi:10.1006/jcss.2000.1727

- Scott, Michael L. (2009). Programming Language Pragmatics (3rd ed.). Morgan Kaufmann Publishers/Elsevier. ISBN 978-0-12-374514-9

- Franceschini, G. (June 2007). "Sorting Stably, in Place, with O(n log n) Comparisons and O(n) Moves". Theory of Computing Systems. 40 (4): 327–353. doi:10.1007/s00224-006-1311-1

- Tausworthe, Robert C (1977). Standardized Development of Computer Software Part 1 Methods. Englewood Cliffs NJ: Prentice–Hall, Inc. ISBN 0-13-842195-1

- Brejová, B. (15 September 2001). "Analyzing variants of Shellsort". Inform. Process. Lett. 79 (5): 223–227. doi:10.1016/S0020-0190(00)00223-4

- Naik, Ashish V.; Regan, Kenneth W.; Sivakumar, D. (1995). "On Quasilinear Time Complexity Theory" (PDF). Theoretical Computer Science. 148: 325–349. doi:10.1016/0304-3975(95)00031-q. Retrieved 23 February 2015

- Impagliazzo, R.; Paturi, R.; Zane, F. (2001). "Which problems have strongly exponential complexity?". Journal of Computer and System Sciences. 63 (4): 512–530. doi:10.1006/jcss.2001.1774

- Ajtai, M.; Komlós, J.; Szemerédi, E. (1983). An O(n log n) sorting network. STOC '83. Proceedings of the fifteenth annual ACM symposium on Theory of computing. pp. 1–9. ISBN 0-89791-099-0. doi:10.1145/800061.808726

- Wang, Xiang-Sheng; Wong, Roderick (2012). "Asymptotics of orthogonal polynomials via recurrence relations". Anal. Appl. 10 (2): 215–235. doi:10.1142/S0219530512500108

- Arora, Sanjeev; Barak, Boaz (2009). Computational complexity. A modern approach. Cambridge University Press. ISBN 978-0-521-42426-4. Zbl 1193.68112

- Hume; Sunday (1991). "Fast String Searching". Software: Practice and Experience. 21 (11): 1221–1248. doi:10.1002/spe.4380211105

3

An Integrated Study of Search Algorithms

Science and technology has undergone rapid developments in the past decade which has resulted in the discovery of significant techniques in the field of search algorithms and hashing. Search algorithm helps in recovering information from data structures. Hashing is a method to optimize searching, inserting, deleting, and sorting functions by storing data in an array. Two notable techniques of hashing are chaining and rehashing. This chapter will provide an integrated understanding of search algorithms.

Search Algorithm

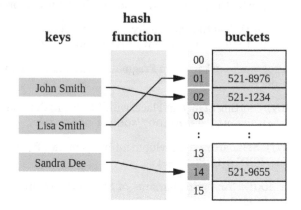

Visual representation of a hash table, a data structure that allows for fast retrieval of information.

In computer science, a search algorithm is an algorithm that retrieves information stored within some data structure. Data structures can include linked lists, arrays, search trees, hash tables, or various other storage methods. The appropriate search algorithm often depends on the data structure being searched. Searching also encompasses algorithms that query the data structure, such as the SQL SELECT command.

Search algorithms can be classified based on their mechanism of searching. Linear search algorithms check every record for the one associated with a target key in a linear fashion. Binary, or half interval searches, repeatedly target the center of the search structure and divide the search space in half. Comparison search algorithms improve on linear searching by successively eliminating records based on comparisons of the keys until the target record is found, and can be applied on data structures with a defined order. Digital search algorithms work based on the properties of digits in data structures that use numerical keys. Finally, hashing directly maps keys to records based on a hash function. Searches outside of a linear search require that the data be sorted in some way.

Search functions are also evaluated on the basis of their complexity, or maximum theoretical run time. Binary search functions, for example, have a maximum complexity of $O(\log(n))$, or logarithmic time. This means that the maximum number of operations needed to find the search target is a logarithmic function of the size of the search space.

Classes

For Virtual Search Spaces

Algorithms for searching virtual spaces are used in constraint satisfaction problem, where the goal is to find a set of value assignments to certain variables that will satisfy specific mathematical equations and inequations / inequalities. They are also used when the goal is to find a variable assignment that will maximize or minimize a certain function of those variables. Algorithms for these problems include the basic brute-force search (also called "naïve" or "uninformed" search), and a variety of heuristics that try to exploit partial knowledge about structure of the space, such as linear relaxation, constraint generation, and constraint propagation.

An important subclass are the local search methods, that view the elements of the search space as the vertices of a graph, with edges defined by a set of heuristics applicable to the case; and scan the space by moving from item to item along the edges, for example according to the steepest descent or best-first criterion, or in a stochastic search. This category includes a great variety of general metaheuristic methods, such as simulated annealing, tabu search, A-teams, and genetic programming, that combine arbitrary heuristics in specific ways.

This class also includes various tree search algorithms, that view the elements as vertices of a tree, and traverse that tree in some special order. Examples of the latter include the exhaustive methods such as depth-first search and breadth-first search, as well as various heuristic-based search tree pruning methods such as backtracking and branch and bound. Unlike general metaheuristics, which at best work only in a probabilistic sense, many of these tree-search methods are guaranteed to find the exact or optimal solution, if given enough time. This is called "completeness".

Another important sub-class consists of algorithms for exploring the game tree of multiple-player games, such as chess or backgammon, whose nodes consist of all possible game situations that could result from the current situation. The goal in these problems is to find the move that provides the best chance of a win, taking into account all possible moves of the opponent(s). Similar problems occur when humans or machines have to make successive decisions whose outcomes are not entirely under one's control, such as in robot guidance or in marketing, financial, or military strategy planning. This kind of problem — combinatorial search — has been extensively studied in the context of artificial intelligence. Examples of algorithms for this class are the minimax algorithm, alpha–beta pruning, * Informational search and the A* algorithm.

For Sub-structures of a Given Structure

The name "combinatorial search" is generally used for algorithms that look for a specific sub-structure of a given discrete structure, such as a graph, a string, a finite group, and so on. The term combinatorial optimization is typically used when the goal is to find a sub-structure with a maximum (or minimum) value of some parameter. (Since the sub-structure is usually represented in the computer by a set of integer variables with constraints, these problems can be viewed as special cases of constraint satisfaction or discrete optimization; but they are usually formulated and solved in a more abstract setting where the internal representation is not explicitly mentioned.)

An important and extensively studied subclass are the graph algorithms, in particular graph traversal algorithms, for finding specific sub-structures in a given graph — such as subgraphs, paths, circuits, and so on. Examples include Dijkstra's algorithm, Kruskal's algorithm, the nearest neighbour algorithm, and Prim's algorithm.

Another important subclass of this category are the string searching algorithms, that search for patterns within strings. Two famous examples are the Boyer–Moore and Knuth–Morris–Pratt algorithms, and several algorithms based on the suffix tree data structure.

Search for the Maximum of a Function

In 1953, American statistician Jack Kiefer devised Fibonacci search which can be used to find the maximum of a unimodal function and has many other applications in computer science.

For Quantum Computers

There are also search methods designed for quantum computers, like Corley's algorithm, that are theoretically faster than linear or brute-force search even without the help of data structures or heuristics.

Linear Search

In computer science, linear search or sequential search is a method for finding a target value within a list. It sequentially checks each element of the list for the target value until a match is found or until all the elements have been searched.

Linear search runs in at worst linear time and makes at most n comparisons, where n is the length of the list. If each element is equally likely to be searched, then linear search has an average case of $n/2$ comparisons, but the average case can be affected if the search probabilities for each element vary. Linear search is rarely practical because other search algorithms and schemes, such as the binary search algorithm and hash tables, allow significantly faster searching for all but short lists.

Algorithm

Linear search sequentially checks each element of the list until it finds an element that matches the target value. If the algorithm reaches the end of the list, the search terminates unsuccessfully.

Basic Algorithm

Given a list L of n elements with values or records $L_0 \ldots L_{n-1}$, and target value T, the following subroutine uses linear search to find the index of the target T in L.

1. Set i to 0.

2. If $L_i = T$, the search terminates successfully; return i.

3. Increase i by 1.

4. If $i < n$, go to step 2. Otherwise, the search terminates unsuccessfully.

With a Sentinel

The basic algorithm above makes two comparisons per iteration: one to check if L_i equals t, and the other to check if i still points to a valid index of the list. By adding an extra record L_n to the list (a sentinel value) that equals the target, the second comparison can be eliminated until the end of the search, making the algorithm faster. The search will reach the sentinel if the target is not contained within the list.

1. Set i to 0.

2. If $L_i = T$, go to step 4.

3. Increase i by 1 and go to step 2.

4. If $i < n$, the search terminates successfully; return i. Else, the search terminates unsuccessfully.

In an Ordered Table

If the list is ordered such that $L_0 \le L_1 \ldots \le L_{n-1}$, the search can establish the absence of the target more quickly by concluding the search once L_i exceeds the target. This variation requires a sentinel that is greater than the target.

1. Set i to 0.

2. If $L_i \ge T$, go to step 4.

3. Increase i by 1 and go to step 2.

4. If $L_i = T$, the search terminates successfully; return i. Else, the search terminates unsuccessfully.

Analysis

For a list with n items, the best case is when the value is equal to the first element of the list, in which case only one comparison is needed. The worst case is when the value is not in the list (or occurs only once at the end of the list), in which case n comparisons are needed.

If the value being sought occurs k times in the list, and all orderings of the list are equally likely, the expected number of comparisons is

$$\begin{cases} n & \text{if } k = 0 \\ \dfrac{n+1}{k+1} & \text{if } 1 \le k \le n. \end{cases}$$

For example, if the value being sought occurs once in the list, and all orderings of the list are equally likely, the expected number of comparisons is $\dfrac{n+1}{2}$. However, if it is *known* that it occurs once, then at most $n - 1$ comparisons are needed, and the expected number of comparisons is

$$\frac{(n+2)(n-1)}{2n}$$

(for example, for $n = 2$ this is 1, corresponding to a single if-then-else construct).

Either way, asymptotically the worst-case cost and the expected cost of linear search are both $O(n)$.

Non-uniform Probabilities

The performance of linear search improves if the desired value is more likely to be near the beginning of the list than to its end. Therefore, if some values are much more likely to be searched than others, it is desirable to place them at the beginning of the list.

In particular, when the list items are arranged in order of decreasing probability, and these probabilities are geometrically distributed, the cost of linear search is only $O(1)$. If the table size n is large enough, linear search will be faster than binary search, whose cost is $O(\log n)$.

Application

Linear search is usually very simple to implement, and is practical when the list has only a few elements, or when performing a single search in an unordered list.

When many values have to be searched in the same list, it often pays to pre-process the list in order to use a faster method. For example, one may sort the list and use binary search, or build any efficient search data structure from it. Should the content of the list change frequently, repeated re-organization may be more trouble than it is worth.

As a result, even though in theory other search algorithms may be faster than linear search (for instance binary search), in practice even on medium-sized arrays (around 100 items or less) it might be infeasible to use anything else. On larger arrays, it only makes sense to use other, faster search methods if the data is large enough, because the initial time to prepare (sort) the data is comparable to many linear searches.

 Linear search is the most simple of all searching techniques. It is also called sequential search. To find an element with key value='key',every element of the list is checked for key value='k' sequentially one by one.If such an element with key=k is found out, then the search is stopped. But if we eventually reach the end of the list & still the required element is not found then also we terminate the search as an unsuccessful one.

The linear search can be applied for both unsorted & sorted list.

- Linear search for Unsorted list
- Linear search for sorted list

In case of unsorted list, we have to search the entire list every time i.e.we have to keep on searching the list till we find the required element or we reach the end of the list.this is because as elements are not in any order,so any element can be found just anywhere.

Algorithm

```
linear search(int x[],int n,int key)

{

 int i,flag = 0;

 for(i=0;i < n ;  i++)

  {

  if(x[i]==key)

  {

  flag=1;

  break;

  }

  }

  if(flag==0)

  return(-1);

  else

 return(1);

}
```

Complexity

The number of comparisons in this case is n-1.So it is of o(n). The implementation af algo is simple but the efficiency is not good. Everytime we have to search the whole array (if the element with required value is not found out).

The efficiency of linear search can be increased if we take a previously sorted array say in ascending order. Now in this case, the basic algorithm remains the same as we have done in case of an unsorted array but the only difference is we do not have to search the entire array everytime. Whenever we encounter an element say y greater than the key to be searched, we conclude that there is no such element which is equal to the key, in the list. This is because all the elements in the list are in ascending order and all elements to the right of y will be greater or equal to y, ie greater than the key. So there is no point in continuing the search even if the end of the list has not been reached and the required element has not been found.

```
Linear search( int x[], int n, int key)

{
```

```
int i, flag=0;

for(i=0; i < n && x[i] <= key; i++)

{

if(x[i]==key)

{

flag=1;

break;

}

}

if(flag==1)  /* Unsuccessful Search*/

return(-1);

else return(1); /*Successful search*/

}
```

Illustrative Explanation

The array to be sorted is as follows:

21 35 41 65 72

It is sorted in ascending order. Now let key = 40. At first 21 is checked as [x]=21.

It is smaller than 40. So next element is checked which is 35 that is also smaller than 40. So now 41 is checked.But 41 > 40 & all elements to the right of 41 are also greater than 40.So we terminate the search as an unsuccessful one and we may not have to search the entire list.

Complexity

Searching is NOT more efficient when key is in present in the list in case when the search key value lies between the minimum and the maximum element in the list. The Complexity of linear search both in case of sorted and unsorted list is the same. The average complexity for linear search for sorted list is better than that in unsorted list since the search need not continue beyond an element with higher value than the search value.

Binary Search

The most efficient method of searching a sequential file is binary search. This method is applicable to elements of a sorted list only. In this method, to search an element we compare it with the center element of the list. If it matches, then the search is successful and it is terminated. But if it does not match, the list is divided into two halves. The first half consists of 0th element to the center element whereas the second list consists of the element next to the center element to the last element. Now It is obvious that all elements in first half will be < or = to the center element and all element elements in the second half will be > than the center element. If the element to be searched is greater than the center element then searching will be done in the second half, otherwise in the first half.

Same process of comparing the element to be searched with the center element & if not found then dividing the elements into two halves is repeated for the first or second half. This process is repeated till the required element is found or the division of half parts gives a single element.

Algorithm for Binary Search

Illustrative Explanation

Let the array to be sorted is as follows:

```
11  23  31  33  65  68  71  89  100
```

Now let the element to be searched ie `key = 31` At first `hi=8  low=0` so `mid=4` and `x[mid]=` 65 is the center element but `65 > 31`. So now `hi = 4-1=3`. Now `mid= (0 + 3)/2 = 1`, so `x[mid]= 23 < 31`. So again `low= 1 + 1 = 2`. Now `mid = (3 + 2)/2 = 2` & `x[mid]= 31 = key`. So the search is successful. Similarly had the key been 32 it would have been an unsuccessful search.

Complexity

This is highly efficient than linear search. Each comparision in the binary search reduces the no. of possible candidates by a factor of 2. So the maximum no. of key comparisions is equal to $\log(2,n)$ approx. So the complexity of binary search is $O(\log n)$.

Limitations

Binary search algorithm can only be used if the list to be searched is in array form and not linked list. This is because the algorithm uses the fact that the indices of the array elements are consecutive integers. This makes this algorithm useless for lists with many insertions and deletions which can be implemented only when the list is in the form of a linked list.

But this can be overcome using *padded list* .

Hash Function

A hash function is any function that can be used to map data of arbitrary size to data of fixed size. The values returned by a hash function are called hash values, hash codes, digests, or simply hashes. One use is a data structure called a hash table, widely used in computer software for rapid data lookup. Hash functions accelerate table or database lookup by detecting duplicated records in a large file. An example is finding similar stretches in DNA sequences. They are also useful in cryptography. A cryptographic hash function allows one to easily verify that some input data maps to a given hash value, but if the input data is unknown, it is deliberately difficult to reconstruct it (or equivalent alternatives) by knowing the stored hash value. This is used for assuring integrity of transmitted data, and is the building block for HMACs, which provide message authentication.

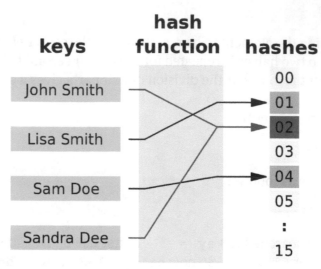

A hash function that maps names to integers from 0 to 15. There is a collision between keys "John Smith" and "Sandra Dee".

Hash functions are related to (and often confused with) checksums, check digits, fingerprints, lossy compression, randomization functions, error-correcting codes, and ciphers. Although these concepts overlap to some extent, each has its own uses and requirements and is designed and optimized differently. The Hash Keeper database maintained by the American National Drug Intelligence Center, for instance, is more aptly described as a catalogue of file fingerprints than of hash values.

Uses

Hash Tables

Hash functions are used in hash tables, to quickly locate a data record (e.g., a dictionary definition) given its search key (the headword). Specifically, the hash function is used to map the search key to an index; the index gives the place in the hash table where the corresponding record should be stored. Hash tables, in turn, are used to implement associative arrays and dynamic sets.

Typically, the domain of a hash function (the set of possible keys) is larger than its range (the number of different table indices), and so it will map several different keys to the same index. Therefore, each slot of a hash table is associated with (implicitly or explicitly) a set of records, rather than a single record. For this reason, each slot of a hash table is often called a *bucket*, and hash values are also called *bucket indices*.

Thus, the hash function only hints at the record's location — it tells where one should start looking for it. Still, in a half-full table, a good hash function will typically narrow the search down to only one or two entries.

Caches

Hash functions are also used to build caches for large data sets stored in slow media. A cache is generally simpler than a hashed search table, since any collision can be resolved by discarding or writing back the older of the two colliding items. This is also used in file comparison.

Bloom Filters

Hash functions are an essential ingredient of the Bloom filter, a space-efficient probabilistic data structure that is used to test whether an element is a member of a set.

Finding Duplicate Records

When storing records in a large unsorted file, one may use a hash function to map each record to an index into a table T, and to collect in each bucket $T[i]$ a list of the numbers of all records with the same hash value i. Once the table is complete, any two duplicate records will end up in the same bucket. The duplicates can then be found by scanning every bucket $T[i]$ which contains two or more members, fetching those records, and comparing them. With a table of appropriate size, this method is likely to be much faster than any alternative approach (such as sorting the file and comparing all consecutive pairs).

Protecting Data

A hash value can be used to uniquely identify secret information. This requires that the hash function is collision-resistant, which means that it is very hard to find data that will generate the same hash value. These functions are categorized into cryptographic hash functions and provably secure hash functions. Functions in the second category are the most secure but also too slow for most practical purposes. Collision resistance is accomplished in part by generating very large hash values. For example, SHA-1, one of the most widely used cryptographic hash functions, generates 160 bit values.

Finding Similar Records

Hash functions can also be used to locate table records whose key is similar, but not identical, to a given key; or pairs of records in a large file which have similar keys. For that purpose, one needs a hash function that maps similar keys to hash values that differ by at most m, where m is a small integer (say, 1 or 2). If one builds a table T of all record numbers, using such a hash function, then similar records will end up in the same bucket, or in nearby buckets. Then one need only check the records in each bucket $T[i]$ against those in buckets $T[i+k]$ where k ranges between $-m$ and m.

This class includes the so-called acoustic fingerprint algorithms, that are used to locate similar-sounding entries in large collection of audio files. For this application, the hash function must be as insensitive as possible to data capture or transmission errors, and to trivial changes such as timing and volume changes, compression, etc.

Finding Similar Substrings

The same techniques can be used to find equal or similar stretches in a large collection of strings, such as a document repository or a genomic database. In this case, the input strings are broken into many small pieces, and a hash function is used to detect potentially equal pieces, as above.

The Rabin–Karp algorithm is a relatively fast string searching algorithm that works in O(n) time on average. It is based on the use of hashing to compare strings.

Geometric Hashing

This principle is widely used in computer graphics, computational geometry and many other disciplines, to solve many proximity problems in the plane or in three-dimensional space, such as finding closest pairs in a set of points, similar shapes in a list of shapes, similar images in an image database, and so on. In these applications, the set of all inputs is some sort of metric space, and the hashing function can be interpreted as a partition of that space into a grid of *cells*. The table is often an array with two or more indices (called a *grid file*, *grid index*, *bucket grid*, and similar names), and the hash function returns an index tuple. This special case of hashing is known as geometric hashing or *the grid method*. Geometric hashing is also used in telecommunications (usually under the name vector quantization) to encode and compress multi-dimensional signals.

Standard uses of Hashing in Cryptography

Some standard applications that employ hash functions include authentication, message integrity (using an HMAC (Hashed MAC)), message fingerprinting, data corruption detection, and digital signature efficiency.

Properties

Good hash functions, in the original sense of the term, are usually required to satisfy certain properties listed below. The exact requirements are dependent on the application, for example a hash function well suited to indexing data will probably be a poor choice for a cryptographic hash function.

Determinism

A hash procedure must be deterministic—meaning that for a given input value it must always generate the same hash value. In other words, it must be a function of the data to be hashed, in the mathematical sense of the term. This requirement excludes hash functions that depend on external variable parameters, such as pseudo-random number generators or the time of day. It also excludes functions that depend on the memory address of the object being hashed in cases that the address may change during execution (as may happen on systems that use certain methods of garbage collection), although sometimes rehashing of the item is possible.

The determinism is in the context of the reuse of the function. For example, Python adds the feature that hash functions make use of a randomized seed that is generated once when the Python process starts in addition to the input to be hashed. The Python hash is still a valid hash function when used in within a single run. But if the values are persisted (for example, written to disk) they can no longer be treated as valid hash values, since in the next run the random value might differ.

Uniformity

A good hash function should map the expected inputs as evenly as possible over its output range. That is, every hash value in the output range should be generated with roughly the same probability. The reason for this last requirement is that the cost of hashing-based methods goes up sharply as the number of *collisions*—pairs of inputs that are mapped to the same hash value—increases. If some hash values are more likely to occur than others, a larger fraction of the lookup operations will have to search through a larger set of colliding table entries.

Note that this criterion only requires the value to be *uniformly distributed*, not *random* in any sense. A good randomizing function is (barring computational efficiency concerns) generally a good choice as a hash function, but the converse need not be true.

Hash tables often contain only a small subset of the valid inputs. For instance, a club membership list may contain only a hundred or so member names, out of the very large set of all possible names. In these cases, the uniformity criterion should hold for almost all typical subsets of entries that may be found in the table, not just for the global set of all possible entries.

In other words, if a typical set of m records is hashed to n table slots, the probability of a bucket receiving many more than m/n records should be vanishingly small. In particular, if m is less than n, very few buckets should have more than one or two records. (In an ideal "perfect hash function", no bucket should have more than one record; but a small number of collisions is virtually inevitable, even if n is much larger than m).

When testing a hash function, the uniformity of the distribution of hash values can be evaluated by the chi-squared test.

Defined Range

It is often desirable that the output of a hash function have fixed size. If, for example, the output is constrained to 32-bit integer values, the hash values can be used to index into an array. Such hashing is commonly used to accelerate data searches. On the other hand, cryptographic hash functions produce much larger hash values, in order to ensure the computational complexity of brute-force inversion. For example, SHA-1, one of the most widely used cryptographic hash functions, produces a 160-bit value.

Producing fixed-length output from variable length input can be accomplished by breaking the input data into chunks of specific size. Hash functions used for data searches use some arithmetic expression which iteratively processes chunks of the input (such as the characters in a string) to produce the hash value. In cryptographic hash functions, these chunks are processed by a one-way compression function, with the last chunk being padded if necessary. In this case, their size, which is called *block size*, is much bigger than the size of the hash value. For example, in SHA-1, the hash value is 160 bits and the block size 512 bits.

Variable Range

In many applications, the range of hash values may be different for each run of the program, or may change along the same run (for instance, when a hash table needs to be expanded). In those situations, one needs a hash function which takes two parameters—the input data z, and the number n of allowed hash values.

A common solution is to compute a fixed hash function with a very large range (say, 0 to $2^{32} - 1$), divide the result by n, and use the division's remainder. If n is itself a power of 2, this can be done by bit masking and bit shifting. When this approach is used, the hash function must be chosen so that the result has fairly uniform distribution between 0 and $n - 1$, for any value of n that may occur in the application. Depending on the function, the remainder may be uniform only for certain values of n, e.g. odd or prime numbers.

We can allow the table size n to not be a power of 2 and still not have to perform any remainder or division operation, as these computations are sometimes costly. For example, let n be significantly less than 2^b. Consider a pseudorandom number generator (PRNG) function $P(key)$ that is uniform on the interval $[0, 2^b - 1]$. A hash function uniform on the interval $[0, n-1]$ is $n\,P(key)/2^b$. We can replace the division by a (possibly faster) right bit shift: $nP(key) >> b$.

Variable Range with Minimal Movement (Dynamic Hash Function)

When the hash function is used to store values in a hash table that outlives the run of the program, and the hash table needs to be expanded or shrunk, the hash table is referred to as a dynamic hash table.

A hash function that will relocate the minimum number of records when the table is – where z is the key being hashed and n is the number of allowed hash values – such that $H(z,n + 1) = H(z,n)$ with probability close to $n/(n + 1)$.

Linear hashing and spiral storage are examples of dynamic hash functions that execute in constant time but relax the property of uniformity to achieve the minimal movement property.

Extendible hashing uses a dynamic hash function that requires space proportional to n to compute the hash function, and it becomes a function of the previous keys that have been inserted.

Several algorithms that preserve the uniformity property but require time proportional to n to compute the value of $H(z,n)$ have been invented.

Data Normalization

In some applications, the input data may contain features that are irrelevant for comparison purposes. For example, when looking up a personal name, it may be desirable to ignore the distinction between upper and lower case letters. For such data, one must use a hash function that is compatible with the data equivalence criterion being used: that is, any two inputs that are considered equivalent must yield the same hash value. This can be accomplished by normalizing the input before hashing it, as by upper-casing all letters.

Continuity

"A hash function that is used to search for similar (as opposed to equivalent) data must be as continuous as possible; two inputs that differ by a little should be mapped to equal or nearly equal hash values."

Note that continuity is usually considered a fatal flaw for checksums, cryptographic hash functions, and other related concepts. Continuity is desirable for hash functions only in some applications, such as hash tables used in Nearest neighbor search.

Non-invertible

In cryptographic applications, hash functions are typically expected to be practically non-invertible, meaning that it is not realistic to reconstruct the input datum x from its hash value $h(x)$ alone without spending great amounts of computing time.

Hash Function Algorithms

For most types of hashing functions, the choice of the function depends strongly on the nature of the input data, and their probability distribution in the intended application.

Trivial Hash Function

If the data to be hashed is small enough, one can use the data itself (reinterpreted as an integer) as the hashed value. The cost of computing this "trivial" (identity) hash function is effectively zero. This hash function is perfect, as it maps each input to a distinct hash value.

The meaning of "small enough" depends on the size of the type that is used as the hashed value. For example, in Java, the hash code is a 32-bit integer. Thus the 32-bit integer `Integer` and 32-bit floating-point Float objects can simply use the value directly; whereas the 64-bit integer `Long` and 64-bit floating-point Double cannot use this method.

Other types of data can also use this perfect hashing scheme. For example, when mapping character strings between upper and lower case, one can use the binary encoding of each character, interpreted as an integer, to index a table that gives the alternative form of that character ("A" for "a", "8" for "8", etc.). If each character is stored in 8 bits (as in extended ASCII or ISO Latin 1), the table has only $2^8 = 256$ entries; in the case of Unicode characters, the table would have $17 \times 2^{16} = 1114112$ entries.

The same technique can be used to map two-letter country codes like "us" or "za" to country names ($26^2 = 676$ table entries), 5-digit zip codes like 13083 to city names (100000 entries), etc. Invalid data values (such as the country code "xx" or the zip code 00000) may be left undefined in the table or mapped to some appropriate "null" value.

Perfect Hashing

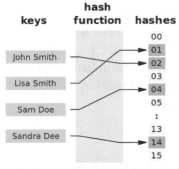

A perfect hash function for the four names shown.

A hash function that is injective—that is, maps each valid input to a different hash value—is said to be perfect. With such a function one can directly locate the desired entry in a hash table, without any additional searching.

Minimal Perfect Hashing

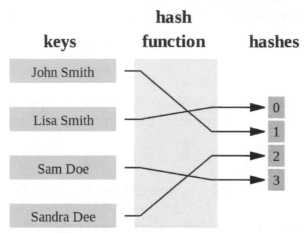

A minimal perfect hash function for the four names shown.

A perfect hash function for n keys is said to be minimal if its range consists of n *consecutive* integers, usually from 0 to $n-1$. Besides providing single-step lookup, a minimal perfect hash function also yields a compact hash table, without any vacant slots. Minimal perfect hash functions are much harder to find than perfect ones with a wider range.

Hashing Uniformly Distributed Data

If the inputs are bounded-length strings and each input may independently occur with uniform probability (such as telephone numbers, car license plates, invoice numbers, etc.), then a hash function needs to map roughly the same number of inputs to each hash value. For instance, suppose that each input is an integer z in the range 0 to $N-1$, and the output must be an integer h in the range 0 to $n-1$, where N is much larger than n. Then the hash function could be $h = z \bmod n$ (the remainder of z divided by n), or $h = (z \times n) \div N$ (the value z scaled down by n/N and truncated to an integer), or many other formulas.

Hashing Data with Other Distributions

These simple formulas will not do if the input values are not equally likely, or are not independent. For instance, most patrons of a supermarket will live in the same geographic area, so their telephone numbers are likely to begin with the same 3 to 4 digits. In that case, if m is 10000 or so, the division formula $(z \times m) \div M$, which depends mainly on the leading digits, will generate a lot of collisions; whereas the remainder formula $z \bmod m$, which is quite sensitive to the trailing digits, may still yield a fairly even distribution.

Hashing Variable-length Data

When the data values are long (or variable-length) character strings—such as personal names, web page addresses, or mail messages—their distribution is usually very uneven, with complicated dependencies. For example, text in any natural language has highly non-uniform distributions of characters, and character pairs, very characteristic of the language. For such data, it is prudent to use a hash function that depends on all characters of the string—and depends on each character in a different way.

In cryptographic hash functions, a Merkle–Damgård construction is usually used. In general, the scheme for hashing such data is to break the input into a sequence of small units (bits, bytes, words, etc.) and combine all the units b [1], b [2], ..., $b[m]$ sequentially, as follows

```
S ← S0;                    // Initialize the state.

for k in 1, 2, ..., m do   // Scan the input data units:

  S ← F(S, b[k]);          // Combine data unit k into the state.

return G(S, n)             // Extract the hash value from the state.
```

This schema is also used in many text checksum and fingerprint algorithms. The state variable S may be a 32- or 64-bit unsigned integer; in that case, $S0$ can be 0, and $G(S,n)$ can be just $S \bmod n$. The best choice of F is a complex issue and depends on the nature of the data. If the units $b[k]$ are single bits, then $F(S,b)$ could be, for instance

```
if highbit(S) = 0 then

   return 2 * S + b

 else

   return (2 * S + b) ^ P
```

Here *highbit(S)* denotes the most significant bit of S; the '*' operator denotes unsigned integer multiplication with lost overflow; '^' is the bitwise exclusive or operation applied to words; and P is a suitable fixed word.

Special-purpose Hash Functions

In many cases, one can design a special-purpose (heuristic) hash function that yields many fewer collisions than a good general-purpose hash function. For example, suppose that the input data are file names such as FILE0000.CHK, FILE0001.CHK, FILE0002.CHK, etc., with mostly sequential numbers. For such data, a function that extracts the numeric part k of the file name and returns k mod n would be nearly optimal. Needless to say, a function that is exceptionally good for a specific kind of data may have dismal performance on data with different distribution.

Rolling Hash

In some applications, such as substring search, one must compute a hash function h for every k-character substring of a given n-character string t; where k is a fixed integer, and n is k. The straightforward solution, which is to extract every such substring s of t and compute $h(s)$ separately, requires a number of operations proportional to $k \cdot n$. However, with the proper choice of h, one can use the technique of rolling hash to compute all those hashes with an effort proportional to $k + n$.

Universal Hashing

A universal hashing scheme is a randomized algorithm that selects a hashing function h among a family of such functions, in such a way that the probability of a collision of any two distinct keys is $1/n$, where n is the number of distinct hash values desired—independently of the two keys. Universal hashing ensures (in a probabilistic sense) that the hash function application will behave as well as if it were using a random function, for any distribution of the input data. It will, however, have more collisions than perfect hashing and may require more operations than a special-purpose hash function.

Hashing with Checksum Functions

One can adapt certain checksum or fingerprinting algorithms for use as hash functions. Some of those algorithms will map arbitrary long string data z, with any typical real-world distribution—no matter how non-uniform and dependent—to a 32-bit or 64-bit string, from which one can extract a hash value in 0 through $n - 1$.

This method may produce a sufficiently uniform distribution of hash values, as long as the hash range size n is small compared to the range of the checksum or fingerprint function. However, some checksums fare poorly in the avalanche test, which may be a concern in some applications. In particular, the popular CRC32 checksum provides only 16 bits (the higher half of the result) that are usable for hashing. Moreover, each bit of the input has a deterministic effect on each bit of the CRC32, that is one can tell without looking at the rest of the input, which bits of the output will flip if the input bit is flipped; so care must be taken to use all 32 bits when computing the hash from the checksum.

Multiplicative Hashing

Multiplicative hashing is a simple type of hash function often used by teachers introducing students to hash tables. Multiplicative hash functions are simple and fast, but have higher collision rates in hash tables than more sophisticated hash functions.

In many applications, such as hash tables, collisions make the system a little slower but are otherwise harmless. In such systems, it is often better to use hash functions based on multiplication—such as MurmurHash and the SBoxHash—or even simpler hash functions such as CRC32—and tolerate more collisions; rather than use a more complex hash function that avoids many of those collisions but takes longer to compute. Multiplicative hashing is susceptible to a "common mistake" that leads to poor diffusion—higher-value input bits do not affect lower-value output bits.

Hashing with Cryptographic Hash Functions

Some cryptographic hash functions, such as SHA-1, have even stronger uniformity guarantees than checksums or fingerprints, and thus can provide very good general-purpose hashing functions.

In ordinary applications, this advantage may be too small to offset their much higher cost. However, this method can provide uniformly distributed hashes even when the keys are chosen by a malicious agent. This feature may help to protect services against denial of service attacks.

Hashing by Nonlinear Table Lookup

Tables of random numbers (such as 256 random 32-bit integers) can provide high-quality nonlinear functions to be used as hash functions or for other purposes such as cryptography. The key to be hashed is split into 8-bit (one-byte) parts, and each part is used as an index for the nonlinear table. The table values are then added by arithmetic or XOR addition to the hash output value. Because the table is just 1024 bytes in size, it fits into the cache of modern microprocessors and allows very fast execution of the hashing algorithm. As the table value is on average much longer than 8 bits, one bit of input affects nearly all output bits.

This algorithm has proven to be very fast and of high quality for hashing purposes (especially hashing of integer-number keys).

Efficient Hashing of Strings

Modern microprocessors will allow for much faster processing, if 8-bit character strings are not hashed by processing one character at a time, but by interpreting the string as an array of 32 bit or 64 bit integers and hashing/accumulating these "wide word" integer values by means of arithmetic operations (e.g. multiplication by constant and bit-shifting). The remaining characters of the string which are smaller than the word length of the CPU must be handled differently (e.g. being processed one character at a time).

This approach has proven to speed up hash code generation by a factor of five or more on modern microprocessors of a word size of 64 bit.

Another approach is to convert strings to a 32 or 64 bit numeric value and then apply a hash function. One method that avoids the problem of strings having great similarity ("Aaaaaaaaaa" and "Aaaaaaaaab") is to use a Cyclic redundancy check (CRC) of the string to compute a 32- or 64-bit value. While it is possible that two different strings will have the same CRC, the likelihood is very small and only requires that one check the actual string found to determine whether one has an exact match. CRCs will be different for strings such as "Aaaaaaaaaa" and "Aaaaaaaaab". Although, CRC codes can be used as hash values they are not cryptographically secure since they are not collision-resistant.

Locality-Sensitive Hashing

Locality-sensitive hashing (LSH) is a method of performing probabilistic dimension reduction of high-dimensional data. The basic idea is to hash the input items so that similar items are mapped to the same buckets with high probability (the number of buckets being much smaller than the universe of possible input items). This is different from the conventional hash functions, such as those used in cryptography, as in this case the goal is to maximize the probability of "collision" of similar items rather than to avoid collisions.

One example of LSH is MinHash algorithm used for finding similar documents (such as web-pages):

Let h be a hash function that maps the members of A and B to distinct integers, and for any set S define $h_{min}(S)$ to be the member x of S with the minimum value of $h(x)$. Then $h_{min}(A) =$

$h_{min}(B)$ exactly when the minimum hash value of the union $A \cup B$ lies in the intersection $A \cap B$. Therefore,

$$Pr[h_{min}(A) = h_{min}(B)] = J(A,B).$$ where J is Jaccard index.

In other words, if r is a random variable that is one when $h_{min}(A) = h_{min}(B)$ and zero otherwise, then r is an unbiased estimator of $J(A,B)$, although it has too high a variance to be useful on its own. The idea of the MinHash scheme is to reduce the variance by averaging together several variables constructed in the same way.

Origins of the Term

The term "hash" offers a natural analogy with its non-technical meaning (to "chop" or "make a mess" out of something), given how hash functions scramble their input data to derive their output. In his research for the precise origin of the term, Donald Knuth notes that, while Hans Peter Luhn of IBM appears to have been the first to use the concept of a hash function in a memo dated January 1953, the term itself would only appear in published literature in the late 1960s, on Herbert Hellerman's *Digital Computer System Principles*, even though it was already widespread jargon by then.

List of Hash Functions

- Coalesced hashing
- Cuckoo hashing
- Hopscotch hashing
- NIST hash function competition
- MD5
- Bernstein hash
- Fowler-Noll-Vo hash function (32, 64, 128, 256, 512, or 1024 bits)
- Jenkins hash function (32 bits)
- Pearson hashing (64 bits)
- Zobrist hashing

Hashing Techniques

Introduction

Hashing is a method to store data in an array so that sorting, searching, inserting and deleting data is fast. For this every record needs unique key.

The basic idea is not to search for the correct position of a record with comparisons but to compute the position within the array. The function that returns the position is called the 'hash function' and the array is called a 'hash table'.

Why Hashing?

In the other type of searching, we have seen that the record is stored in a table and it is necessary to pass through some number of keys before finding the desired one. While we know that the efficient search technique is one which minimizesthese comparisons. Thus we need a search technique in which there is no unnecessary comparisons.

If we want to access a key in a single retrieval, then the location of the record within the table must depend only on the key, not on the location of other keys(as in other type of searching i.e. tree). The most efficient way to organize such a table is an array.It was possible only with hashing.

Hash Clash

Suppose two keys k1 and k2 are such that h(k1) equals h(k2).When a record with key two keys can't get the same position.such a situation is called hash collision or hash clash.

Methods of Dealing with Hash Clash

There are three basic methods of dealing with hash clash. They are:

1. Chaining

2. Rehashing

3. Separate Chaining.

Chaining

It builds a link list of all items whose keys has the same value. During search,this sorted linked list is traversed sequentially fro the desired key.It involves adding an extra link field to each table position. There are three types of chaining

1. Standard Coalsced Hashing

2. General Coalsced Hashing

3. Varied insertion coalsced Hashing

Standard Coalsced Hashing

It is the simplest of chaining methods. It reduces the average number of probes for an unsuccessful search. It efficiently does the deletion without affecting the efficiency

General Coalsced Hashing

It is the generalization of standard coalesced chaining method. In this method, we add extra positions to the hash table that can be used to list the nodes in the time of collision.

Varied Insertion Coalsced Hashing

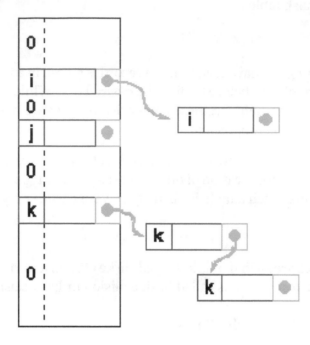

It is the combination of standard and general coalesced hashing. Under this method, the colliding item is inserted to the list immediately following the hash position unless the list forming from that position containing a cellar element.

Solving Hash Clashes by Linear Probing

The simplest method is that when a clash occurs, insert the record in the next available place in the table. For example in the table the next position 646 is empty. So we can insert the record with key 012345645 in this place which is still empty. Similarly if the record with key %1000 = 646 appears, it will be inserted in next empty space. This technique is called linear probing and is an example for resolving hash clashes called rehashing or open addressing.

Working of Linear Probing Algorithm

It works like this: If array location h(key) is already occupied by a record with a different key, rh is applied to the value of h(key) to find the other location where the record may be placed. If position rh(h(key))is also occupied,it too is rehashed to see if rh(rh(h(key))) is available. This process continues until an empty location is found. Thus we can write a search and insert algorithm using hashing as follows:

Algorithm

```
void insert( key, r )

typekey key; dataarray r;

   {
```

```
extern int n;

int i, last;

i = hashfunction( key ) ;

last = (i+m-1) % m;

 while ( i!=last && !empty(r[i]) && !deleted(r[i]) && r[i].k!=key )

 i = (i+1) % m;

  if (empty(r[i]) || deleted(r[i]))

   {

    /*** insert here ***/

   r[i].k = key;

   n++;

   }

 else Error /*** table full, or key already in table ***/;

}
```

Disadvantages of Linear Probing

It may happen, however, that the loop executes forever. There are two possible reasons for this. First, the table may be full so that it is impossible to insert any new record. This situation can be detected by keeping an account of the number of records in the table.

When the count equals the table size, no further insertion should be done. The other reason may be that the table is not full, too. In this type, suppose all the odd positions are emptyAnd the even positions are full and we want to insert in the even position by rh(i)=(i+2)%1000 used as a hash function. Of course, it is very unlikely that all the odd positions are empty and all the even positions are full.

However the rehash function rh(i)=(i+200)%1000 is used, each key can be placed in one of the five positions only. Here the loop can run infinitely, too.

Separate Chaining

As we have seen earlier, we can't insert items more than the table size. In some cases, we allocate space much more than required resulting in wastage of space. In order to tackle all these problems, we have a separate method of resolving clashes called separate chaining. It keeps a distinct link list for all records whose keys hash into a particular value. In this method, the items that end with a particular number (unit position) is placed in a particular link list as shown in the figure. The 10's, 100's not taken into account. The pointer to the node points to the next node and when there is no more nodes, the pointer points to NULL value.

Advantages of Seperate Chaining

1. No worries of filling up the table whatever be the number of items.

2. The list items need not be contiguous storage

3. It allows traversal of items in hash key order.

Situation of Hash Clash

What would happen if we want to insert a new part number 012345645 in the table .Using he hash function key %1000 we get 645.Therefore for the part belongs in position 645.However record for the part is already being occupied by 011345645.Therefore the record with the key 012345645 must be inserted somewhere in the table resulting in hash clash.This is illustrated in the given table:

Position	Key	Record
0	258001201	
2	698321903	
3	986453204	
.		
.		
450	256894450	
451	158965451	
.		
.		
647	214563647	
648	782154648	
649	325649649	
.		
.		
997	011239997	
998	231452998	
999	011232999	

Double Hashing

A method of open addressing for a hash table in which a collision is resolved by searching the table for an empty place at intervals given by a different hash function, thus minimizing clustering. Double Hashing is another method of collision resolution, but unlike the linear collision resolution, double hashing uses a second hashing function that normally limits multiple collisions. The idea is that if two values hash to the same spot in the table, a constant can be calculated from the initial value using the second hashing function that can then be used to change the sequence of locations in the table, but still have access to the entire table.

Algorithm for double hashing

```
void insert( key, r )

typekey key; dataarray r;

{

extern int n;

int i, inc, last;

i = hashfunction( key ) ;

inc = increment( key );

last = (i+(m-1)*inc) % m;

while ( i!=last && !empty(r[i]) && !deleted(r[i]) && r[i].k!=key )

i = (i+inc) % m;

if ( empty(r[i]) || deleted(r[i]) )

{

/*** insert here ***/

r[i].k = key;

n++;

}

else Error /*** table full, or key already in table ***/;

}
```

Clustering

There are mainly two types of clustering:

Primary clustering

When the entire array is empty, it is equally likely that a record is inserted at any position in the array. However, once entries have been inserted and several hash clashes have been resolved, it doesn't remain true. For, example in the given above table, it is five times as likely for the record to be inserted at the position 994 as the position 401. This is because any record whose key hashes into 990, 991, 992, 993 or 994 will be placed in 994, whereas only a record whose key hashes into 401 will be placed there. This phenomenon where two keys that hash into different values compete with each other in successive rehashes is called primary clustering.

Cause of Primary Clustering

Any rehash function that depends solely on the index to be rehashed causes primary clustering

Ways of Eleminating Primary Clustering

One way of eliminating primary clustering is to allow the rehash function to depend on the number of times that the function is applied to a particular hash value. Another way is to use random permutation of the number between 1 and e, where e is (table size -1, the largest index of the table). One more method is to allow rehash to depend on the hash value. All these methods allow key that hash into different locations to follow separate rehash paths.

Secondary Clustering

In this type, different keys that hash to the same value follow same rehash path.

Ways to Eliminate Secondary Clustering

All types of clustering can be eliminated by double hashing, which involves the use of two hash function h1(key) and h2(key).h1 is known as primary hash function and is allowed first to get the position where the key will be inserted. If that position is occupied already, the rehash function rh(i,key) = (i+h2(key))%table size is used successively until an empty position is found. As long as h2(key1) doesn't equal h2(key2),records with keys h1 and h2 don't compete for the same position. Therefore one should choose functions h1 and h2 that distributes the hashes and rehashes uniformly in the table and also minimizes clustering.

Deleting an Item from the Hash Table

It is very difficult to delete an item from the hash table that uses rehashes for search and insertion. Suppose that a record r is placed at some specific location. We want to insert some other record r1 on the same location. We will have to insert the record in the next empty location to the specified original location. Suppose that the record r which was there at the specified location is deleted.

Now, we want to search the record r1, as the location with record r is now empty, it will erroneously conclude that the record r1 is absent from the table. One possible solution to this problem is that the deleted record must be marked "deleted" rather than "empty" and the search must continue whenever a "deleted" position is encountered. But this is possible only when there are small numbers of deletions otherwise an unsuccessful search will have to search the entire table since most of the positions will be marked "deleted" rather than "empty".

Dynamic and Extendible Hashing

One of the serious drawbacks associated with hashing of external storage is its being insufficiently flexible. The contents of the external storage structure tend to grow and shrink unpredictably. The entire hash table structuring method that we have examined has a sharp space/time trade-off. Either the table uses a large amount of space for efficient access which results in wastage of large space an or it uses a small amount of space and accommodates growth very poorly and sharply increasing the access time fro overflow elements. So in order to tackle the above stated problems, we would like to develop a scheme that doesn't utilize too much extra space when a file is small but permits efficient access when it grows larger. Two such schemes are dynamic hashing and Extendible hashing.

Dynamic Hashing

Dynamic hashing is a hash table that grows to handle more items. The associated hash function must change as the table grows. Some schemes may shrink the table to save space when items are deleted.

Extendible Hashing

A hash table in which the hash function is the last few bits of the key and the table refer to buckets. Table entries with the same final bits may use the same bucket. If a bucket overflows, it splits, and if only one entry referred to it, the table doubles in size. If a bucket is emptied by deletion, entries using it are changed to refer to an adjoining bucket, and the table may be halved.

Hash Table Reordering

When a hash table is nearly full, many items given by their hash keys are not at their specified location. Thus, we have to make a lot of key comparisons before finding such items. If an item is not in the table, entire hash table has to be searched. Then, we come to the conclusion that the key is not in the table. In order to tackle this situation, many techniques came forward.

Amble and Knuth Method

In this method, all the records that hash into same locations are placed in descending order (assuming that the NULLKEY is the smallest one). Suppose we want to search a key, we need not rehash repeatedly until an empty slot is found. As soon as an item whose key is less than the search key is found in the table, we come to the conclusion that the search key is not in the table. At the time of insertion, if we want to insert a key k, if the rehash accesses a key smaller than k, the associated record with k replaces it and the insertion process continues with the replaced key.

The ordered hash table method can be used only in the technique in which a rehash depends only on the index and the key not in the technique in which a rehash function depends on the no of items the item is rehashed (unless that number is kept in the table).

Advantages of Amble and Knuth's Method

It reduces significantly the number of key comparisons necessary to determine that a key doesn't exist in the table.

Disadvantages of Amble and Knuth's Method

1. It doesn't change the average number of key comparisons required to find a key that is in the table

2. The unsuccessful search needs same average number of probes as the successful search.

3. Average number of probes in insertion is not reduced in ordered table.

Brent's Method

This technique involves rehashing the search argument until an empty slot is found. Then each of the keys in rehash path is itself rehashed to determine if placing one of those keys in an empty slot would require fewer rehashes. If this is the case the search argument replaces the existing key in the table and the existing key is inserted in its empty rehash slot.

Binary Tree Hashing

Another method of reordering the hash table was developed by Gonnet and Munro and is called as binary tree hashing. It is seen as an improvement to Brent's algorithm. In this method, we assume to use double hashing. Whenever a key is inserted in the hash table, an almost complete binary tree is constructed. Figure below illustrates an example of such a tree in which the nodes are arranged according to the array representation of an almost complete binary tree.node(0) is the root and node(2*i+1)and node(2*i+2) are the left and right children of node(i) respectively. Each node of the tree contains an index into the hash table. In the explanation, node(i) will be referred to as index(i) and the key at that position is referred to as k(-1).

How to Construct a Tree

Firstly, we define the youngest right ancestor of node(i) or yra(i) as the node number of the father of the youngest son i.e. the right son. In the given figure, yra(12) is 1, since it is the left son of its father node(6) and its father is also a left child. So the youngest ancestor of node(12) is node(3) and is father is node(1). Similarly, yra(10) is 2 and yra(18) is 4 and yra(14) is 3. if node(i) is the right son, yra(i) is defined as the node number of its father (i-1)/2. Thus, yra(15) is 7 and yra(13) is 6. If node(i) has no ancestor i.e. is a right son, yra(i) is defined as (-1). Thus, yra(16) is -1. The binary tree is constructed according to the node number. The table construction continues until a NULLKEY and an empty position is found in the table.

How to Calculate Yra (i)

As we have seen above, the entire algorithm depends on the routine yra(i). Fortunately, yra(i) can be calculated very easily. It can be derived directly using this method. Find the binary representation of (i+1). Delete all the trailing zero bits along with one bit preceding them. Subtract 1 from the result and you will get the resulting binary number to get the value of yra(i).

Examples

1. yra(11):

11+1=12

Binary representation: 1100.

Removing 100, we get 1, which is binary representation of 1.

Therefore, yra(11)=0.

2.   yra(17):

17+1=18

Binary representation: 10010.

Removing 10, we get 100, which is binary representation of 4.

Therefore, yra(11)=3.

3.   yra(15):

15+1=16

Binary representation: 010000.

Removing 10000, we get 0, which is binary representation of 0.

Therefore, yra(11)=-1.

How to Insert a Key in the Table

Once the tree has been constructed, the keys along the path from the root to the last node are reordered in the hash table. Let, i be initialized to the last node of the tree. If yra(i) is non-zero, k(yra(i)) and its associated record are shifted from the table[index(yra(i))] to table[index(i)] and I is reset to yra(i). It is repeated until yra(i) is -1 at which point insertion is complete.

Example of Insertion

Suppose yra(21)=10 and index(10) is j, the key and record from j is shifted to u which is the right child. Then suppose yra(10) is 2, the record and key from position b is shifted to j which is the right child of index b.Finally since yra(2) is -1, key is inserted in position b.

Advantage of Binary Search Tree

Binary tree hashing yields results that are even closer to optimal than Brent's.

References

- Konheim, Alan (2010). "7. HASHING FOR STORAGE: DATA MANAGEMENT". Hashing in Computer Science: Fifty Years of Slicing and Dicing. Wiley-Interscience. ISBN 9780470344736
- Horvath, Adam. "Binary search and linear search performance on the .NET and Mono platform". Retrieved 19 April 2013

- Menezes, Alfred J.; van Oorschot, Paul C.; Vanstone, Scott A (1996). Handbook of Applied Cryptography. CRC Press. ISBN 0849385237

- Knuth, Donald E. (2000). Sorting and searching (2. ed., 6. printing, newly updated and rev. ed.). Boston [u.a.]: Addison-Wesley. pp. 547–548. ISBN 0-201-89685-0

- Cam-Winget, Nancy; Housley, Russ; Wagner, David; Walker, Jesse (May 2003). "Security Flaws in 802.11 Data Link Protocols". Communications of the ACM. 46 (5): 35–39. doi:10.1145/769800.769823

- Knuth, Donald (1997). "Section 6.1: Sequential Searching,". Sorting and Searching. The Art of Computer Programming. 3 (3rd ed.). Addison-Wesley. pp. 396–408. ISBN 0-201-89685-0

4

Tree Data Structure: An Integrated Study

The major categories of trees in data structure are dealt with great details in the section. It focuses on binary tree, its operation, representation and transversal. Binary tree is a type of tree that has a distinct node and can have a maximum of two children. Other type of tree discussed here is the search tree. It helps in finding out specific keys from a set. The chapter strategically encompasses and incorporates the major components and key concepts of data structures, providing a complete understanding.

Tree (Data Structure)

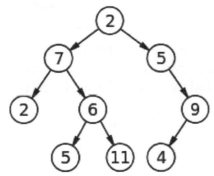

A simple unordered tree; in this diagram, the node labeled 7 has two children, labeled 2 and 6, and one parent, labeled 2. The root node, at the top, has no parent.

In computer science, a tree is a widely used abstract data type (ADT)—or data structure implementing this ADT—that simulates a hierarchical tree structure, with a root value and subtrees of children with a parent node, represented as a set of linked nodes.

A tree data structure can be defined recursively (locally) as a collection of nodes (starting at a root node), where each node is a data structure consisting of a value, together with a list of references to nodes (the "children"), with the constraints that no reference is duplicated, and none points to the root.

Alternatively, a tree can be defined abstractly as a whole (globally) as an ordered tree, with a value assigned to each node. Both these perspectives are useful: while a tree can be analyzed mathematically as a whole, when actually represented as a data structure it is usually represented and worked with separately by node (rather than as a list of nodes and an adjacency list of edges between nodes, as one may represent a digraph, for instance). For example, looking at a tree as a whole, one can talk about "the parent node" of a given node, but in general as a data structure a given node only contains the list of its children, but does not contain a reference to its parent (if any).

Definition

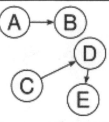

Not a tree: two non-connected parts, A→B and C→D→E. There is more than one root.

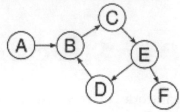

Not a tree: cycle B→C→E→D→B. B has more than one parent (inbound edge).

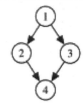

Not a tree: undirected cycle 1-2-4-3. 4 has more than one parent (inbound edge).

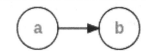

Each linear list is trivially a tree

Not a tree: cycle A→A. A is the root but it also has a parent.

A tree is a data structure made up of nodes or vertices and edges without having any cycle. The tree with no nodes is called the null or empty tree. A tree that is not empty consists of a root node and potentially many levels of additional nodes that form a hierarchy.

Terminology used in Trees

Root

> The top node in a tree.

Child

> A node directly connected to another node when moving away from the Root.

Parent

> The converse notion of a *child*.

Siblings

> A group of nodes with the same parent.

Descendant

> A node reachable by repeated proceeding from parent to child.

Ancestor

> A node reachable by repeated proceeding from child to parent.

Leaf

(less commonly called External node)

> A node with no children.

Branch

Internal node

> A node with at least one child.

Degree

> The number of sub trees of a node.

Edge

> The connection between one node and another.

Path

> A sequence of nodes and edges connecting a node with a descendant.

Level

> The level of a node is defined by 1 + (the number of connections between the node and the root).

Height of node

> The height of a node is the number of edges on the longest path between that node and a leaf.

Height of tree

> The height of a tree is the height of its root node.

Depth

> The depth of a node is the number of edges from the tree's root node to the node.

Forest

> A forest is a set of n ≥ 0 disjoint trees.

Data type vs. Data Structure

There is a distinction between a tree as an abstract data type and as a concrete data structure, analogous to the distinction between a list and a linked list. As a data type, a tree has a value and children, and the children are themselves trees; the value and children of the tree are interpreted as the value of the root node and the subtrees of the children of the root node. To allow finite trees, one must either allow the list of children to be empty (in which case trees can be required to be non-empty, an "empty tree" instead being represented by a forest of zero trees), or allow trees to be empty, in which case the list of children can be of fixed size (branching factor, especially 2 or "binary"), if desired.

As a data structure, a linked tree is a group of nodes, where each node has a value and a list of references to other nodes (its children). This data structure actually defines a directed graph,[a] because it may have loops or several references to the same node, just as a linked list may have a loop. Thus there is also the requirement that no two references point to the same node (that each node has at most a single parent, and in fact exactly one parent, except for the root), and a tree that violates this is "corrupt".

Due to the use of *references* to trees in the linked tree data structure, trees are often discussed implicitly assuming that they are being represented by references to the root node, as this is often how they are actually implemented. For example, rather than an empty tree, one may have a null reference: a tree is always non-empty, but a reference to a tree may be null.

Recursive

Recursively, as a data type a tree is defined as a value (of some data type, possibly empty), together with a list of trees (possibly an empty list), the subtrees of its children; symbolically:

```
t: v [t, ..., t[k]]
```

(A tree *t* consists of a value *v* and a list of other trees.)

More elegantly, via mutual recursion, of which a tree is one of the most basic examples, a tree can be defined in terms of a forest (a list of trees), where a tree consists of a value and a forest (the subtrees of its children):

```
f: [t, ..., t[k]]
```

```
t: v f
```

Note that this definition is in terms of values, and is appropriate in functional languages (it assumes referential transparency); different trees have no connections, as they are simply lists of values.

As a data structure, a tree is defined as a node (the root), which itself consists of a value (of some data type, possibly empty), together with a list of references to other nodes (list possibly empty, references possibly null); symbolically:

```
n: v [&n, ..., &n[k]]
```

(A node *n* consists of a value *v* and a list of references to other nodes.)

This data structure defines a directed graph and for it to be a tree one must add a condition on its global structure (its topology), namely that at most one reference can point to any given node (a node has at most a single parent), and no node in the tree point to the root. In fact, every node (other than the root) must have exactly one parent, and the root must have no parents.

Indeed, given a list of nodes, and for each node a list of references to its children, one cannot tell if this structure is a tree or not without analyzing its global structure and that it is in fact topologically a tree, as defined below.

Type Theory

As an ADT, the abstract tree type T with values of some type E is defined, using the abstract forest type F (list of trees), by the functions:

value: $T \rightarrow E$

children: $T \rightarrow F$

nil: $() \rightarrow F$

node: $E \times F \rightarrow T$

with the axioms:

value(node(e, f)) = e

children(node(e, f)) = f

In terms of type theory, a tree is an inductive type defined by the constructors *nil* (empty forest) and *node* (tree with root node with given value and children).

Mathematical

Viewed as a whole, a tree data structure is an ordered tree, generally with values attached to each node. Concretely, it is (if required to be non-empty):

- A rooted tree with the "away from root" direction (a more narrow term is an "arborescence"), meaning:

    o   A directed graph,

    o   whose underlying undirected graph is a tree (any two vertices are connected by exactly one simple path),

    o   with a distinguished root (one vertex is designated as the root),

    o   which determines the direction on the edges (arrows point away from the root; given an edge, the node that the edge points from is called the *parent* and the node that the edge points to is called the *child*),

together with:

- an ordering on the child nodes of a given node, and

- a value (of some data type) at each node.

Often trees have a fixed (more properly, bounded) branching factor (outdegree), particularly always having two child nodes (possibly empty, hence *at most* two *non-empty* child nodes), hence a "binary tree".

Allowing empty trees makes some definitions simpler, some more complicated: a rooted tree must be non-empty, hence if empty trees are allowed the above definition instead becomes "an empty tree, or a rooted tree such that ...". On the other hand, empty trees simplify defining fixed branching factor: with empty trees allowed, a binary tree is a tree such that every node has exactly two children, each of which is a tree (possibly empty).The complete sets of operations on tree must include fork operation.

Terminology

A node is a structure which may contain a value or condition, or represent a separate data structure (which could be a tree of its own). Each node in a tree has zero or more child nodes, which are below it in the tree (by convention, trees are drawn growing downwards). A node that has a child is called the child's parent node (or *ancestor node*, or superior). A node has at most one parent.

An internal node (also known as an inner node, inode for short, or branch node) is any node of a tree that has child nodes. Similarly, an external node (also known as an outer node, leaf node, or terminal node) is any node that does not have child nodes.

The topmost node in a tree is called the root node. Depending on definition, a tree may be required to have a root node (in which case all trees are non-empty), or may be allowed to be empty, in which case it does not necessarily have a root node. Being the topmost node, the root node will not have a parent. It is the node at which algorithms on the tree begin, since as a data structure, one can only pass from parents to children. Note that some algorithms (such as post-order depth-first search) begin at the root, but first visit leaf nodes (access the value of leaf nodes), only visit the root last (i.e., they first access the children of the root, but only access the *value* of the root last). All other nodes can be reached from it by following edges or links. (In the formal definition, each such path is also unique.) In diagrams, the root node is conventionally drawn at the top. In some trees, such as heaps, the root node has special properties. Every node in a tree can be seen as the root node of the subtree rooted at that node.

The height of a node is the length of the longest downward path to a leaf from that node. The height of the root is the height of the tree. The depth of a node is the length of the path to its root (i.e., its *root path*). This is commonly needed in the manipulation of the various self-balancing trees, AVL Trees in particular. The root node has depth zero, leaf nodes have height zero, and a tree with only a single node (hence both a root and leaf) has depth and height zero. Conventionally, an empty tree (tree with no nodes, if such are allowed) has height −1.

A subtree of a tree T is a tree consisting of a node in T and all of its descendants in T.[c] Nodes thus correspond to subtrees (each node corresponds to the subtree of itself and all its descendants) – the subtree corresponding to the root node is the entire tree, and each node is the root node of the subtree it determines; the subtree corresponding to any other node is called a proper subtree (by analogy to a proper subset).

Drawing Trees

Trees are often drawn in the plane. Ordered trees can be represented essentially uniquely in the plane, and are hence called *plane trees,* as follows: if one fixes a conventional order (say, counter-clockwise), and arranges the child nodes in that order (first incoming parent edge, then first child edge, etc.), this yields an embedding of the tree in the plane, unique up to ambient isotopy. Conversely, such an embedding determines an ordering of the child nodes.

If one places the root at the top (parents above children, as in a family tree) and places all nodes that are a given distance from the root (in terms of number of edges: the "level" of a tree) on a given horizontal line, one obtains a standard drawing of the tree. Given a binary tree, the first child is on the left (the "left node"), and the second child is on the right (the "right node").

Representations

There are many different ways to represent trees; common representations represent the nodes as dynamically allocated records with pointers to their children, their parents, or both, or as items in an array, with relationships between them determined by their positions in the array (e.g., binary heap).

Indeed, a binary tree can be implemented as a list of lists (a list where the values are lists): the head of a list (the value of the first term) is the left child (subtree), while the tail (the list of second and subsequent terms) is the right child (subtree). This can be modified to allow values as well, as in Lisp S-expressions, where the head (value of first term) is the value of the node, the head of the tail (value of second term) is the left child, and the tail of the tail (list of third and subsequent terms) is the right child.

In general a node in a tree will not have pointers to its parents, but this information can be included (expanding the data structure to also include a pointer to the parent) or stored separately. Alternatively, upward links can be included in the child node data, as in a threaded binary tree.

Generalizations

Digraphs

If edges (to child nodes) are thought of as references, then a tree is a special case of a digraph, and the tree data structure can be generalized to represent directed graphs by removing the constraints that a node may have at most one parent, and that no cycles are allowed. Edges are still abstractly considered as pairs of nodes, however, the terms *parent* and *child* are usually replaced by different terminology (for example, *source* and *target*). Different implementation strategies exist: a digraph can be represented by the same local data structure as a tree (node with value and list of children), assuming that "list of children" is a list of references, or globally by such structures as adjacency lists.

In graph theory, a tree is a connected acyclic graph; unless stated otherwise, in graph theory trees and graphs are assumed undirected. There is no one-to-one correspondence between such trees and trees as data structure. We can take an arbitrary undirected tree, arbitrarily pick one of its vertices as the *root*, make all its edges directed by making them point away from the root node –

producing an arborescence – and assign an order to all the nodes. The result corresponds to a tree data structure. Picking a different root or different ordering produces a different one.

Given a node in a tree, its children define an ordered forest (the union of subtrees given by all the children, or equivalently taking the subtree given by the node itself and erasing the root). Just as subtrees are natural for recursion (as in a depth-first search), forests are natural for corecursion (as in a breadth-first search).

Via mutual recursion, a forest can be defined as a list of trees (represented by root nodes), where a node (of a tree) consists of a value and a forest (its children):

```
f: [n, ..., n[k]]
```

```
n: v f
```

Traversal Methods

Stepping through the items of a tree, by means of the connections between parents and children, is called walking the tree, and the action is a walk of the tree. Often, an operation might be performed when a pointer arrives at a particular node. A walk in which each parent node is traversed before its children is called a pre-order walk; a walk in which the children are traversed before their respective parents are traversed is called a post-order walk; a walk in which a node's left subtree, then the node itself, and finally its right subtree are traversed is called an in-order traversal. (This last scenario, referring to exactly two subtrees, a left subtree and a right subtree, assumes specifically a binary tree.) A level-order walk effectively performs a breadth-first search over the entirety of a tree; nodes are traversed level by level, where the root node is visited first, followed by its direct child nodes and their siblings, followed by its grandchild nodes and their siblings, etc., until all nodes in the tree have been traversed.

Common Operations

- Enumerating all the items

- Enumerating a section of a tree

- Searching for an item

- Adding a new item at a certain position on the tree

- Deleting an item

- Pruning: Removing a whole section of a tree

- Grafting: Adding a whole section to a tree

- Finding the root for any node

Common uses

- Representing hierarchical data

- Storing data in a way that makes it efficiently searchable (see binary search tree and tree traversal)

- Representing sorted lists of data

- As a workflow for compositing digital images for visual effects

Binary Tree

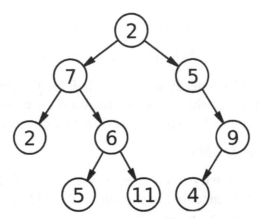

A labeled binary tree of size 9 and height 3, with a root node whose value is 2.
The above tree is unbalanced and not sorted.

In computer science, a binary tree is a tree data structure in which each node has at most two children, which are referred to as the *left child* and the *right child*. A recursive definition using just set theory notions is that a (non-empty) binary tree is a triple (L, S, R), where L and R are binary trees or the empty set and S is a singleton set. Some authors allow the binary tree to be the empty set as well.

From a graph theory perspective, binary (and K-ary) trees as defined here are actually arborescences. A binary tree may thus be also called a bifurcating arborescence—a term which appears in some very old programming books, before the modern computer science terminology prevailed. It is also possible to interpret a binary tree as an undirected, rather than a directed graph, in which case a binary tree is an ordered, rooted tree. Some authors use rooted binary tree instead of *binary tree* to emphasize the fact that the tree is rooted, but as defined above, a binary tree is always rooted. A binary tree is a special case of an ordered K-ary tree, where k is 2.

In computing, binary trees are seldom used solely for their structure. Much more typical is to define a labeling function on the nodes, which associates some value to each node. Binary trees labelled this way are used to implement binary search trees and binary heaps, and are used for efficient searching and sorting. The designation of non-root nodes as left or right child even when there is only one child present matters in some of these applications, in particular it is significant in binary search trees. In mathematics, what is termed *binary tree* can vary significantly from author to author. Some use the definition commonly used in computer science, but others define it as every non-leaf having exactly two children and don't necessarily order (as left/right) the children either.

Definitions

Recursive Definition

Another way of defining a *full* binary tree is a recursive definition. A full binary tree is either:

- A single vertex.

- A graph formed by taking two (full) binary trees, adding a vertex, and adding an edge directed from the new vertex to the root of each binary tree.

This also does not establish the order of children, but does fix a specific root node.

To actually define a binary tree in general, we must allow for the possibility that only one of the children may be empty. An artifact, which in some textbooks is called an *extended binary tree* is needed for that purpose. An extended binary tree is thus recursively defined as:

- the empty set is an extended binary tree

- if T_1 and T_2 are extended binary trees, then denote by $T_1 \cdot T_2$ the extended binary tree obtained by adding a root r connected to the left to T_1 and to the right to T_2 by adding edges when these sub-trees are non-empty.

Another way of imagining this construction (and understanding the terminology) is to consider instead of the empty set a different type of node—for instance square nodes if the regular ones are circles.

Using Graph Theory Concepts

A binary tree is a rooted tree that is also an ordered tree (a.k.a. plane tree) in which every node has at most two children. A rooted tree naturally imparts a notion of levels (distance from the root), thus for every node a notion of children may be defined as the nodes connected to it a level below. Ordering of these children (e.g., by drawing them on a plane) makes possible to distinguish left child from right child. But this still doesn't distinguish between a node with left but not a right child from a one with right but no left child.

The necessary distinction can be made by first partitioning the edges, i.e., defining the binary tree as triplet (V, E_1, E_2), where $(V, E_1 \cup E_2)$ is a rooted tree (equivalently arborescence) and $E_1 \cap E_2$ is empty, and also requiring that for all $j \in \{1, 2\}$ every node has at most one E_j child. A more informal way of making the distinction is to say, quoting the Encyclopedia of Mathematics, that "every node has a left child, a right child, neither, or both" and to specify that these "are all different" binary trees.

Types of Binary Trees

Tree terminology is not well-standardized and so varies in the literature.

- A rooted binary tree has a root node and every node has at most two children.

- A full binary tree (sometimes referred to as a proper or plane binary tree) is a tree in which every node in the tree has either 0 or 2 children.

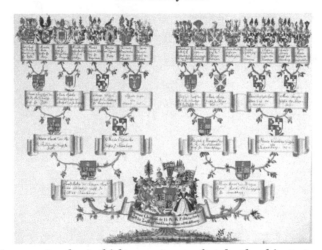

A full binary tree.

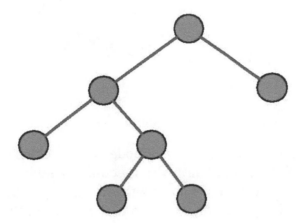

An ancestry chart which maps to a perfect depth-4 binary tree.

- A perfect binary tree is a binary tree in which all interior nodes have two children *and* all leaves have the same *depth* or same *level*. (This is ambiguously also called a complete binary tree.) An example of a perfect binary tree is the ancestry chart of a person to a given depth, as each person has exactly two biological parents (one mother and one father).

- In a complete binary tree every level, *except possibly the last*, is completely filled, and all nodes in the last level are as far left as possible. It can have between 1 and 2^h nodes at the last level h. An alternative definition is a perfect tree whose rightmost leaves (perhaps all) have been removed. Some authors use the term complete to refer instead to a perfect binary tree as defined above, in which case they call this type of tree an almost complete binary tree or nearly complete binary tree. A complete binary tree can be efficiently represented using an array.

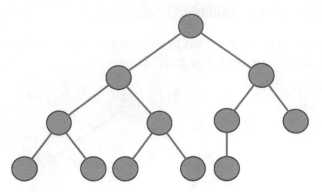

A complete binary tree.

- In the infinite complete binary tree, every node has two children (and so the set of levels is countably infinite). The set of all nodes is countably infinite, but the set of all infinite paths from the root is uncountable, having the cardinality of the continuum. These paths correspond by an order-preserving bijection to the points of the Cantor set, or (using the example of a Stern–Brocot tree) to the set of positive irrational numbers.

- A balanced binary tree has the minimum possible maximum height (a.k.a. depth) for the leaf nodes, because for any given number of leaf nodes, the leaf nodes are placed at the greatest height possible.

```
h Balanced                          Unbalanced, h = (n + 1)/2 - 1

 0: ABCDE                            ABCDE

    /    \                          /    \

 1: ABCD   E                         ABCD   E

    /  \                            /   \

 2: AB   CD                          ABC  D

   / \ / \                          /   \

 3: A  B  C  D                       AB   C

                                    / \

 4:                                  A   B
```

One common balanced tree structure is a binary tree structure in which the left and right subtrees of every node differ in height by no more than 1. One may also consider binary trees where no leaf is much farther away from the root than any other leaf. (Different balancing schemes allow different definitions of "much farther".)

- A degenerate (or pathological) tree is where each parent node has only one associated child node. This means that performance-wise, the tree will behave like a linked list data structure.

Properties of Binary Trees

- The number of nodes n in a full binary tree, is at least $n = 2h+1$ and at most $n = 2^{h+1}-1$, where h is the height of the tree. A tree consisting of only a root node has a height of 0.

- The number of leaf nodes l in a perfect binary tree, is $l = (n+1)/2$ because the number of non-leaf (a.k.a. internal) nodes $n-l = \sum_{k=0}^{\log_2(l)-1} 2^k = 2^{\log_2(l)} - 1 = l - 1$.

- This means that a perfect binary tree with l leaves has $n = 2l - 1$ nodes.

- In a balanced full binary tree, $h = \langle \log_2(l) \rangle + 1 = \langle \log_2((n+1)/2) \rangle + 1 = \langle \log_2(n+1) \rangle$.

- In a perfect full binary tree, $l = 2^h$ thus $n = 2^{h+1} - 1$.

- The maximum possible number of null links (i.e., absent children of the nodes) in a complete binary tree of n nodes is $(n+1)$, where only 1 node exists in bottom-most level to the far left.

- The number of internal nodes in a complete binary tree of n nodes is $\langle n/2 \rangle$.

- For any non-empty binary tree with n_0 leaf nodes and n_2 nodes of degree 2, $n_0 = n_2 + 1$.

Combinatorics

In combinatorics one considers the problem of counting the number of full binary trees of a given size. Here the trees have no values attached to their nodes (this would just multiply the number of possible trees by an easily determined factor), and trees are distinguished only by their structure; however the left and right child of any node are distinguished (if they are different trees, then interchanging them will produce a tree distinct from the original one). The size of the tree is taken to be the number n of internal nodes (those with two children); the other nodes are leaf nodes and there are $n + 1$ of them. The number of such binary trees of size n is equal to the number of ways of fully parenthesizing a string of $n + 1$ symbols (representing leaves) separated by n binary operators (representing internal nodes), so as to determine the argument subexpressions of each operator. For instance for $n = 3$ one has to parenthesize a string like $X * X * X * X$, which is possible in five ways:

$$((X*X)*X)*X, \quad (X*(X*X))*X, \quad (X*X)*(X*X), \quad X*((X*X)*X), \quad X*(X*(X*X)).$$

The correspondence to binary trees should be obvious, and the addition of redundant parentheses (around an already parenthesized expression or around the full expression) is disallowed (or at least not counted as producing a new possibility).

There is a unique binary tree of size 0 (consisting of a single leaf), and any other binary tree is characterized by the pair of its left and right children; if these have sizes i and j respectively, the full tree has size $i + j + 1$. Therefore, the number C_n of binary trees of size n has the following recursive description $C_0 = 1$, and $C_n = \sum_{i=0}^{n-1} C_i C_{n-1-i}$ for any positive integer n. It follows that C_n is the Catalan number of index n.

The above parenthesized strings should not be confused with the set of words of length $2n$ in the Dyck language, which consist only of parentheses in such a way that they are properly balanced.

The number of such strings satisfies the same recursive description (each Dyck word of length $2n$ is determined by the Dyck subword enclosed by the initial '(' and its matching ')' together with the Dyck subword remaining after that closing parenthesis, whose lengths $2i$ and $2j$ satisfy $i + j + 1 = n$); this number is therefore also the Catalan number C_n. So there are also five Dyck words of length 6:

$$()()(),\qquad ()(()),\qquad (())(),\qquad (()()),\qquad ((())).$$

These Dyck words do not correspond to binary trees in the same way. Instead, they are related by the following recursively defined bijection: the Dyck word equal to the empty string corresponds to the binary tree of size 0 with only one leaf. Any other Dyck word can be written as $(w_1) w_2$, where w_1, w_2 are themselves (possibly empty) Dyck words and where the two written parentheses are matched. The bijection is then defined by letting the words w_1 and w_2 correspond to the binary trees that are the left and right children of the root.

A bijective correspondence can also be defined as follows: enclose the Dyck word in an extra pair of parentheses, so that the result can be interpreted as a Lisp list expression (with the empty list () as only occurring atom); then the dotted-pair expression for that proper list is a fully parenthesized expression (with NIL as symbol and '.' as operator) describing the corresponding binary tree (which is in fact the internal representation of the proper list).

The ability to represent binary trees as strings of symbols and parentheses implies that binary trees can represent the elements of a free magma on a singleton set.

Methods for Storing Binary Trees

Binary trees can be constructed from programming language primitives in several ways.

Nodes and References

In a language with records and references, binary trees are typically constructed by having a tree node structure which contains some data and references to its left child and its right child. Sometimes it also contains a reference to its unique parent. If a node has fewer than two children, some of the child pointers may be set to a special null value, or to a special sentinel node.

This method of storing binary trees wastes a fair bit of memory, as the pointers will be null (or point to the sentinel) more than half the time; a more conservative representation alternative is threaded binary tree.

In languages with tagged unions such as ML, a tree node is often a tagged union of two types of nodes, one of which is a 3-tuple of data, left child, and right child, and the other of which is a "leaf" node, which contains no data and functions much like the null value in a language with pointers. For example, the following line of code in OCaml (an ML dialect) defines a binary tree that stores a character in each node.

```
type chr_tree = Empty | Node of char * chr_tree * chr_tree
```

Arrays

Binary trees can also be stored in breadth-first order as an implicit data structure in arrays, and if the tree is a complete binary tree, this method wastes no space. In this compact arrangement, if a node has an index i, its children are found at indices $2i+1$ (for the left child) and $2i+2$ (for the right), while its parent (if any) is found at index $\lfloor \frac{i-1}{2} \rfloor$ (assuming the root has index zero). This method benefits from more compact storage and better locality of reference, particularly during a preorder traversal. However, it is expensive to grow and wastes space proportional to $2^h - n$ for a tree of depth h with n nodes.

This method of storage is often used for binary heaps. No space is wasted because nodes are added in breadth-first order.

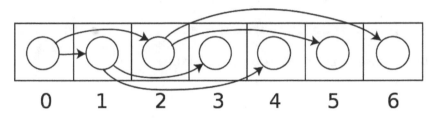

Encodings

Succinct Encodings

A succinct data structure is one which occupies close to minimum possible space, as established by information theoretical lower bounds. The number of different binary trees on n nodes is C_n, the nth Catalan number (assuming we view trees with identical *structure* as identical). For large n, this is about 4^n; thus we need at least about $\log_2 4^n = 2n$ bits to encode it. A succinct binary tree therefore would occupy $2n + o(n)$ bits.

One simple representation which meets this bound is to visit the nodes of the tree in preorder, outputting "1" for an internal node and "0" for a leaf. [1] If the tree contains data, we can simply simultaneously store it in a consecutive array in preorder. This function accomplishes this:

```
function EncodeSuccinct(node n, bitstring structure, array data) {

  if n = nil then

  append 0 to structure;

  else

  append 1 to structure;

  append n.data to data;

  EncodeSuccinct(n.left, structure, data);

  EncodeSuccinct(n.right, structure, data);

}
```

The string *structure* has only $2n+1$ bits in the end, where n is the number of (internal) nodes; we don't even have to store its length. To show that no information is lost, we can convert the output back to the original tree like this:

```
function DecodeSuccinct(bitstring structure, array data) {

  remove first bit of structure and put it in b

  if b = 1 then

  create a new node n

  remove first element of data and put it in n.data

  n.left = DecodeSuccinct(structure, data)

  n.right = DecodeSuccinct(structure, data)

  return n

  else

  return nil

}
```

More sophisticated succinct representations allow not only compact storage of trees but even useful operations on those trees directly while they're still in their succinct form.

Encoding General Trees as Binary Trees

There is a one-to-one mapping between general ordered trees and binary trees, which in particular is used by Lisp to represent general ordered trees as binary trees. To convert a general ordered tree to binary tree, we only need to represent the general tree in left-child right-sibling way. The result of this representation will automatically be a binary tree, if viewed from a different perspective. Each node *N* in the ordered tree corresponds to a node *N'* in the binary tree; the *left* child of *N'* is the node corresponding to the first child of *N*, and the *right* child of *N'* is the node corresponding to *N*'s next sibling --- that is, the next node in order among the children of the parent of *N*. This binary tree representation of a general order tree is sometimes also referred to as a left-child right-sibling binary tree (LCRS tree), or a doubly chained tree, or a Filial-Heir chain.

One way of thinking about this is that each node's children are in a linked list, chained together with their *right* fields, and the node only has a pointer to the beginning or head of this list, through its *left* field.

For example, in the tree on the left, A has the 6 children {B,C,D,E,F,G}. It can be converted into the binary tree on the right.

The binary tree can be thought of as the original tree tilted sideways, with the black left edges representing *first child* and the blue right edges representing *next sibling*. The leaves of the tree on the left would be written in Lisp as:

(((N O) I J) C D ((P) (Q)) F (M))

which would be implemented in memory as the binary tree on the right, without any letters on those nodes that have a left child.

Common Operations

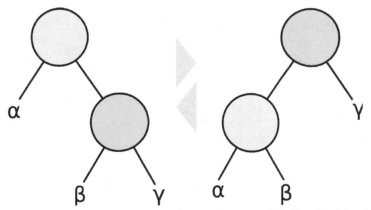

Tree rotations are very common internal operations on self-balancing binary trees.

There are a variety of different operations that can be performed on binary trees. Some are mutator operations, while others simply return useful information about the tree.

Insertion

Nodes can be inserted into binary trees in between two other nodes or added after a leaf node. In binary trees, a node that is inserted is specified as to which child it is.

Leaf Nodes

To add a new node after leaf node A, A assigns the new node as one of its children and the new node assigns node A as its parent.

Internal Nodes

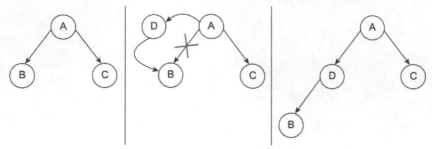

The process of inserting a node into a binary tree.

Insertion on internal nodes is slightly more complex than on leaf nodes. Say that the internal node is node A and that node B is the child of A. (If the insertion is to insert a right child, then B is the right child of A, and similarly with a left child insertion.) A assigns its child to the new node and the new node assigns its parent to A. Then the new node assigns its child to B and B assigns its parent as the new node.

Deletion

Deletion is the process whereby a node is removed from the tree. Only certain nodes in a binary tree can be removed unambiguously.

Node with Zero or One Children

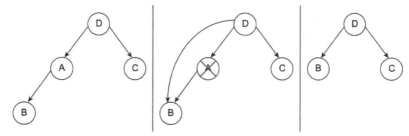

The process of deleting an internal node in a binary tree.

Suppose that the node to delete is node A. If A has no children, deletion is accomplished by setting the child of A's parent to null. If A has one child, set the parent of A's child to A's parent and set the child of A's parent to A's child.

Node with Two Children

In a binary tree, a node with two children cannot be deleted unambiguously. However, in certain binary trees (including binary search trees) these nodes *can* be deleted, though with a rearrangement of the tree structure.

Traversal

Pre-order, in-order, and post-order traversal visit each node in a tree by recursively visiting each node in the left and right subtrees of the root.

Depth-first Order

In depth-first order, we always attempt to visit the node farthest from the root node that we can, but with the caveat that it must be a child of a node we have already visited. Unlike a depth-first search on graphs, there is no need to remember all the nodes we have visited, because a tree cannot contain cycles. Pre-order is a special case of this.

Breadth-first Order

Contrasting with depth-first order is breadth-first order, which always attempts to visit the node closest to the root that it has not already visited.

In a complete binary tree, a node's breadth-index ($i - (2^d - 1)$) can be used as traversal instructions from the root. Reading bitwise from left to right, starting at bit $d - 1$, where d is the node's distance from the root ($d = \lfloor \log_2(i+1) \rfloor$) and the node in question is not the root itself ($d > 0$). When the breadth-index is masked at bit $d - 1$, the bit values 0 and 1 mean to step either left or right, respectively. The process continues by successively checking the next bit to the right until there are no more. The rightmost bit indicates the final traversal from the desired node's parent to the node itself. There is a time-space trade-off between iterating a complete binary tree this way versus each node having pointer/s to its sibling/s.

Representation of Binary Tree

The structure of each node of a binary tree contains one data field and two pointers, each for the right & left child. Each child being a node has also the same structure.

The structure of a node is shown below.

Value	
left	right

The structure defining a node of binary tree in C is as follows.

```
Struct node

{

struct node *lc ; /* points to the left child */

int data; /* data field */

struct node *rc; /* points to the right child */

}
```

There are two ways for representation of binary tree.

1.   Linked List representation of a Binary tree

```
Struct node
```

```
{
struct node * lc;
int data;
struct node * rc;
};
struct node * buildtree(int);/* builds the tree*/
void inorder(struct node *);/* Traverses the tree in inorder*/
int
a[]={ 3,5,9,6,8,20,10,/0,/0,9,/0,/0,/0,/0,/0,/0,/0,/0,/0,/0,/0};
void main( )
{
struct node * root;
root= buildtree(0);
printf("\n Inorder Traversal");
inorder(root);
getch( );
}
struct node * buildtree(int n);
struct node * temp=NULL;
if( a[n] != NULL)
{
temp = (struct node *) malloc(sizeof(struct node));
temp-> lc=buildtree(2n + 1);
temp-> data= a[n];
temp-> rc=buildtree(2n + 2);
}
return temp;
}
```

```
void inorder(struct node * root);

{

if(root != NULL)

{

if(root!= NULL)

{

inorder(roo-> lc);

printf("%d\t",root->data);

inorder(root->rc);

}

}
```

Binary trees can be represented by links where each node contains the address of the left child and the right child. If any node has its left or right child empty then it will have in its respective link field, a null value. A leaf node has null value in both of its links.

The structure defining a node of binary tree in C is as follows.

Struct node

{

struct node *lc ; /* points to the left child */

int data; /* data field */

struct node *rc; /* points to the right child */

}

2.   Array representation of a Binary tree

A single array can be used to represent a binary tree.

For these nodes are numbered / indexed according to a scheme giving 0 to root. Then all the nodes are numbered from left to right level by level from top to bottom. Empty nodes are also numbered. Then each node having an index i is put into the array as its ith element.

In the figure shown below the nodes of binary tree are numbered according to the given scheme.

The following program implements the above binary tree in an array form. And then traverses the tree in inorder traversal.

Program Implementing a binary tree.

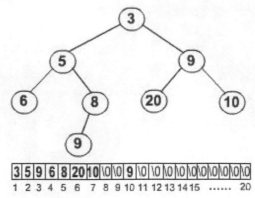

Text description of the above figure.

Operations on a Binary Tree

- Searching
- Insertion
- Deletion
- Traversal
- Sort

Searching

Searching a binary tree for a specific value is a process that can be performed recursively because of the order in which values are stored. At first examining the root. If the value is equals the root, the value exists in the tree. If it is less than the root, then it must be in the left subtree, so we recursively search the left subtree in the same manner. Similarly, if it is greater than the root, then it must be in the right subtree, so we recursively search the right subtree. If we reach a leaf and have not found the value, then the item does not lie in the tree at all.

Here is the search algorithm

```
search_btree(node, key):

if node is None:

return None // key not found

if key < node.key:

return search_btree(node.left, key)

else if key > node.key:

return search_btree(node.right, key)

else : // key is equal to node key

return node.value // found key
```

Insertion

The way to insert a new node in the tree, its value is first compared with the value of the root. If its value is less than the root's, it is then compared with the value of the root's left child. If its value is greater, it is compared with the root's right child. This process continues, until the new node is compared with a leaf node, and then it is added as this node's right or left child, depending on its value.

Another way is examine the root and recursively insert the new node to the left subtree if the new value is less than or equal to the root, or the right subtree if the new value is greater than the root.

Deletion

There are several cases to be considered:

- Deleting a leaf: If the key to be deleted has an empty left or right subtree, Deleting the key is easy, we can simply remove it from the tree.

- Deleting a node with one child: Delete the key and fill up this place with its child.

- Deleting a node with two children: Suppose the key to be deleted is called K. We replace the key K with either its in-order successor (the left-most child of the right subtree) or the in-order predecessor (the right-most child of the left subtree). we find either the in-order successor or predecessor, swap it with K, and then delete it. Since either of these nodes must have less than two children (otherwise it cannot be the in-order successor or predecessor), it can be deleted using the previous two cases.

Sort

A binary tree can be used to implement a simple but inefficient sorting algorithm. We insert all the values we wish to sort into a new ordered data structure.

Traversal of a Binary Tree

Traversal of a binary tree means to visit each node in the tree exactly once. The tree traversal is used in all the applications of it.

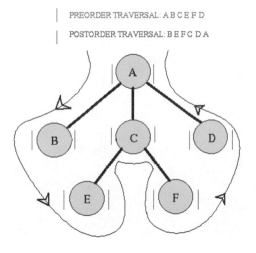

PREORDER TRAVERSAL: A B C E F D

POSTORDER TRAVERSAL: B E F C D A

In a linear list nodes are visited from first to last, but a tree being a non linear one we need definite rules. There are a no. of ways to traverse a tree. All of them differ only in the order in which they visit the nodes.

The three main methods of traversing a tree are:

- Inorder Traversal

- Preorder Traversal

- Postorder Traversal

In all of them we do not require to do anything to traverse an empty tree. All the traversal methods are based on recursive functions since a binary tree is itself recursive as every child of a node in a binary tree is itself a binary tree.

To traverse a non empty tree in inorder the following steps are followed recursively.

- Visit the Root

- Traverse the left subtree

- Traverse the right subtree

The inorder traversal of the tree shown below is as follows.

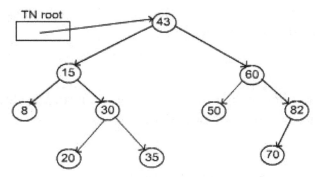

Inorder: 8, 15, 20, 30, 35, 43, 50, 60, 70, 82

Algorithm for inorder traversal.

Algorithm

The algorithm for inorder traversal is as follows.

```
Struct node
{
struct node * lc;
int data;
struct node * rc;
};
```

```
void inorder(struct node * root);

{

if(root != NULL)

{

inorder(roo-> lc);

printf("%d\t",root->data);

\inorder(root->rc);

}

}
```

So the function calls itself recursively and carries on the traversal.

Search Tree

In computer science, a search tree is a tree data structure used for locating specific keys from within a set. In order for a tree to function as a search tree, the key for each node must be greater than any keys in subtrees on the left and less than any keys in subtrees on the right.

The advantage of search trees is their efficient search time given the tree is reasonably balanced, which is to say the leaves at either end are of comparable depths. Various search-tree data structures exist, several of which also allow efficient insertion and deletion of elements, which operations then have to maintain tree balance.

Search trees are often used to implement an associative array. The search tree algorithm uses the key from the key-value pair to find a location, and then the application stores the entire key–value pair at that location.

Types of Trees

Binary Search Tree

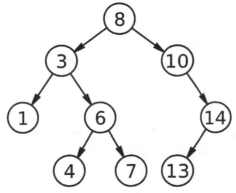

Binary search tree.

A Binary Search Tree is a node-based data structure where each node contains a key and two subtrees, the left and right. For all nodes, the left subtree's key must be less than the node's key, and the right subtree's key must be greater than the node's key. These subtrees must all qualify as binary search trees.

The time complexity for searching a binary search tree in the average case is O(log n).

B-tree

B-trees are generalizations of binary search trees in that they can have a variable number of sub-trees at each node. While child-nodes have a pre-defined range, they will not necessarily be filled with data, meaning B-trees can potentially waste some space. The advantage is that B-trees do not need to be re-balanced as frequently as other self-balancing trees.

Due to the variable range of their node length, B-trees are optimized for systems that read large blocks of data. They are also commonly used in databases.

The time complexity for searching a B-tree is O(log n).

(a,b)-tree

An (a,b)-tree is a search tree where all of its leaves are the same depth. Each node has at least a children and at most b children, while the root has at least 2 children and at most b children.

a and b can be decided with the following formula:

$$2 \leq a \leq \frac{(b+1)}{2}$$

The time complexity for searching an (a,b)-tree is O(log n).

Ternary Search Tree

A ternary search tree is a type of trie that can have 3 nodes: a lo kid, an equal kid, and a hi kid. Each node stores a single character and the tree itself is ordered the same way a binary search tree is, with the exception of a possible third node.

Searching a ternary search tree involves passing in a string to test whether any path contains it.

The time complexity for searching a ternary search tree is O(log n).

Searching Algorithms

Searching for a Specific Key

Assuming the tree is ordered, we can take a key and attempt to locate it within the tree. The following algorithms are generalized for binary search trees, but the same idea can be applied to trees of other formats.

Recursive

```
search-recursive(key, node)

  if node is NULL

      return EMPTY_TREE

  if key < node.key

      return search-recursive(key, node.left)

  else if key > node.key

      return search-recursive(key, node.right)

  else

      return node
```

Iterative

```
searchIterative(key, node)

    currentNode := node

    while currentNode is not NULL

        if currentNode.key = key

            return currentNode

    else if currentNode.key > key

        currentNode := currentNode.left

    else

        currentNode := currentNode.right
```

Searching for Min and Max

In a sorted tree, the minimum is located at the node farthest left, while the maximum is located at the node farthest right.

Minimum

```
findMinimum(node)

    if node is NULL

        return EMPTY_TREE

    min := node
```

```
while min.left is not NULL

  min := min.left

return min.key
```

Maximum

```
findMaximum(node)

    if node is NULL

        return EMPTY_TREE

    max := node

    while max.right is not NULL

        max := max.right

    return max.key
```

Binary Search Tree

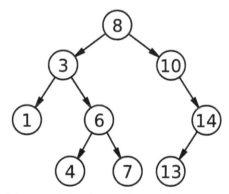

A binary search tree of size 9 and depth 3, with 8 at the root. The leaves are not drawn.

In computer science, binary search trees (BST), sometimes called ordered or sorted binary trees, are a particular type of container: data structures that store "items" (such as numbers, names etc.) in memory. They allow fast lookup, addition and removal of items, and can be used to implement either dynamic sets of items, or lookup tables that allow finding an item by its *key* (e.g., finding the phone number of a person by name).

Binary search trees keep their keys in sorted order, so that lookup and other operations can use the principle of binary search: when looking for a key in a tree (or a place to insert a new key), they traverse the tree from root to leaf, making comparisons to keys stored in the nodes of the tree and deciding, based on the comparison, to continue searching in the left or right subtrees. On average, this means that each comparison allows the operations to skip about half of the tree, so that each lookup, insertion or deletion takes time proportional to the logarithm of the number of items stored in the tree. This is much better than the linear time required to find items by key in an (unsorted) array, but slower than the corresponding operations on hash tables.

Several variants of the binary search tree have been studied in computer science; this article deals primarily with the basic type, making references to more advanced types when appropriate.

Definition

A binary search tree is a rooted binary tree, whose internal nodes each store a key (and optionally, an associated value) and each have two distinguished sub-trees, commonly denoted *left* and *right*. The tree additionally satisfies the binary search tree property, which states that the key in each node must be greater than or equal to any key stored in the left sub-tree, and less than or equal to any key stored in the right sub-tree. (The leaves (final nodes) of the tree contain no key and have no structure to distinguish them from one another. Leaves are commonly represented by a special `leaf` or `nil` symbol, a `NULL` pointer, etc.).

Generally, the information represented by each node is a record rather than a single data element. However, for sequencing purposes, nodes are compared according to their keys rather than any part of their associated records.

The major advantage of binary search trees over other data structures is that the related sorting algorithms and search algorithms such as in-order traversal can be very efficient; they are also easy to code.

Binary search trees are a fundamental data structure used to construct more abstract data structures such as sets, multisets, and associative arrays. Some of their disadvantages are as follows:

- The shape of the binary search tree depends entirely on the order of insertions and deletions, and can become degenerate.

- When inserting or searching for an element in a binary search tree, the key of each visited node has to be compared with the key of the element to be inserted or found.

- The keys in the binary search tree may be long and the run time may increase.

- After a long intermixed sequence of random insertion and deletion, the expected height of the tree approaches square root of the number of keys, $\sqrt{n}$, which grows much faster than $\log n$.

Order Relation

Binary search requires an order relation by which every element (item) can be compared with every other element in the sense of a total preorder. The part of the element which effectively takes place in the comparison is called its *key*. Whether duplicates, i.e. different elements with same key, shall be allowed in the tree or not, does not depend on the order relation, but on the application only.

In the context of binary search trees a total preorder is realized most flexibly by means of a three-way comparison subroutine.

Operations

Binary search trees support three main operations: insertion of elements, deletion of elements, and lookup (checking whether a key is present).

Searching

Searching a binary search tree for a specific key can be programmed recursively or iteratively.

We begin by examining the root node. If the tree is *null*, the key we are searching for does not exist in the tree. Otherwise, if the key equals that of the root, the search is successful and we return the node. If the key is less than that of the root, we search the left subtree. Similarly, if the key is greater than that of the root, we search the right subtree. This process is repeated until the key is found or the remaining subtree is *null*. If the searched key is not found after a *null* subtree is reached, then the key is not present in the tree. This is easily expressed as a recursive algorithm (implemented in Python):

```
1 def search_recursively(key, node):

2     if node is None or node.key == key:

3         return node

4     elif key < node.key:

5         return search_recursively(key, node.left)

6     else: # key > node.key

7         return search_recursively(key, node.right)
```

The same algorithm can be implemented iteratively:

```
1 def search_iteratively(key, node):

2     current_node = node

3     while current_node is not None:

4         if key == current_node.key:

5             return current_node

6         elif key < current_node.key:

7             current_node = current_node.left

8         else: # key > current_node.key:

9             current_node = current_node.right

10    return None
```

These two examples rely on the order relation being a total order.

If the order relation is only a total preorder a reasonable extension of the functionality is the following: also in case of equality search down to the leaves in a direction specifiable by the user. A binary tree sort equipped with such a comparison function becomes stable.

Because in the worst case this algorithm must search from the root of the tree to the leaf farthest from the root, the search operation takes time proportional to the tree's *height*. On average, binary search trees with n nodes have $O(\log n)$ height. However, in the worst case, binary search trees can have $O(n)$ height, when the unbalanced tree resembles a linked list (degenerate tree).

Insertion

Insertion begins as a search would begin; if the key is not equal to that of the root, we search the left or right subtrees as before. Eventually, we will reach an external node and add the new key-value pair (here encoded as a record 'newNode') as its right or left child, depending on the node's key. In other words, we examine the root and recursively insert the new node to the left subtree if its key is less than that of the root, or the right subtree if its key is greater than or equal to the root.

Here's how a typical binary search tree insertion might be performed in a binary tree in C++:

```cpp
Node* insert(Node*& root, int key, int value) {

  if (!root)

    root = new Node(key, value);

  else if (key < root->key)

    root->left = insert(root->left, key, value);

  else // key >= root->key

    root->right = insert(root->right, key, value);

  return root;

}
```

The above *destructive* procedural variant modifies the tree in place. It uses only constant heap space (and the iterative version uses constant stack space as well), but the prior version of the tree is lost. Alternatively, as in the following Python example, we can reconstruct all ancestors of the inserted node; any reference to the original tree root remains valid, making the tree a persistent data structure:

```python
def binary_tree_insert(node, key, value):

    if node is None:

        return NodeTree(None, key, value, None)

    if key == node.key:

        return NodeTree(node.left, key, value, node.right)
```

```
if key < node.key:

    return NodeTree(binary_tree_insert(node.left, key, value), node.
key, node.value, node.right)

else:

    return NodeTree(node.left, node.key, node.value, binary_tree_in-
sert(node.right, key, value))
```

The part that is rebuilt uses O(log n) space in the average case and O(n) in the worst case.

In either version, this operation requires time proportional to the height of the tree in the worst case, which is O(log n) time in the average case over all trees, but O(n) time in the worst case.

Another way to explain insertion is that in order to insert a new node in the tree, its key is first compared with that of the root. If its key is less than the root's, it is then compared with the key of the root's left child. If its key is greater, it is compared with the root's right child. This process continues, until the new node is compared with a leaf node, and then it is added as this node's right or left child, depending on its key: if the key is less than the leaf's key, then it is inserted as the leaf's left child, otherwise as the leaf's right child.

There are other ways of inserting nodes into a binary tree, but this is the only way of inserting nodes at the leaves and at the same time preserving the BST structure.

Deletion

When removing a node from a binary *search* tree it is mandatory to maintain the in-order sequence of the nodes. There are many possibilities to do this. However, the following method which has been proposed by T. Hibbard in 1962 guarantees that the heights of the subject subtrees are changed by at most one. There are three possible cases to consider:

- Deleting a node with no children: simply remove the node from the tree.

- Deleting a node with one child: remove the node and replace it with its child.

- Deleting a node with two children: call the node to be deleted D. Do not delete D. Instead, choose either its in-order predecessor node or its in-order successor node as replacement node E (s. figure). Copy the user values of E to D. If E does not have a child simply remove E from its previous parent G. If E has a child, say F, it is a right child. Replace E with F at E's parent.

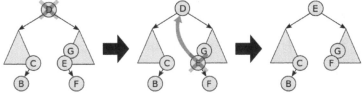

Deleting a node with two children from a binary search tree. First the leftmost node in the right subtree, the in-order successor E, is identified. Its value is copied into the node D being deleted. The in-order successor can then be easily deleted because it has at most one child. The same method works symmetrically using the in-order predecessor C.

In all cases, when D happens to be the root, make the replacement node root again.

Broadly speaking, nodes with children are harder to delete. As with all binary trees, a node's in-order successor is its right subtree's left-most child, and a node's in-order predecessor is the left subtree's right-most child. In either case, this node will have only one or no child at all. Delete it according to one of the two simpler cases above.

Consistently using the in-order successor or the in-order predecessor for every instance of the two-child case can lead to an unbalanced tree, so some implementations select one or the other at different times.

Runtime analysis: Although this operation does not always traverse the tree down to a leaf, this is always a possibility; thus in the worst case it requires time proportional to the height of the tree. It does not require more even when the node has two children, since it still follows a single path and does not visit any node twice.

```python
def find_min(self):  # Gets minimum node in a subtree

    current_node = self

    while current_node.left_child:

        current_node = current_node.left_child

    return current_node

def replace_node_in_parent(self, new_value=None):

    if self.parent:

        if self == self.parent.left_child:

            self.parent.left_child = new_value

    else:

            self.parent.right_child = new_value

    if new_value:

        new_value.parent = self.parent

def binary_tree_delete(self, key):

    if key < self.key:

        self.left_child.binary_tree_delete(key)

    elif key > self.key:

        self.right_child.binary_tree_delete(key)

    else: # delete the key here

        if self.left_child and self.right_child: # if both children are
```

```
present

          successor = self.right_child.find_min()

          self.key = successor.key

          successor.binary_tree_delete(successor.key)

    elif self.left_child:  # if the node has only a *left* child

        self.replace_node_in_parent(self.left_child)

    elif self.right_child: # if the node has only a *right* child

        self.replace_node_in_parent(self.right_child)

    else: # this node has no children

        self.replace_node_in_parent(None)
```

Traversal

Once the binary search tree has been created, its elements can be retrieved in-order by recursively traversing the left subtree of the root node, accessing the node itself, then recursively traversing the right subtree of the node, continuing this pattern with each node in the tree as it's recursively accessed. As with all binary trees, one may conduct a pre-order traversal or a post-order traversal, but neither are likely to be useful for binary *search* trees. An in-order traversal of a binary search tree will always result in a sorted list of node items (numbers, strings or other comparable items).

The code for in-order traversal in Python is given below. It will call callback (some function the programmer wishes to call on the node's value, such as printing to the screen) for every node in the tree.

```python
def traverse_binary_tree(node, callback):

    if node is None:

        return

    traverse_binary_tree(node.leftChild, callback)

    callback(node.value)

    traverse_binary_tree(node.rightChild, callback)
```

Traversal requires $O(n)$ time, since it must visit every node. This algorithm is also $O(n)$, so it is asymptotically optimal.

Traversal can also be implemented iteratively. For certain applications, e.g. greater equal search, approximative search, an operation for *single step (iterative) traversal* can be very useful. This is, of course, implemented without the callback construct and takes $O(1)$ on average and $O(\log n)$ in the worst case.

Verification

Sometimes we already have a binary tree, and we need to determine whether it is a BST. This problem has a simple recursive solution.

The BST property—every node on the right subtree has to be larger than the current node and every node on the left subtree has to be smaller than (or equal to - should not be the case as only unique values should be in the tree - this also poses the question as to if such nodes should be left or right of this parent) the current node—is the key to figuring out whether a tree is a BST or not. The greedy algorithm – simply traverse the tree, at every node check whether the node contains a value larger than the value at the left child and smaller than the value on the right child – does not work for all cases. Consider the following tree:

```
  20
 /  \
10   30
    /  \
   5    40
```

In the tree above, each node meets the condition that the node contains a value larger than its left child and smaller than its right child hold, and yet it is not a BST: the value 5 is on the right subtree of the node containing 20, a violation of the BST property.

Instead of making a decision based solely on the values of a node and its children, we also need information flowing down from the parent as well. In the case of the tree above, if we could remember about the node containing the value 20, we would see that the node with value 5 is violating the BST property contract.

So the condition we need to check at each node is:

- if the node is the left child of its parent, then it must be smaller than (or equal to) the parent and it must pass down the value from its parent to its right subtree to make sure none of the nodes in that subtree is greater than the parent.

- if the node is the right child of its parent, then it must be larger than the parent and it must pass down the value from its parent to its left subtree to make sure none of the nodes in that subtree is lesser than the parent.

A recursive solution in C can explain this further:

```c
struct TreeNode {
    int key;
    int value;
    struct TreeNode *left;
```

```
    struct TreeNode *right;
};

bool isBST(struct TreeNode *node, int minKey, int maxKey) {

    if(node == NULL) return true;

    if(node->key < minKey || node->key > maxKey) return false;

    return isBST(node->left, minKey, node->key-1) && isBST(node->right,
node->key+1, maxKey);

}
```

node->key+1 and node->key-1 are done to allow only distinct elements in BST.

If we want same elements to also be present, then we can use only node->key in both places.

The initial call to this function can be something like this:

```
if(isBST(root, INT_MIN, INT_MAX)) {

    puts("This is a BST.");

} else {

  puts("This is NOT a BST!");

}
```

Essentially we keep creating a valid range (starting from [MIN_VALUE, MAX_VALUE]) and keep shrinking it down for each node as we go down recursively.

As pointed out in section #Traversal, an in-order traversal of a binary *search* tree returns the nodes sorted. Thus we only need to keep the last visited node while traversing the tree and check whether its key is smaller (or smaller/equal, if duplicates are to be allowed in the tree) compared to the current key.

Examples of Applications

Some examples shall illustrate the use of above basic building blocks.

Sort

A binary search tree can be used to implement a simple sorting algorithm. Similar to heapsort, we insert all the values we wish to sort into a new ordered data structure—in this case a binary search tree—and then traverse it in order.

The worst-case time of build_binary_tree is $O(n^2)$—if you feed it a sorted list of values, it chains them into a linked list with no left subtrees. For example, build_binary_tree([1, 2, 3, 4, 5]) yields the tree (1 (2 (3 (4 (5))))).

There are several schemes for overcoming this flaw with simple binary trees; the most common is the self-balancing binary search tree. If this same procedure is done using such a tree, the overall worst-case time is O(n log n), which is asymptotically optimal for a comparison sort. In practice, the added overhead in time and space for a tree-based sort (particularly for node allocation) make it inferior to other asymptotically optimal sorts such as heapsort for static list sorting. On the other hand, it is one of the most efficient methods of *incremental sorting*, adding items to a list over time while keeping the list sorted at all times.

Priority Queue Operations

Binary search trees can serve as priority queues: structures that allow insertion of arbitrary key as well as lookup and deletion of the minimum (or maximum) key. Insertion works as previously explained. *Find-min* walks the tree, following left pointers as far as it can without hitting a leaf:

```
// Precondition: T is not a leaf

function find-min(T):

    while hasLeft(T):

        T ? left(T)

    return key(T)
```

Find-max is analogous: follow right pointers as far as possible. *Delete-min* (*max*) can simply look up the minimum (maximum), then delete it. This way, insertion and deletion both take logarithmic time, just as they do in a binary heap, but unlike a binary heap and most other priority queue implementations, a single tree can support all of *find-min*, *find-max*, *delete-min* and *delete-max* at the same time, making binary search trees suitable as double-ended priority queues.

Types

There are many types of binary search trees. AVL trees and red-black trees are both forms of self-balancing binary search trees. A splay tree is a binary search tree that automatically moves frequently accessed elements nearer to the root. In a treap (*tree heap*), each node also holds a (randomly chosen) priority and the parent node has higher priority than its children. Tango trees are trees optimized for fast searches. T-trees are binary search trees optimized to reduce storage space overhead, widely used for in-memory databases

A degenerate tree is a tree where for each parent node, there is only one associated child node. It is unbalanced and, in the worst case, performance degrades to that of a linked list. If your add node function does not handle re-balancing, then you can easily construct a degenerate tree by feeding it with data that is already sorted. What this means is that in a performance measurement, the tree will essentially behave like a linked list data structure.

Performance Comparisons

D. A. Heger (2004) presented a performance comparison of binary search trees. Treap was found to have the best average performance, while red-black tree was found to have the smallest amount of performance variations.

Optimal Binary Search Trees

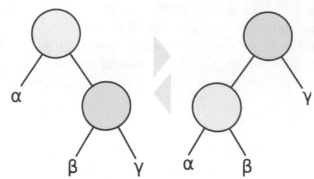

Tree rotations are very common internal operations in binary trees to keep perfect,
or near-to-perfect, internal balance in the tree.

If we do not plan on modifying a search tree, and we know exactly how often each item will be accessed, we can construct an *optimal binary search tree*, which is a search tree where the average cost of looking up an item (the *expected search cost*) is minimized.

Even if we only have estimates of the search costs, such a system can considerably speed up lookups on average. For example, if you have a BST of English words used in a spell checker, you might balance the tree based on word frequency in text corpora, placing words like *the* near the root and words like *agerasia* near the leaves. Such a tree might be compared with Huffman trees, which similarly seek to place frequently used items near the root in order to produce a dense information encoding; however, Huffman trees store data elements only in leaves, and these elements need not be ordered.

If we do not know the sequence in which the elements in the tree will be accessed in advance, we can use splay trees which are asymptotically as good as any static search tree we can construct for any particular sequence of lookup operations.

Alphabetic trees are Huffman trees with the additional constraint on order, or, equivalently, search trees with the modification that all elements are stored in the leaves. Faster algorithms exist for *optimal alphabetic binary trees* (OABTs).

Self-balancing Binary Search Tree

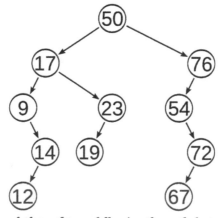

An example of an unbalanced tree; following the path from the root to a node
takes an average of 3.27 node accesses.

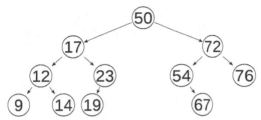

The same tree after being height-balanced; the average path effort decreased to 3.00 node accesses.

In computer science, a self-balancing (or height-balanced) binary search tree is any node-based binary search tree that automatically keeps its height (maximal number of levels below the root) small in the face of arbitrary item insertions and deletions.

These structures provide efficient implementations for mutable ordered lists, and can be used for other abstract data structures such as associative arrays, priority queues and sets.

The red–black tree, which is a type of self-balancing binary search tree, was called symmetric binary B-tree and was renamed but can still be confused with the generic concept of self-balancing binary search tree because of the initials.

Overview

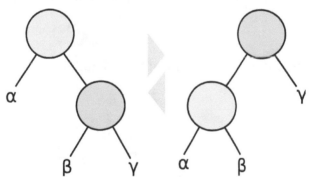

Tree rotations are very common internal operations on self-balancing binary trees to keep perfect or near-to-perfect balance.

Most operations on a binary search tree (BST) take time directly proportional to the height of the tree, so it is desirable to keep the height small. A binary tree with height h can contain at most $2^0+2^1+\cdots+2^h = 2^{h+1}-1$ nodes. It follows that for a tree with n nodes and height h:

$$n \leq 2^{h+1} - 1$$

And that implies:

$$h \geq [\log_2(n+1)-1] \geq [\log_2 n]..$$

In other words, the minimum height of a tree with n nodes is $\log_2(n)$, rounded down; that is, $[\log_2 n]$.

However, the simplest algorithms for BST item insertion may yield a tree with height n in rather common situations. For example, when the items are inserted in sorted key order, the tree degenerates into a linked list with n nodes. The difference in performance between the two situations may be enormous: for $n = 1,000,000$, for example, the minimum height is $\lfloor \log_2(1,000,000) \rfloor = 19.$.

If the data items are known ahead of time, the height can be kept small, in the average sense, by adding values in a random order, resulting in a random binary search tree. However, there are many situations (such as online algorithms) where this randomization is not viable.

Self-balancing binary trees solve this problem by performing transformations on the tree (such as tree rotations) at key insertion times, in order to keep the height proportional to $\log_2(n)$. Although a certain overhead is involved, it may be justified in the long run by ensuring fast execution of later operations.

Maintaining the height always at its minimum value $\lfloor \log_2(n) \rfloor$ is not always viable; it can be proven that any insertion algorithm which did so would have an excessive overhead. Therefore, most self-balanced BST algorithms keep the height within a constant factor of this lower bound.

In the asymptotic ("Big-O") sense, a self-balancing BST structure containing n items allows the lookup, insertion, and removal of an item in $O(\log n)$ worst-case time, and ordered enumeration of all items in $O(n)$ time. For some implementations these are per-operation time bounds, while for others they are amortized bounds over a sequence of operations. These times are asymptotically optimal among all data structures that manipulate the key only through comparisons.

Implementations

Popular data structures implementing this type of tree include:

- 2-3 tree
- AA tree
- AVL tree
- Red-black tree
- Scapegoat tree
- Splay tree
- Treap

Applications

Self-balancing binary search trees can be used in a natural way to construct and maintain ordered lists, such as priority queues. They can also be used for associative arrays; key-value pairs are simply inserted with an ordering based on the key alone. In this capacity, self-balancing BSTs have a number of advantages and disadvantages over their main competitor, hash tables. One advantage of self-balancing BSTs is that they allow fast (indeed, asymptotically optimal) enumeration of the items *in key order*, which hash tables do not provide. One disadvantage is that their lookup algorithms get more complicated when there may be multiple items with the same key. Self-balancing BSTs have better worst-case lookup performance than hash tables ($O(\log n)$ compared to $O(n)$), but have worse average-case performance ($O(\log n)$ compared to $O(1)$).

Self-balancing BSTs can be used to implement any algorithm that requires mutable ordered lists, to achieve optimal worst-case asymptotic performance. For example, if binary tree sort is implemented with a self-balanced BST, we have a very simple-to-describe yet asymptotically optimal $O(n \log n)$ sorting algorithm. Similarly, many algorithms in computational geometry exploit variations on self-balancing BSTs to solve problems such as the line segment intersection problem and the point location problem efficiently. (For average-case performance, however, self-balanced BSTs may be less efficient than other solutions. Binary tree sort, in particular, is likely to be slower than merge sort, quicksort, or heapsort, because of the tree-balancing overhead as well as cache access patterns.)

Self-balancing BSTs are flexible data structures, in that it's easy to extend them to efficiently record additional information or perform new operations. For example, one can record the number of nodes in each subtree having a certain property, allowing one to count the number of nodes in a certain key range with that property in $O(\log n)$ time. These extensions can be used, for example, to optimize database queries or other list-processing algorithms.

AVL Tree

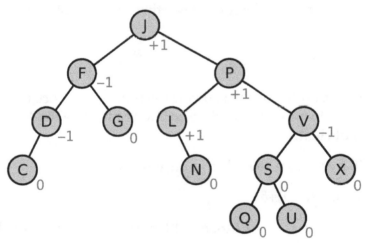

(A) AVL tree with balance factors (green).

In computer science, an AVL tree is a self-balancing binary search tree. It was the first such data structure to be invented. In an AVL tree, the heights of the two child subtrees of any node differ by at most one; if at any time they differ by more than one, rebalancing is done to restore this property. Lookup, insertion, and deletion all take $O(\log n)$ time in both the average and worst cases, where n is the number of nodes in the tree prior to the operation. Insertions and deletions may require the tree to be rebalanced by one or more tree rotations.

The AVL tree is named after its two Soviet inventors, Georgy Adelson-Velsky and Evgenii Landis, who published it in their 1962 paper "An algorithm for the organization of information".

AVL trees are often compared with red–black trees because both support the same set of operations and take $O(\log n)$ time for the basic operations. For lookup-intensive applications, AVL trees are faster than red–black trees because they are more strictly balanced. Similar to red–black trees, AVL trees are height-balanced. Both are, in general, neither weight-balanced nor μ-balanced for any $\mu \leq \frac{1}{2}$; that is, sibling nodes can have hugely differing numbers of descendants.

Definition

Balance Factor

In a binary tree the *balance factor* of a node N is defined to be the height difference

$$\text{BalanceFactor(N)} := \text{Height(LeftSubtree(N))} - \text{Height(RightSubtree(N))}$$

of its two child subtrees. A binary tree is defined to be an *AVL tree* if the invariant

$$\text{BalanceFactor(N)} \in \{-1, 0, +1\}$$

holds for every node N in the tree.

A node N with BalanceFactor(N) < 0 is called "left-heavy", one with BalanceFactor(N) > 0 is called "right-heavy", and one with BalanceFactor(N) = 0 is sometimes simply called "balanced".

Remark

In the sequel, because there is a one-to-one correspondence between nodes and the subtrees rooted by them, we sometimes leave it to the context whether the name of an object stands for the node or the subtree.

Properties

Balance factors can be kept up-to-date by knowing the previous balance factors and the change in height – it is not necessary to know the absolute height. For holding the AVL balance information, two bits per node are sufficient.

The height h of an AVL tree with n nodes lies in the interval:

$$\log_2(n+1) \le h < c \log_2(n+2) + b$$

with the golden ratio $\varphi := (1+\sqrt{5})/_2 \approx 1.618$, $c := 1/\log_2 \varphi \approx 1.44$, and $b := 5/_2 \log_2 5 - 2 \approx -0.328$. This is because an AVL tree of height h contains at least $F_{h+2} - 1$ nodes where $\{F_h\}$ is the Fibonacci sequence with the seed values $F_1 = 1$, $F_2 = 1$.

Operations

Read-only operations of an AVL tree involve carrying out the same actions as would be carried out on an unbalanced binary search tree, but modifications have to observe and restore the height balance of the subtrees.

Searching

Searching for a specific key in an AVL tree can be done the same way as that of a normal unbalanced binary search tree. In order for search to work effectively it has to employ a comparison function which establishes a total order (or at least a total preorder) on the set of keys. The number of comparisons required for successful search is limited by the height h and for unsuccessful search is very close to h, so both are in O(log n).

Traversal

Once a node has been found in an AVL tree, the *next* or *previous* node can be accessed in amortized constant time. Some instances of exploring these "nearby" nodes require traversing up to $h \propto \log(n)$ links (particularly when navigating from the rightmost leaf of the root's left subtree to the root or from the root to the leftmost leaf of the root's right subtree; in the AVL tree figure, moving from node P to the *next but one* node Q takes 3 steps). However, exploring all n nodes of the tree in this manner would visit each link exactly twice: one downward visit to enter the subtree rooted by that node, another visit upward to leave that node's subtree after having explored it. And since there are $n-1$ links in any tree, the amortized cost is found to be $2 \times (n-1)/n$, or approximately 2.

Insert

When inserting an element into an AVL tree, you initially follow the same process as inserting into a Binary Search Tree. After inserting a node, it is necessary to check each of the node's ancestors for consistency with the invariants of AVL trees: this is called "retracing". This is achieved by considering the balance factor of each node.

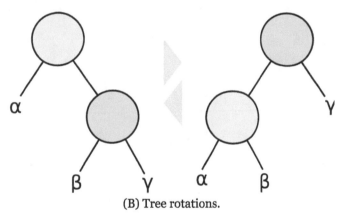

(B) Tree rotations.

Since with a single insertion the height of an AVL subtree cannot increase by more than one, the temporary balance factor of a node after an insertion will be in the range $[-2,+2]$. For each node checked, if the temporary balance factor remains in the range from -1 to $+1$ then only an update of the balance factor and no rotation is necessary. However, if the temporary balance factor becomes less than -1 or greater than $+1$, the subtree rooted at this node is AVL unbalanced, and a rotation is needed.

By inserting the new node Z as a child of node X the height of that subtree Z increases from 0 to 1.

Invariant of the retracing loop for an insertion

The height of the subtree rooted by Z has increased by 1. It is already in AVL shape.

```
 for (X = parent(Z); X != null; X = parent(Z)) { // Loop (possibly up to
the root)

    // BalanceFactor(X) has to be updated:

  if (Z == right_child(X)) { // The right subtree increases
```

```
    if (BalanceFactor(X) > 0) { // X is right-heavy

        // ===> the temporary BalanceFactor(X) == +2

        // ===> rebalancing is required.

        G = parent(X); // Save parent of X around rotations

         if (BalanceFactor(Z) < 0)                    // Right Left Case (fig D)


              N = rotate_RightLeft(X,Z);    // Double rotation: Right(Z)
then Left(X)

              else                          // Right Right Case   (fig C)


              N = rotate_Left(X,Z);     // Single rotation Left(X)

       // After rotation adapt parent link

   }

    else {

        if (BalanceFactor(X) < 0) {

          BalanceFactor(X) = 0; // Z's height increase is absorbed at X.

          break; // Leave the loop

        }

        BalanceFactor(X) = +1;

        Z=X; // Height(Z) increases by 1

        continue;

    }

}

else { // Z == left_child(X): the left subtree increases

    if (BalanceFactor(X) < 0) { // X is left-heavy

        // ===> the temporary BalanceFactor(X) == -2

        // ===> rebalancing is required.

        G = parent(X); // Save parent of X around rotations
```

```
       if (BalanceFactor(Z) > 0)        // Left Right Case
         N = rotate_LeftRight(X,Z);    // Double rotation: Left(Z)
then Right(X)
           else                         // Left Left Case
       N = rotate_Right(X,Z);         // Single rotation Right(X)
           // After rotation adapt parent link
   }
   else {
       if (BalanceFactor(X) > 0) {
           BalanceFactor(X) = 0; // Z's height increase is absorbed at X.
            break; // Leave the loop
       }
       BalanceFactor(X) = -1;
       Z=X; // Height(Z) increases by 1
       continue;
     }
   }
   // After a rotation adapt parent link:
   // N is the new root of the rotated subtree
   // Height does not change: Height(N) == old Height(X)
 parent(N) = G;
 if (G != null) {
    if (X == left_child(G))
    left_child(G) = N;
  else
    right_child(G) = N;
  break;
 }
```

```
else {

  tree->root = N; // N is the new root of the total tree

  break;

}

// There is no fall thru, only break; or continue;

}

// Unless loop is left via break, the height of the total tree increases
by 1.
```

In order to update the balance factors of all nodes, first observe that all nodes requiring correction lie from child to parent along the path of the inserted leaf. If the above procedure is applied to nodes along this path, starting from the leaf, then every node in the tree will again have a balance factor of −1, 0, or 1.

The retracing can stop if the balance factor becomes 0 implying that the height of that subtree remains unchanged.

If the balance factor becomes ±1 then the height of the subtree increases by one and the retracing needs to continue.

If the balance factor temporarily becomes ±2, this has to be repaired by an appropriate rotation after which the subtree has the same height as before (and its root the balance factor 0).

The time required is $O(\log n)$ for lookup, plus a maximum of $O(\log n)$ retracing levels ($O(1)$ on average) on the way back to the root, so the operation can be completed in $O(\log n)$ time.

Delete

There, the effective deletion of the subject node or the replacement node decreases the height of the corresponding child tree either from 1 to 0 or from 2 to 1, if that node had a child.

Starting at this subtree, it is necessary to check each of the ancestors for consistency with the invariants of AVL trees. This is called "retracing".

Since with a single deletion the height of an AVL subtree cannot decrease by more than one, the temporary balance factor of a node will be in the range from −2 to +2. If the balance factor remains in the range from −1 to +1 it can be adjusted in accord with the AVL rules. If it becomes ±2 then the subtree is unbalanced and needs to be rotated.

Invariant of the Retracing Loop for a Deletion

The height of the subtree rooted by N has decreased by 1. It is already in AVL shape.

```
for (X = parent(N); X != null; X = G) { // Loop (possibly up to the root)

    G = parent(X); // Save parent of X around rotations
```

```
   // BalanceFactor(X) has not yet been updated!
  if (N == left_child(X)) { // the left subtree decreases
     if (BalanceFactor(X) > 0) { // X is right-heavy
        // ===> the temporary BalanceFactor(X) == +2
       // ===> rebalancing is required.
       Z = right_child(X); // Sibling of N (higher by 2)
       b = BalanceFactor(Z);
      if (b < 0)                              // Right Left Case (fig D)


            N = rotate_RightLeft(X,Z); // Double rotation: Right(Z)
then Left(X)
          else                            // Right Right Case   (fig C)


            N = rotate_Left(X,Z);    // Single rotation Left(X)
        // After rotation adapt parent link
  }
   else {
     if (BalanceFactor(X) == 0) {
       BalanceFactor(X) = +1; // N's height decrease is absorbed at X.
       break; // Leave the loop
     }
     N = X;
     BalanceFactor(N) = 0; // Height(N) decreases by 1
     continue;
   }
 }
 else { // (N == right_child(X)): The right subtree decreases
    if (BalanceFactor(X) < 0) { // X is left-heavy
```

```
            // ===> the temporary BalanceFactor(X) == -2

          // ===> rebalancing is required.

          Z = left_child(X); // Sibling of N (higher by 2)

          b = BalanceFactor(Z);

        if (b > 0)      // Left Right Case

            N = rotate_LeftRight(X,Z); // Double rotation: Left(Z)
then Right(X)

            else                      // Left Left Case
          N = rotate_Right(X,Z);    // Single rotation Right(X)

          // After rotation adapt parent link

    }

    else {

      if (BalanceFactor(X) == 0) {

          BalanceFactor(X) = -1; // N's height decrease is absorbed
at X.

          break; // Leave the loop

      }

      N = X;

      BalanceFactor(N) = 0; // Height(N) decreases by 1

      continue;

        }

    }

  // After a rotation adapt parent link:

  // N is the new root of the rotated subtree

  parent(N) = G;

  if (G != null) {

      if (X == left_child(G))

          left_child(G) = N;
```

```
    else

        right_child(G) = N;

    if (b == 0)

        break; // Height does not change: Leave the loop

}

else {

    tree->root = N; // N is the new root of the total tree

    continue;

}

  // Height(N) decreases by 1 (== old Height(X)-1)

}

// Unless loop is left via break, the height of the total tree decreases
by 1.
```

The retracing can stop if the balance factor becomes ±1 meaning that the height of that subtree remains unchanged.

If the balance factor becomes 0 then the height of the subtree decreases by one and the retracing needs to continue.

If the balance factor temporarily becomes ±2, this has to be repaired by an appropriate rotation. It depends on the balance factor of the sibling Z (the higher child tree) whether the height of the subtree decreases by one or does not change (the latter, if Z has the balance factor 0).

The time required is $O(\log n)$ for lookup, plus a maximum of $O(\log n)$ retracing levels ($O(1)$ on average) on the way back to the root, so the operation can be completed in $O(\log n)$ time.

Set Operations and Bulk Operations

In addition to the single-element insert, delete and lookup operations, several set operations have been defined on AVL trees: union, intersection and set difference. Then fast *bulk* operations on insertions or deletions can be implemented based on these set functions. These set operations rely on two helper operations, *Split* and *Join*. With the new operations, the implementation of AVL trees can be more efficient and highly-parallelizable.

- *Join*: The function *Join* is on two AVL trees t_1 and t_2 and a key k and will return a tree containing all elements in t_1, t_2 as well as k. It requires k to be greater than all keys in t_1 and smaller than all keys in t_2. If the two trees differ by height at most one, *Join* simply create a new node with left subtree t_1, root k and right subtree t_2. Otherwise, suppose that t_1 is higher than t_2 for more than one (the other case is symmetric). *Join* follows the right spine of t_1 until a node c which is balanced with t_2. At this point a new node with left child c, root k and right child t_1 is created to replace c. The new node satisfies the AVL invariant, and its height is one greater than c. The increase in height can increase the height of its ancestors, possibly invalidating the AVL invariant of those nodes. This can be fixed either with a double rotation if invalid at the parent or a single left rotation if invalid higher in the tree, in both cases restoring the height for any further ancestor nodes. *Join* will therefore require at most two rotations. The cost of this function is the difference of the heights between the two input trees.

- *Split*: To split an AVL tree into two smaller trees, those smaller than key x, and those larger than key x, first draw a path from the root by inserting x into the AVL. After this insertion, all values less than x will be found on the left of the path, and all values greater than x will be found on the right. By applying *Join*, all the subtrees on the left side are merged bottom-up using keys on the path as intermediate nodes from bottom to top to form the left tree, and the right part is asymmetric. The cost of *Split* is order of $O(n)$, the height of the tree.

The union of two AVLs t_1 and t_2 representing sets A and B, is an AVL t that represents $A \cup B$. The following recursive function computes this union:

```
function union(t₁, t₂):

    if t₁ = nil:

        return t₂

    if t₂ = nil:

        return t₁

    t<, t> ← split t₂ on t₁.root

    return join(t₁.root,union(left(t₁), t<),union(right(t₁), t>))
```

Here, *Split* is presumed to return two trees: one holding the keys less its input key, one holding the greater keys. (The algorithm is non-destructive, but an in-place destructive version exists as well.)

The algorithm for intersection or difference is similar, but requires the *Join2* helper routine that is the same as *Join* but without the middle key. Based on the new functions for union, intersection or difference, either one key or multiple keys can be inserted to or deleted from the AVL tree. Since *Split* calls *Join* but does not deal with the balancing criteria of AVL trees directly, such an implementation is usually called the "join-based" implementation.

The complexity of each of union, intersection and difference is $O\left(m\log\left(\frac{n}{m}+1\right)\right)$ for AVLs of sizes m and $n(\geq m)$. More importantly, since the recursive calls to union, intersection or difference are independent of each other, they can be executed in parallel with a parallel depth $O(\log m \log n)$. When $m = 1$, the join-based implementation has the same computational DAG as single-element insertion and deletion.

Rebalancing

If during a modifying operation (e.g. insert, delete) a (temporary) height difference of more than one arises between two child subtrees, the parent subtree has to be "rebalanced". The given repair tools are the so-called tree rotations, because they move the keys only "vertically", so that the ("horizontal") in-order sequence of the keys is fully preserved (which is essential for a binary-search tree).

Let Z be the child higher by 2. Two flavors of rotations are required: simple and double. Rebalancing can be accomplished by a simple rotation (see figure C) if the inner child of Z, that is the child with a child direction opposite to that of Z, (t_{23} in figure C, Y in figure D) is *not higher* than its sibling, the outer child t_4 in both figures. This situation is called "Right Right" or "Left Left" in the literature.

On the other hand, if the inner child (t_{23} in figure C, Y in figure D) of Z *is* higher than t_4 then rebalancing can be accomplished by a double rotation (see figure D). This situation is called "Right Left" because X is right- and Z left-heavy (or "Left Right" if X is left- and Z is right-heavy). From a mere graph-theoretic point of view, the two rotations of a double are just single rotations. But they encounter and have to maintain other configurations of balance factors. So, in effect, it is simpler – and more efficient – to specialize, just as in the original paper, where the double rotation is called Большое вращение (lit. *big turn*) as opposed to the simple rotation which is called Малое вращение (lit. *little turn*). But there are alternatives: one could e.g. update all the balance factors in a separate walk from leaf to root.

The cost of a rotation, both simple and double, is constant.

For both flavors of rotations a mirrored version, i.e. `rotate_Right` or `rotate_LeftRight`, respectively, is required as well.

Simple Rotation

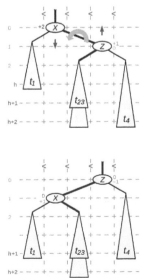

(C) Simple rotation
rotate_Left(X,Z).

Figure C shows a Right Right situation. In its upper half, node X has two child trees with a balance factor of +2. Moreover, the inner child t_{23} of Z is not higher than its sibling t_4. This can happen by a height increase of subtree t_4 or by a height decrease of subtree t_1. In the latter case, also the pale situation where t_{23} has the same height as t_4 may occur.

The result of the left rotation is shown in the lower half of the figure. Three links (thick edges in figure C) and two balance factors are to be updated.

As the figure shows, before an insertion, the leaf layer was at level h+1, temporarily at level h+2 and after the rotation again at level h+1. In case of a deletion, the leaf layer was at level h+2, where it is again, when t_{23} and t_4 were of same height. Otherwise the leaf layer reaches level h+1, so that the height of the rotated tree decreases.

Code Snippet of a Simple Left Rotation

```
Input: X = root of subtree to be rotated left
       Z = its right child, not left-heavy
          with height == Height(LeftSubtree(X))+2

Result:     new root of rebalanced subtree

 node* rotate_Left(node* X,node* Z) {

     // Z is by 2 higher than its sibling

     t23 = left_child(Z); // Inner child of Z

     right_child(X) = t23;

     if (t23 != null)

         parent(t23) = X;

     left_child(Z) = X;

     parent(X) = Z;

     // 1st case, BalanceFactor(Z) == 0, only happens with deletion, not
insertion:

        if (BalanceFactor(Z) == 0) { // t23 has been of same height as t4

            BalanceFactor(X) = +1;   // t23 now higher

            BalanceFactor(Z) = -1;   // t4 now lower than X

     } else // 2nd case happens with insertion or deletion:

     {

            BalanceFactor(X) = 0;

            BalanceFactor(Z) = 0;

     }
```

```
   return Z; // return new root of rotated subtree

}
```

Double Rotation

Figure D shows a Right Left situation. In its upper third, node X has two child trees with a balance factor of +2. But unlike figure C, the inner child Y of Z is higher than its sibling t_4. This can happen by a height increase of subtree t_2 or t_3 (with the consequence that they are of different height) or by a height decrease of subtree t_1. In the latter case, it may also occur that t_2 and t_3 are of same height.

The result of the first, the right, rotation is shown in the middle third of the figure. (With respect to the balance factors, this rotation is not of the same kind as the other AVL single rotations, because the height difference between Y and t_4 is only 1.) The result of the final left rotation is shown in the lower third of the figure. Five links (thick edges in figure D) and three balance factors are to be updated.

As the figure shows, before an insertion, the leaf layer was at level h+1, temporarily at level h+2 and after the double rotation again at level h+1. In case of a deletion, the leaf layer was at level h+2 and after the double rotation it is at level h+1, so that the height of the rotated tree decreases.

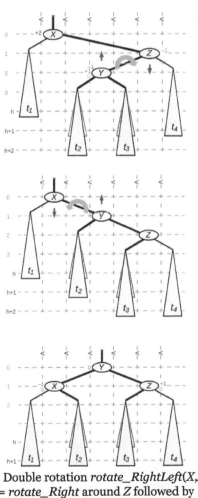

(D) Double rotation *rotate_RightLeft(X,Z)*
= *rotate_Right* around *Z* followed by
rotate_Left around *X*.

Code snippet of a right-left double rotation

Input: X = root of subtree to be rotated

Z = its right child, left-heavy

with height == Height(LeftSubtree(X))+2

Result: new root of rebalanced subtree

```
node* rotate_RightLeft(node* X,node* Z) {
// Z is by 2 higher than its sibling
Y = left_child(Z); // Inner child of Z
// Y is by 1 higher than sibling
t3 = right_child(Y);
left_child(Z) = t3;
if (t3 != null)
  parent(t3) = Z;
right_child(Y) = Z;
parent(Z) = Y;
t2 = left_child(Y);
right_child(X) = t2;
if (t2 != null)
  parent(t2) = X;
left_child(Y) = X;
parent(X) = Y;
// 1st case, BalanceFactor(Y) > 0, happens with insertion or deletion:
if (BalanceFactor(Y) > 0) { // t3 was higher
    BalanceFactor(X) = -1;    // t1 now higher
    BalanceFactor(Z) = 0;
} else // 2nd case, BalanceFactor(Y) == 0, only happens with deletion,
not insertion:
if (BalanceFactor(Y) == 0) {
    BalanceFactor(X) = 0;
    BalanceFactor(Z) = 0;
```

```
} else // 3rd case happens with insertion or deletion:

{       // t2 was higher

    BalanceFactor(X) = 0;

    BalanceFactor(Z) = +1; // t4 now higher

}

BalanceFactor(Y) = 0;

return Y; // return new root of rotated subtree

}
```

Comparison to Other Structures

Both AVL trees and red–black (RB) trees are self-balancing binary search trees and they are related mathematically. Indeed, every AVL tree can be colored red–black, but there are RB trees which are not AVL balanced. For maintaining the AVL resp. RB tree's invariants, rotations play an important role. In the worst case, even without rotations, AVL or RB insertions or deletions require $O(\log n)$ inspections and/or updates to AVL balance factors resp. RB colors. RB insertions and deletions and AVL insertions require from zero to three tail-recursive rotations and run in amortized $O(1)$ time, thus equally constant on average. AVL deletions requiring $O(\log n)$ rotations in the worst case are also $O(1)$ on average. RB trees require storing one bit of information (the color) in each node, while AVL trees mostly use two bits for the balance factor, although, when stored at the children, one bit with meaning «lower than sibling» suffices. The bigger difference between the two data structures is their height limit.

For a tree of size $n \geq 1$

- an AVL tree's height is at most

$$\begin{aligned} h \ &\leqq c\log_2(n+d)+b \\ &< c\log_2(n+2)+b \end{aligned}$$

where $\varphi := \dfrac{1+\sqrt{5}}{2} \approx 1.618$ the golden ratio,

$$c := \frac{1}{\log_2 \varphi} \approx 1.440, \quad b := \frac{c}{2}\log_2 5 - 2 \approx -0.328, \text{ and } \quad d := 1 + \frac{1}{\varphi^4 \sqrt{5}} \approx 1.065 \cdot$$

- an RB tree's height is at most

$$h \ \leqq 2\log_2(n+1).$$

AVL trees are more rigidly balanced than RB trees with an asymptotic relation $^{\text{AVL}}\!/_{\text{RB}} \approx 0.720$ of the maximal heights. For insertions and deletions, Ben Pfaff shows in 79 measurements a relation of $^{\text{AVL}}\!/_{\text{RB}}$ between 0.677 and 1.077 with median ≈ 0.947 and geometric mean ≈ 0.910.

Representation of Avl Tree

In order to represent a node of an AVL Tree, we need four fields :- One for data, two for storing address of left and right child and one is required to hold the balance factor. The balance factor is calculated by subtracting the right sub-tree from the height of left sub - tree.

The structure of AVL Tree can be represented by : -

```
Struct AVL

   {

      struct AVL *left;

      int data;

      struct AVL *right;

      int balfact;

   };
```

Determination of Balance Factor

The value of balance factor may be -1, 0 or 1.

Any value other than these represent that the tree is not an AVL Tree

1. If the value of balance factor is -1, it shows that the height of right sub-tree is one more than the height of the left sub-tree with respect to the given node.

2. If the value of balance factor is 0, it shows that the height of right sub-tree is equal to the height of the left Sub-tree with respect to the given node.

3. If the value of balance factor is 1, it shows that the height of right sub-tree is one less than the height of the left sub-tree with respect to the given node.

Invention and Definition

It was invented in the year 1962 by two Russian mathematicians named G.M. Adelson-Velskii and E.M. Landis and so named AVL Tree.

It is a binary tree in which difference of height of two sub-trees with respect to a node never differ by more than one(1).

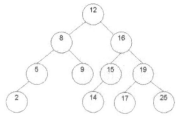

Diagram showing AVL Tree

Insertion of a Node in Avl Tree

Insertion can be done by finding an appropriate place for the node to be inserted. But this can disturb the balance of the tree if the difference of height of sub-trees with respect to a node exceeds the value one. If the insertion is done as a child of non-leaf node then it will not affect the balance, as the height doesn't increase. But if the insertion is done as a child of leaf node, then it can bring the real disturbance in the balance of the tree.

This depends on whether the node is inserted to the left sub-tree or the right sub-tree, which in turn changes the balance factor. If the node to be inserted is inserted as a node of a sub-tree of smaller height then there will be no effect. If the height of both the left and right sub-tree is same then insertionto any of them doesn't affect the balance of AVL Tree. But if it is inserted as a node of sub-tree of larger height, then the balance will be disturbed.

To rebalance the tree, the nodes need to be properly adjusted. So, after insertion of a new node the tree is traversed starting from the new node to the node where the balance has been disturbed. The nodes are adjusted in such a way that the balance is regained.

Algorithm for Insertion in Avl Tree

```
int avl_insert(node *treep, value_t target)

{
/* insert the target into the tree, returning 1 on success or 0 if it

* already existed

*/
    node tree = *treep;

    node *path_top = treep;

     while (tree && target != tree->value)

     {
     direction next_step = (target > tree->value);

     if (!Balanced(tree)) path_top = treep;

     treep = &tree->next[next_step];

     tree = *treep;

     }
   if (tree) return 0;

     tree = malloc(sizeof(*tree));
```

```
    tree->next = tree->next[1] = NULL;

    tree->longer = NEITHER;

    tree->value = target;

    *treep = tree;

    avl_rebalance(path_top, target);

 return 1;

    }
```

Algorithm for Rebalancing in Insertion

```
void

avl_rebalance_path(node path, value_t target)

    {

/* Each node in path is currently balanced. Until we find target, mark each
node as longer in the direction of rget because we know we have inserted
target there */

    while (path && target != path->value) {

    direction next_step = (target > path->value);

    path->longer = next_step;

    path = path->next[next_step];

    }

    }

 void avl_rebalance(node *path_top, value_t target)

  {

  node path = *path_top;

  direction first, second, third;

  if (Balanced(path)) {

  avl_rebalance_path(path, target);

  return;

  }

  first = (target > path->value);
```

```
        if (path->longer != first) {

        /* took the shorter path */

        path->longer = NEITHER;

        avl_rebalance_path(path->next[first], target);

        return;

        }

/* took the longer path, need to rotate */

second = (target > path->next[first]->value);

    if (first == second) {

/* just a two-point rotate */

        path = avl_rotate_2(path_top, first);

        avl_rebalance_path(path, target);

        return;

        }

/* fine details of the 3 point rotate depend on the third step. However
there may not be a third step, if the third point of the rotation is the
newly inserted point. In that case we record the third step as NEITHER */

path = path->next[first]->next[second];

    if (target == path->value) third = NEITHER;

        else third = (target > path->value);

            path = avl_rotate_3(path_top, first, third);

            avl_rebalance_path(path, target);

        }
```

Deletion

A node in AVL Tree is deleted as it is deleted in the binary search tree. The only difference is that we have to do rebalancing which is done similar to that of insertion of a node in AVL Tree. The algorithm for deletion and rebalancing is given below:

Algorithm for Deletion in Avl Tree

```
int avl_delete(node *treep, value_t target)

    {
```

```
/* delete the target from the tree, returning 1 on success or 0 if it
wasn't found */
    node tree = *treep;

  direction dir;

  node *targetp, targetn;

    while(tree) {

    dir = (target > value);

     if (target == value) targetp = treep;

     if (tree->next[dir] == NULL)

      break;

        if (tree->longer == NEITHER || (tree->longer == 1-dir && tree-
>next[1-dir]->longer == NEITHER))

        path_top = treep;

         treep = &tree->next[dir];

         tree = *treep;

          }

      if (targetp == NULL) return 0;

      targetp = avl_rebalance_del(path_top, target, targetp);

      avl_swap_del(targetp, treep, dir);

      return 1;

    }
```

Algorithm for Rebalancing in Deletion in Avl Tree

```
node *avl_rebalance_del(node *treep, value_t target, node *targetp)

{

  node targetn = *targetp;

  while(1) {

    node tree = *treep;

    direction dir = (target > tree->value);

    if (tree->next[dir] == NULL)

     break;
```

```
    if (Balanced(tree))
     tree->longer = 1-dir;
    else if (tree->longer == dir)
     tree->longer = NEITHER;
    else {
        /* a rotation is needed, and targetp might change */
      if (tree->next[1-dir]->longer == dir)
        avl_rotate_3_shrink(treep, dir);
       else
       avl_rotate_2_shrink(treep, dir);
        if (tree == targetn)
         *targetp = &(*treep)->next[dir];
       }
    treep = &tree->next[dir];
    }
return targetp;
}
```

Rebalancing of Avl Tree

When we insert a node to the taller sub-tree, four cases arise and we have different rebalancing methods to bring it back to a balanced tree form.

Left Rotation

In general if we want to insert a node R (either as left child or right child) to N3 as shown in figure. Here, as we see the balance factor of node P becomes 2. So to rebalance it, we have a technique called left rotation.

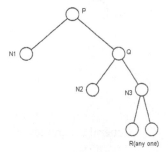

General Diagram

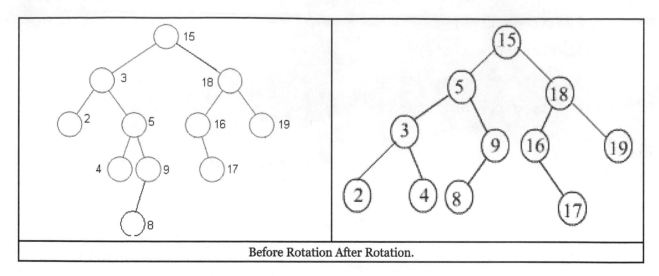

Before Rotation After Rotation.

Explanation of Example

In the given AVL tree when we insert a node 8,it becomes the left child of node 9 and the balance doesn't exist, as the balance factor of node 3 becomes -2. So, we try to rebalance it. In order to do so, we do left rotation at node 3. Now node 5 becomes the left child of the root. Node 9 and node 3 becomes the right and left child of node 5 respectively. Node 2 and node 4 becomes the left and right child of node 3 respectively. Lastly, node 8 becomes the left child of node 9. Hence, the balance is once again attained and we get AVL Tree after the left rotation.

Right Rotation

In general if we want to insert a node R (either as left or right child) to N1 as shown in figure. Here, as we see the balance factor of node P becomes 2. So to rebalance it, we have a technique called right rotation.

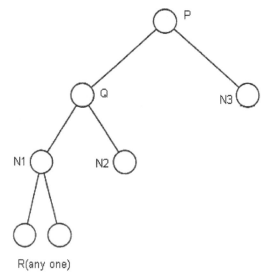

General Diagram.

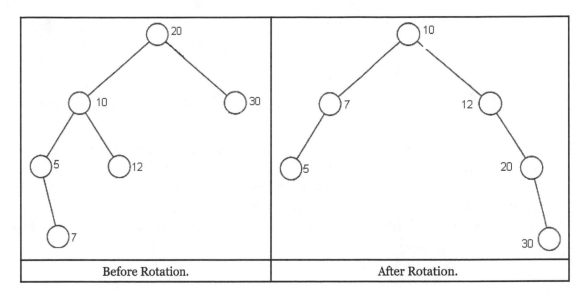

| Before Rotation. | After Rotation. |

Explanation of Example

In the given AVL tree when we insert a node 7,it becomes the right child of node 5 and the balance doesn't exist, as the balance factor of node 20 becomes 2. So, we try to rebalance it. In order to do so, we do right rotation at node 20. Now node 10 becomes the root. Node 12 and node 7 becomes the right and left child of root respectively. Node 20 becomes the right child of node 12. Node 30 becomes the right child of node 20. Lastly, node 5 becomes the left child of node 7. Hence, the balance is once again attained and we get AVL Tree after the right rotation.

References

- Rowan Garnier; John Taylor (2009). Discrete Mathematics: Proofs, Structures and Applications, Third Edition. CRC Press. p. 620. ISBN 978-1-4398-1280-8

- Paul E. Black (2015-04-13). "AVL tree". Dictionary of Algorithms and Data Structures. National Institute of Standards and Technology. Retrieved 2016-07-02

- Kenneth Rosen (2011). Discrete Mathematics and Its Applications 7th edition. McGraw-Hill Science. pp. 352–353. ISBN 978-0-07-338309-5

- Heger, Dominique A. (2004), "A Disquisition on The Performance Behavior of Binary Search Tree Data Structures" (PDF), European Journal for the Informatics Professional, 5 (5): 67–75

- Knuth, Donald E. (2000). Sorting and searching (2. ed., 6. printing, newly updated and rev. ed.). Boston [u.a.]: Addison-Wesley. p. 459. ISBN 0-201-89685-0

- Gonnet, Gaston. "Optimal Binary Search Trees". Scientific Computation. ETH Zürich. Retrieved 1 December 2013

5

Program Development and Related Processes

The chapter serves as a source to understand program development and the processes related to it. Software development is crafting a software product that involves processes such as programming, testing, bug-fixing etc. In the development stage, source code is written and maintained as well. The section also sheds light on concepts of programming language, source code, debugger, etc. This chapter is an overview of the subject matter incorporating all the major aspects of program development.

Software Development

Software development is the process of computer programming, documenting, testing, and bug fixing involved in creating and maintaining applications and frameworks resulting in a software product. Software development is a process of writing and maintaining the source code, but in a broader sense, it includes all that is involved between the conception of the desired software through to the final manifestation of the software, sometimes in a planned and structured process. Therefore, software development may include research, new development, prototyping, modification, reuse, re-engineering, maintenance, or any other activities that result in software products.

Software can be developed for a variety of purposes, the three most common being to meet specific needs of a specific client/business (the case with custom software), to meet a perceived need of some set of potential users (the case with commercial and open source software), or for personal use (e.g. a scientist may write software to automate a mundane task). Embedded software development, that is, the development of embedded software such as used for controlling consumer products, requires the development process to be integrated with the development of the controlled physical product. System software underlies applications and the programming process itself, and is often developed separately.

The need for better quality control of the software development process has given rise to the discipline of software engineering, which aims to apply the systematic approach exemplified in the engineering paradigm to the process of software development.

There are many approaches to software project management, known as software development life cycle models, methodologies, processes, or models. The waterfall model is a traditional version, contrasted with the more recent innovation of agile software development.

Methodologies

A software development process (also known as a software development methodology, model, or life cycle) is a framework that is used to structure, plan, and control the process of developing information systems. A wide variety of such frameworks has evolved over the years, each with its own recognized strengths and weaknesses. There are several different approaches to software development: some take a more structured, engineering-based approach to developing business solutions, whereas others may take a more incremental approach, where software evolves as it is developed piece-by-piece. One system development methodology is not necessarily suitable for use by all projects. Each of the available methodologies is best suited to specific kinds of projects, based on various technical, organizational, project and team considerations.

Most methodologies share some combination of the following stages of software development:

- Analyzing the problem

- Market research

- Gathering requirements for the proposed business solution

- Devising a plan or design for the software-based solution

- Implementation (coding) of the software

- Testing the software

- Deployment

- Maintenance and bug fixing

These stages are often referred to collectively as the software development lifecycle, or SDLC. Different approaches to software development may carry out these stages in different orders, or devote more or less time to different stages. The level of detail of the documentation produced at each stage of software development may also vary. These stages may also be carried out in turn (a "waterfall" based approach), or they may be repeated over various cycles or iterations (a more "extreme" approach). The more extreme approach usually involves less time spent on planning and documentation, and more time spent on coding and development of automated tests. More "extreme" approaches also promote continuous testing throughout the development lifecycle, as well as having a working (or bug-free) product at all times. More structured or "waterfall" based approaches attempt to assess the majority of risks and develop a detailed plan for the software before implementation (coding) begins, and avoid significant design changes and re-coding in later stages of the software development lifecycle planning.

There are significant advantages and disadvantages to the various methodologies, and the best approach to solving a problem using software will often depend on the type of problem. If the problem is well understood and a solution can be effectively planned out ahead of time, the more "waterfall" based approach may work the best. If, on the other hand, the problem is unique (at least to the development team) and the structure of the software solution cannot be easily envisioned, then a more "extreme" incremental approach may work best.

Software Development Activities

Identification of Need

The sources of ideas for software products are plenteous. These ideas can come from market research including the demographics of potential new customers, existing customers, sales prospects who rejected the product, other internal software development staff, or a creative third party. Ideas for software products are usually first evaluated by marketing personnel for economic feasibility, for fit with existing channels distribution, for possible effects on existing product lines, required features, and for fit with the company's marketing objectives. In a marketing evaluation phase, the cost and time assumptions become evaluated. A decision is reached early in the first phase as to whether, based on the more detailed information generated by the marketing and development staff, the project should be pursued further.

In the book *"Great Software Debates"*, Alan M. Davis states in the chapter *"Requirements"*, subchapter *"The Missing Piece of Software Development"*

Students of engineering learn engineering and are rarely exposed to finance or marketing. Students of marketing learn marketing and are rarely exposed to finance or engineering. Most of us become specialists in just one area. To complicate matters, few of us meet interdisciplinary people in the workforce, so there are few roles to mimic. Yet, software product planning is critical to the development success and absolutely requires knowledge of multiple disciplines.

Because software development may involve compromising or going beyond what is required by the client, a software development project may stray into less technical concerns such as human resources, risk management, intellectual property, budgeting, crisis management, etc. These processes may also cause the role of business development to overlap with software development.

Planning

Planning is an objective of each and every activity, where we want to discover things that belong to the project. An important task in creating a software program is extracting the requirements or requirements analysis. Customers typically have an abstract idea of what they want as an end result but do not know what *software* should do. Skilled and experienced software engineers recognize incomplete, ambiguous, or even contradictory requirements at this point. Frequently demonstrating live code may help reduce the risk that the requirements are incorrect.

Once the general requirements are gathered from the client, an analysis of the scope of the development should be determined and clearly stated. This is often called a scope document.

Certain functionality may be out of scope of the project as a function of cost or as a result of unclear requirements at the start of development. If the development is done externally, this document can be considered a legal document so that if there are ever disputes, any ambiguity of what was promised to the client can be clarified.

Designing

Once the requirements are established, the design of the software can be established in a software design document. This involves a preliminary, or high-level design of the main modules with an overall picture (such as a block diagram) of how the parts fit together. The language, operating system, and hardware components should all be known at this time. Then a detailed or low-level design is created, perhaps with prototyping as proof-of-concept or to firm up requirements.

Implementation, Testing and Documenting

Implementation is the part of the process where software engineers actually program the code for the project.

Software testing is an integral and important phase of the software development process. This part of the process ensures that defects are recognized as soon as possible. In some processes, generally known as test-driven development, tests may be developed just before implementation and serve as a guide for the implementation's correctness.

Documenting the internal design of software for the purpose of future maintenance and enhancement is done throughout development. This may also include the writing of an API, be it external or internal. The software engineering process chosen by the developing team will determine how much internal documentation (if any) is necessary. Plan-driven models (e.g., Waterfall) generally produce more documentation than Agile models.

Deployment and Maintenance

Deployment starts directly after the code is appropriately tested, approved for release, and sold or otherwise distributed into a production environment. This may involve installation, customization (such as by setting parameters to the customer's values), testing, and possibly an extended period of evaluation.

Software training and support is important, as software is only effective if it is used correctly.

Maintaining and enhancing software to cope with newly discovered faults or requirements can take substantial time and effort, as missed requirements may force redesign of the software.

Other

- Performance engineering

Software Development is estimated to be a vastly expanding area. With how rapidly technology is changing, this skill has become more and more needed.

Subtopics

View Model

A view model is a framework that provides the viewpoints on the system and its environment, to be used in the software development process. It is a graphical representation of the underlying semantics of a view.

The purpose of viewpoints and views is to enable human engineers to comprehend very complex systems and to organize the elements of the problem and the solution around domains of expertise. In the engineering of physically intensive systems, viewpoints often correspond to capabilities and responsibilities within the engineering organization.

Most complex system specifications are so extensive that no one individual can fully comprehend all aspects of the specifications. Furthermore, we all have different interests in a given system and different reasons for examining the system's specifications. A business executive will ask different questions of a system make-up than would a system implementer. The concept of viewpoints framework, therefore, is to provide separate viewpoints into the specification of a given complex system. These viewpoints each satisfy an audience with interest in some set of aspects of the system. Associated with each viewpoint is a viewpoint language that optimizes the vocabulary and presentation for the audience of that viewpoint.

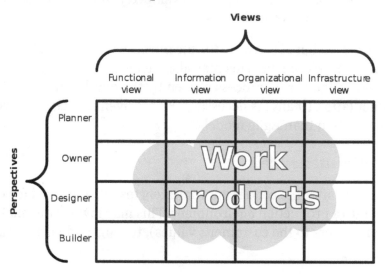

The TEAF Matrix of Views and Perspectives.

Business Process and Data Modelling

Graphical representation of the current state of information provides a very effective means for presenting information to both users and system developers.

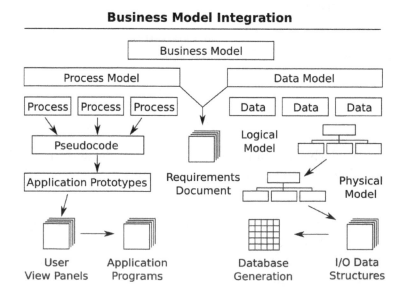

example of the interaction between business process and data models.

- A business model illustrates the functions associated with the business process being modeled and the organizations that perform these functions. By depicting activities and information flows, a foundation is created to visualize, define, understand, and validate the nature of a process.

- A data model provides the details of information to be stored and is of primary use when the final product is the generation of computer software code for an application or the preparation of a functional specification to aid a computer software make-or-buy decision. See the figure for an example of the interaction between business process and data models.

Usually, a model is created after conducting an interview, referred to as business analysis. The interview consists of a facilitator asking a series of questions designed to extract required information that describes a process. The interviewer is called a facilitator to emphasize that it is the participants who provide the information. The facilitator should have some knowledge of the process of interest, but this is not as important as having a structured methodology by which the questions are asked of the process expert. The methodology is important because usually a team of facilitators is collecting information across the facility and the results of the information from all the interviewers must fit together once completed.

The models are developed as defining either the current state of the process, in which case the final product is called the "as-is" snapshot model, or a collection of ideas of what the process should contain, resulting in a "what-can-be" model. Generation of process and data models can be used to determine if the existing processes and information systems are sound and only need minor modifications or enhancements, or if re-engineering is required as a corrective action. The creation of business models is more than a way to view or automate your information process. Analysis can be used to fundamentally reshape the way your business or organization conducts its operations.

Computer-aided Software Engineering

Computer-aided software engineering (CASE), in the field software engineering, is the scientific application of a set of software tools and methods to the development of software which results in high-quality, defect-free, and maintainable software products. It also refers to methods for the development of information systems together with automated tools that can be used in the software development process. The term "computer-aided software engineering" (CASE) can refer to the software used for the automated development of systems software, i.e., computer code. The CASE functions include analysis, design, and programming. CASE tools automate methods for designing, documenting, and producing structured computer code in the desired programming language.

Two key ideas of Computer-aided Software System Engineering (CASE) are:

- Foster computer assistance in software development and or software maintenance processes, and

- An engineering approach to software development and or maintenance.

Typical CASE tools exist for configuration management, data modeling, model transformation, refactoring, source code generation.

Integrated Development Environment

Anjuta, a C and C++ IDE for the GNOME environment.

An integrated development environment (IDE) also known as *integrated design environment* or *integrated debugging environment* is a software application that provides comprehensive facilities to computer programmers for software development. An IDE normally consists of a:

- source code editor,

- compiler and/or interpreter,

- build automation tools, and

- debugger (usually).

IDEs are designed to maximize programmer productivity by providing tight-knit components with similar user interfaces. Typically an IDE is dedicated to a specific programming language, so as to provide a feature set which most closely matches the programming paradigms of the language.

Modeling Language

A modeling language is any artificial language that can be used to express information or knowledge or systems in a structure that is defined by a consistent set of rules. The rules are used for interpretation of the meaning of components in the structure. A modeling language can be graphical or textual. Graphical modeling languages use a diagram techniques with named symbols that represent concepts and lines that connect the symbols and that represent relationships and various other graphical annotation to represent constraints. Textual modeling languages typically use standardised keywords accompanied by parameters to make computer-interpretable expressions.

Examples of graphical modelling languages in the field of software engineering are:

- Business Process Modeling Notation (BPMN, and the XML form BPML) is an example of a process modeling language.

- EXPRESS and EXPRESS-G (ISO 10303-11) is an international standard general-purpose data modeling language.

- Extended Enterprise Modeling Language (EEML) is commonly used for business process modeling across layers.

- Flowchart is a schematic representation of an algorithm or a stepwise process.

- Fundamental Modeling Concepts (FMC) modeling language for software-intensive systems.

- IDEF is a family of modeling languages, the most notable of which include IDEF0 for functional modeling, IDEF1X for information modeling, and IDEF5 for modeling ontologies.

- LePUS3 is an object-oriented visual Design Description Language and a formal specification language that is suitable primarily for modelling large object-oriented (Java, C++, C#) programs and design patterns.

- Specification and Description Language(SDL) is a specification language targeted at the unambiguous specification and description of the behaviour of reactive and distributed systems.

- Unified Modeling Language (UML) is a general-purpose modeling language that is an industry standard for specifying software-intensive systems. UML 2.0, the current version, supports thirteen different diagram techniques and has widespread tool support.

Not all modeling languages are executable, and for those that are, using them doesn't necessarily mean that programmers are no longer needed. On the contrary, executable modeling languages are intended to amplify the productivity of skilled programmers, so that they can address more difficult problems, such as parallel computing and distributed systems.

Programming Paradigm

A programming paradigm is a fundamental style of computer programming, which is not generally dictated by the project management methodology (such as waterfall or agile). Paradigms differ in the concepts and abstractions used to represent the elements of a program (such as objects, functions, variables, constraints) and the steps that comprise a computation (such as assignations, evaluation, continuations, data flows). Sometimes the concepts asserted by the paradigm are utilized cooperatively in high-level system architecture design; in other cases, the programming paradigm's scope is limited to the internal structure of a particular program or module.

A programming language can support multiple paradigms. For example, programs written in C++ or Object Pascal can be purely procedural, or purely object-oriented, or contain elements of both paradigms. Software designers and programmers decide how to use those paradigm elements. In object-oriented programming, programmers can think of a program as a collection of interacting objects, while in functional programming a program can be thought of as a sequence of stateless function evaluations. When programming computers or systems with many processors, process-oriented programming allows programmers to think about applications as sets of concurrent processes acting upon logically shared data structures.

Just as different groups in software engineering advocate different *methodologies*, different programming languages advocate different *programming paradigms*. Some languages are designed to support one paradigm (Smalltalk supports object-oriented programming, Haskell supports functional programming), while other programming languages support multiple paradigms (such as Object Pascal, C++, C#, Visual Basic, Common Lisp, Scheme, Python, Ruby, and Oz).

Many programming paradigms are as well known for what methods they *forbid* as for what they enable. For instance, pure functional programming forbids using side-effects; structured programming forbids using goto statements. Partly for this reason, new paradigms are often regarded as doctrinaire or overly rigid by those accustomed to earlier styles. Avoiding certain methods can make it easier to prove theorems about a program's correctness, or simply to understand its behavior.

Examples of high-level paradigms include:

- Aspect-oriented software development

- Domain-specific modeling

- Model-driven engineering

- Object-oriented programming methodologies

  o Grady Booch's object-oriented design (OOD), also known as object-oriented analysis and design (OOAD). The Booch model includes six diagrams: class, object, state transition, interaction, module, and process.

- Search-based software engineering

- Service-oriented modeling

- Structured programming

- Top-down and bottom-up design

  o Top-down programming: evolved in the 1970s by IBM researcher Harlan Mills (and Niklaus Wirth) in developed structured programming.

Reuse of Solutions

- A software framework is a re-usable design or implementation for a software system or subsystem.

- components (Component-based software engineering)

- API (Application programming interface, Web service)

Software Development Process

In software engineering, a software development methodology (also known as a system development methodology, software development life cycle, software development process, software process) is splitting of software development work into distinct phases (or stages) containing activities with the intent of better planning and management. It is often considered a subset of the systems development life cycle. The methodology may include the pre-definition of specific deliverables and artifacts that are created and completed by a project team to develop or maintain an application.

Common methodologies include waterfall, prototyping, iterative and incremental development, spiral development, rapid application development, extreme programming and various types of agile methodology. Some people consider a life-cycle "model" a more general term for a category of methodologies and a software development "process" a more specific term to refer to a specific process chosen by a specific organization. For example, there are many specific software development processes that fit the spiral life-cycle model.

In Practice

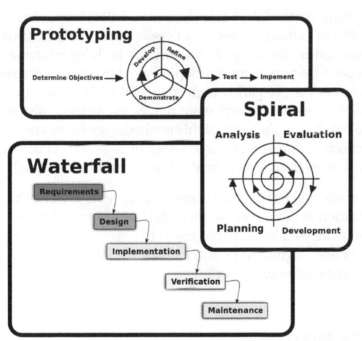

The three basic approaches applied to software development methodology frameworks.

A variety of such frameworks have evolved over the years, each with its own recognized strengths and weaknesses. One software development methodology framework is not necessarily suitable for use by all projects. Each of the available methodology frameworks are best suited to specific kinds of projects, based on various technical, organizational, project and team considerations.

Software development organizations implement process methodologies to ease the process of development. Sometimes, contractors may require methodologies employed, an example is the U.S. defense industry, which requires a rating based on process models to obtain contracts. The international standard for describing the method of selecting, implementing and monitoring the life cycle for software is ISO/IEC 12207.

A decades-long goal has been to find repeatable, predictable processes that improve productivity and quality. Some try to systematize or formalize the seemingly unruly task of designing software.

Others apply project management techniques to designing software. Large numbers of software projects do not meet their expectations in terms of functionality, cost, or delivery schedule.

Organizations may create a Software Engineering Process Group (SEPG), which is the focal point for process improvement. Composed of line practitioners who have varied skills, the group is at the center of the collaborative effort of everyone in the organization who is involved with software engineering process improvement.

A particular development team may also agree to programming environment details, such as which integrated development environment is used, and one or more dominant programming paradigms, programming style rules, or choice of specific software libraries or software frameworks. These details are generally not dictated by the choice of model or general methodology.

History

The software development methodology (also known as SDM) framework didn't emerge until the 1960s. According to Elliott (2004) the systems development life cycle (SDLC) can be considered to be the oldest formalized methodology framework for building information systems. The main idea of the SDLC has been "to pursue the development of information systems in a very deliberate, structured and methodical way, requiring each stage of the life cycle––from inception of the idea to delivery of the final system––to be carried out rigidly and sequentially" within the context of the framework being applied. The main target of this methodology framework in the 1960s was "to develop large scale functional business systems in an age of large scale business conglomerates. Information systems activities revolved around heavy data processing and number crunching routines".

Methodologies, processes, and frameworks range from specific proscriptive steps that can be used directly by an organization in day-to-day work, to flexible frameworks that an organization uses to generate a custom set of steps tailored to the needs of a specific project or group. In some cases a "sponsor" or "maintenance" organization distributes an official set of documents that describe the process. Specific examples include:

1970s

- Structured programming since 1969

- Cap Gemini SDM, originally from PANDATA, the first English translation was published in 1974. SDM stands for System Development Methodology

1980s

- Structured systems analysis and design method (SSADM) from 1980 onwards

- Information Requirement Analysis/Soft systems methodology

1990s

- Object-oriented programming (OOP) developed in the early 1960s, and became a dominant programming approach during the mid-1990s

- Rapid application development (RAD), since 1991

- Dynamic systems development method (DSDM), since 1994

- Scrum, since 1995

- Team software process, since 1998

- Rational Unified Process (RUP), maintained by IBM since 1998

- Extreme programming, since 1999

2000s

- Agile Unified Process (AUP) maintained since 2005 by Scott Ambler

- Disciplined agile delivery (DAD) Supersedes AUP

2010s

- Scaled Agile Framework (SAFe)

- Large-Scale Scrum (LeSS)

It is notable that since DSDM in 1994, all of the methodologies on the above list except RUP have been agile methodologies - yet many organisations, especially governments, still use pre-agile processes (often waterfall or similar). Software process and software quality are closely interrelated; some unexpected facets and effects have been observed in practice.

Since the early 2000s scaling agile delivery processes has become the biggest challenge for teams using agile processes.

Approaches

Several software development approaches have been used since the origin of information technology, in two main categories. Typically an approach or a combination of approaches is chosen by management or a development team.

"Traditional" methodologies such as waterfall that have distinct phases are sometimes known as software development life cycle (SDLC) methodologies, though this term could also be used more generally to refer to any methodology. A "life cycle" approach with distinct phases is in contrast to Agile approaches which define a process of iteration, but where design, construction, and deployment of different pieces can occur simultaneously.

Waterfall Development

The waterfall model is a sequential development approach, in which development is seen as flowing steadily downwards (like a waterfall) through several phases, typically:

- Requirements analysis resulting in a software requirements specification

- Software design

- Implementation

- Testing

- Integration, if there are multiple subsystems

- Deployment (or Installation)

- Maintenance

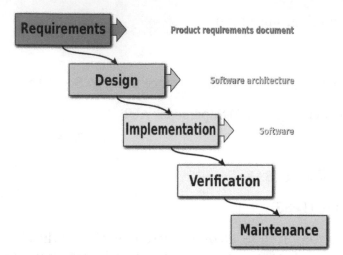

The activities of the software development process represented in the waterfall model.
There are several other models to represent this process.

The first formal description of the method is often cited as an article published by Winston W. Royce in 1970 although Royce did not use the term "waterfall" in this article. The basic principles are:

- Project is divided into sequential phases, with some overlap and splashback acceptable between phases.

- Emphasis is on planning, time schedules, target dates, budgets and implementation of an entire system at one time.

- Tight control is maintained over the life of the project via extensive written documentation, formal reviews, and approval/signoff by the user and information technology management occurring at the end of most phases before beginning the next phase. Written documentation is an explicit deliverable of each phase.

The waterfall model is a traditional engineering approach applied to software engineering. A strict waterfall approach discourages revisiting and revising any prior phase once it is complete. This "inflexibility" in a pure waterfall model has been a source of criticism by supporters of other more "flexible" models. It has been widely blamed for several large-scale government projects running over budget, over time and sometimes failing to deliver on requirements due to the Big Design Up Front approach. Except when contractually required, the waterfall model has been largely superseded by more flexible and versatile methodologies developed specifically for software development.

The waterfall model is sometimes taught with the mnemonic A Dance In The Dark Every Monday, representing Analysis, Design, Implementation, Testing, Documentation and Execution, and Maintenance.

Prototyping

Software prototyping is about creating prototypes, i.e. incomplete versions of the software program being developed.

The basic principles are:

- Prototyping is not a standalone, complete development methodology, but rather an approach to try out particular features in the context of a full methodology (such as incremental, spiral, or rapid application development (RAD)).

- Attempts to reduce inherent project risk by breaking a project into smaller segments and providing more ease-of-change during the development process.

- The client is involved throughout the development process, which increases the likelihood of client acceptance of the final implementation.

- While some prototypes are developed with the expectation that they will be discarded, it is possible in some cases to evolve from prototype to working system.

A basic understanding of the fundamental business problem is necessary to avoid solving the wrong problems, but this is true for all software methodologies.

Incremental Development

Various methods are acceptable for combining linear and iterative systems development methodologies, with the primary objective of each being to reduce inherent project risk by breaking a project into smaller segments and providing more ease-of-change during the development process.

There are three main variants of incremental development:

1. A series of mini-Waterfalls are performed, where all phases of the Waterfall are completed for a small part of a system, before proceeding to the next increment, or

2. Overall requirements are defined before proceeding to evolutionary, mini-Waterfall development of individual increments of a system, or

3. The initial software concept, requirements analysis, and design of architecture and system core are defined via Waterfall, followed by incremental implementation, which culminates in installing the final version, a working system.

Iterative and Incremental Development

Iterative development prescribes the construction of initially small but ever-larger portions of a software project to help all those involved to uncover important issues early before problems or faulty assumptions can lead to disaster.

Spiral Development

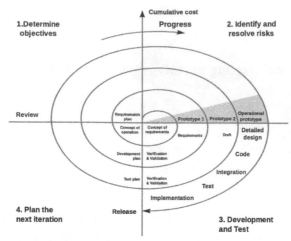

Spiral model (Boehm, 1988).

In 1988, Barry Boehm published a formal software system development "spiral model," which combines some key aspect of the waterfall model and rapid prototyping methodologies, in an effort to combine advantages of top-down and bottom-up concepts. It provided emphasis in a key area many felt had been neglected by other methodologies: deliberate iterative risk analysis, particularly suited to large-scale complex systems.

The basic principles are:

- Focus is on risk assessment and on minimizing project risk by breaking a project into smaller segments and providing more ease-of-change during the development process, as well as providing the opportunity to evaluate risks and weigh consideration of project continuation throughout the life cycle.

- "Each cycle involves a progression through the same sequence of steps, for each part of the product and for each of its levels of elaboration, from an overall concept-of-operation document down to the coding of each individual program."

- Each trip around the spiral traverses four basic quadrants: (1) determine objectives, alternatives, and constraints of the iteration; (2) evaluate alternatives; Identify and resolve risks; (3) develop and verify deliverables from the iteration; and (4) plan the next iteration.

- Begin each cycle with an identification of stakeholders and their "win conditions", and end each cycle with review and commitment.

Rapid Application Development

Rapid application development (RAD) is a software development methodology, which favors iterative development and the rapid construction of prototypes instead of large amounts of up-front planning. The "planning" of software developed using RAD is interleaved with writing the software itself. The lack of extensive pre-planning generally allows software to be written much faster, and makes it easier to change requirements.

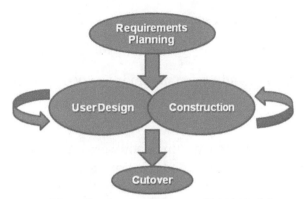

Rapid Application Development (RAD) Model.

The rapid development process starts with the development of preliminary data models and business process models using structured techniques. In the next stage, requirements are verified using prototyping, eventually to refine the data and process models. These stages are repeated iteratively; further development results in "a combined business requirements and technical design statement to be used for constructing new systems".

The term was first used to describe a software development process introduced by James Martin in 1991. According to Whitten (2003), it is a merger of various structured techniques, especially data-driven Information Engineering, with prototyping techniques to accelerate software systems development.

The basic principles of rapid application development are:

- Key objective is for fast development and delivery of a high quality system at a relatively low investment cost.

- Attempts to reduce inherent project risk by breaking a project into smaller segments and providing more ease-of-change during the development process.

- Aims to produce high quality systems quickly, primarily via iterative Prototyping (at any stage of development), active user involvement, and computerized development tools. These tools may include Graphical User Interface (GUI) builders, Computer Aided Software Engineering (CASE) tools, Database Management Systems (DBMS), fourth-generation programming languages, code generators, and object-oriented techniques.

- Key emphasis is on fulfilling the business need, while technological or engineering excellence is of lesser importance.

- Project control involves prioritizing development and defining delivery deadlines or "timeboxes". If the project starts to slip, emphasis is on reducing requirements to fit the timebox, not in increasing the deadline.

- Generally includes joint application design (JAD), where users are intensely involved in system design, via consensus building in either structured workshops, or electronically facilitated interaction.

- Active user involvement is imperative.

- Iteratively produces production software, as opposed to a throwaway prototype.

- Produces documentation necessary to facilitate future development and maintenance.

- Standard systems analysis and design methods can be fitted into this framework.

Agile Development

"Agile software development" refers to a group of software development methodologies based on iterative development, where requirements and solutions evolve via collaboration between self-organizing cross-functional teams. The term was coined in the year 2001 when the Agile Manifesto was formulated.

Agile software development uses iterative development as a basis but advocates a lighter and more people-centric viewpoint than traditional approaches. Agile processes fundamentally incorporate iteration and the continuous feedback that it provides to successively refine and deliver a software system.

There are many agile methodologies, including:

- Dynamic systems development method (DSDM)

- Kanban

- Scrum

Lightweight Methodologies

A lightweight methodology has a small number of rules. Some of these methodologies are also considered "agile".

- Adaptive Software Development by Jim Highsmith, described in his 1999 book *Adaptive Software Development*.

- Crystal Clear family of methodologies with Alistair Cockburn.

- Extreme Programming (XP), promoted by people such as Kent Beck and Martin Fowler. In extreme programming, the phases are carried out in extremely small (or "continuous") steps compared to the older, "batch" processes. The (intentionally incomplete) first pass through the steps might take a day or a week, rather than the months or years of each complete step in the Waterfall model. First, one writes automated tests, to provide concrete goals for development. Next is coding (by programmers working in pairs, a technique known as "pair programming"), which is complete when all the tests pass, and the programmers can't think of any more tests that are needed. Design and architecture emerge from refactoring, and come after coding. The same people who do the coding do design. (Only the last feature — merging design and code — is common to *all* the other agile processes.) The incomplete but functional system is deployed or demonstrated for (some subset of) the users (at least one of which is on the development team). At this point, the practitioners start again on writing tests for the next most important part of the system.

- Feature Driven Development (FDD) developed (1999) by Jeff De Luca and Peter Coad

- ICONIX - UML-based object modeling with use cases, a lightweight precursor to the Rational Unified Process.

Other

Other high-level software project methodologies include:

- Behavior-driven development and business process management.

- Chaos model - The main rule is always resolve the most important issue first.

- Incremental funding methodology - an iterative approach.

- Structured systems analysis and design method - a specific version of waterfall.

- Slow programming, as part of the larger Slow Movement, emphasizes careful and gradual work without (or minimal) time pressures. Slow programming aims to avoid bugs and overly quick release schedules.

- V-Model (software development) - an extension of the waterfall model.

- Unified Process (UP) is an iterative software development methodology framework, based on Unified Modeling Language (UML). UP organizes the development of software into four phases, each consisting of one or more executable iterations of the software at that stage of development: inception, elaboration, construction, and guidelines. Many tools and products exist to facilitate UP implementation. One of the more popular versions of UP is the Rational Unified Process (RUP).

Code and Fix

"Code and fix" is an anti-pattern. Development is not done through a deliberate strategy or methodology. It is often the result of schedule pressure on the software development team. Without much of a design in the way, programmers immediately begin producing code. At some point, testing begins (often late in the development cycle), and the unavoidable bugs must then be fixed - or at least, the most important ones must be fixed - before the product can be shipped.

Process Meta-models

Some "process models" are abstract descriptions for evaluating, comparing, and improving the specific process adopted by an organization.

- ISO/IEC 12207 is the international standard describing the method to select, implement, and monitor the life cycle for software.

- The Capability Maturity Model Integration (CMMI) is one of the leading models and based on best practice. Independent assessments grade organizations on how well they follow their defined processes, not on the quality of those processes or the software produced. CMMI has replaced CMM.

- ISO 9000 describes standards for a formally organized process to manufacture a product and the methods of managing and monitoring progress. Although the standard was originally created for the manufacturing sector, ISO 9000 standards have been applied to software development as well. Like CMMI, certification with ISO 9000 does not guarantee the quality of the end result, only that formalized business processes have been followed.

- ISO/IEC 15504 *Information technology — Process assessment* also known as Software Process Improvement Capability Determination (SPICE), is a "framework for the assessment of software processes". This standard is aimed at setting out a clear model for process comparison. SPICE is used much like CMMI. It models processes to manage, control, guide and monitor software development. This model is then used to measure what a development organization or project team actually does during software development. This information is analyzed to identify weaknesses and drive improvement. It also identifies strengths that can be continued or integrated into common practice for that organization or team.

- SPEM 2.0 by the Object Management Group.

- Soft systems methodology - a general method for improving management processes.

- Method engineering - a general method for improving information system processes.

Formal Methods

Formal methods are mathematical approaches to solving software (and hardware) problems at the requirements, specification, and design levels. Formal methods are most likely to be applied to safety-critical or security-critical software and systems, such as avionics software. Software safety assurance standards, such as DO-178B, DO-178C, and Common Criteria demand formal methods at the highest levels of categorization.

For sequential software, examples of formal methods include the B-Method, the specification languages used in automated theorem proving, RAISE, and the Z notation.

In functional programming, property-based testing has allowed the mathematical specification and testing (if not exhaustive testing) of the expected behaviour of individual functions.

The Object Constraint Language (and specializations such as Java Modeling Language) has allowed object-oriented systems to be formally specified, if not necessarily formally verified.

For concurrent software and systems, Petri nets, process algebra, and finite state machines (which are based on automata theory) allow executable software specification and can be used to build up and validate application behavior.

Another approach to formal methods in software development is to write a specification in some form of logic—usually a variation of first-order logic (FOL)—and then to directly execute the logic as though it were a program. The OWL language, based on Description Logic (DL), is an example. There is also work on mapping some version of English (or another natural language) automatically to and from logic, and executing the logic directly. Examples are Attempto Controlled English, and Internet Business Logic, which do not seek to control the vocabulary or syntax. A feature of systems that support bidirectional English-logic mapping and direct execution of the logic is that they can be made to explain their results, in English, at the business or scientific level.

Programming Language

```
1  /* This line basically imports the "stdio" header file, part of
2   * the standard library. It provides input and output functionality
3   * to the program.
4   */
5  #include <stdio.h>
6
7  /*
8   * Function (method) declaration. This outputs "Hello, world" to
9   * standard output when invoked.
10  */
11 void sayHello() {
12     // printf() in C outputs the specified text (with optional
13     // formatting options) when invoked.
14     printf("Hello, world!");
15 }
16
17 /*
18  * This is a "main function". The compiled program will run the code
19  * defined here.
20  */
21 void main() {
22     // Invoke the sayHello() function.
23     sayHello();
24 }
```

Source code of a simple computer program written in the C programming language, which will output the "Hello, world!" message when compiled and run.

A programming language is a formal computer language designed to communicate instructions to a machine, particularly a computer. Programming languages can be used to create programs to control the behavior of a machine or to express algorithms.

The earliest known programmable machine preceded the invention of the digital computer and is the automatic flute player described in the 9th century by the brothers Musa in Baghdad, "during the Islamic Golden Age". From the early 1800s, "programs" were used to direct the behavior of machines such as Jacquard looms and player pianos. Thousands of different programming languages have been created, mainly in the computer field, and many more still are being created every year. Many programming languages require computation to be specified in an imperative form (i.e., as a sequence of operations to perform) while other languages use other forms of program specification such as the declarative form (i.e. the desired result is specified, not how to achieve it).

The description of a programming language is usually split into the two components of syntax (form) and semantics (meaning). Some languages are defined by a specification document (for example, the C programming language is specified by an ISO Standard) while other languages (such as Perl) have a dominant implementation that is treated as a reference. Some languages have both, with the basic language defined by a standard and extensions taken from the dominant implementation being common.

Definitions

A programming language is a notation for writing programs, which are specifications of a computation or algorithm. Some, but not all, authors restrict the term "programming language" to those languages that can express *all* possible algorithms. Traits often considered important for what constitutes a programming language include:

Function and target

> A *computer programming language* is a language used to write computer programs, which involve a computer performing some kind of computation or algorithm and possibly control external devices such as printers, disk drives, robots, and so on. For example, PostScript programs are frequently created by another program to control a computer printer or display. More generally, a programming language may describe computation on some, possibly abstract, machine. It is generally accepted that a complete specification for a programming language includes a description, possibly idealized, of a machine or processor for that language. In most practical contexts, a programming language involves a computer; consequently, programming languages are usually defined and studied this way. Programming languages differ from natural languages in that natural languages are only used for interaction between people, while programming languages also allow humans to communicate instructions to machines.

Abstractions

> Programming languages usually contain abstractions for defining and manipulating data structures or controlling the flow of execution. The practical necessity that a programming language support adequate abstractions is expressed by the abstraction principle; this principle is sometimes formulated as a recommendation to the programmer to make proper use of such abstractions.

Expressive power

> The theory of computation classifies languages by the computations they are capable of expressing. All Turing complete languages can implement the same set of algorithms. ANSI/ISO SQL-92 and Charity are examples of languages that are not Turing complete, yet often called programming languages.

Markup languages like XML, HTML, or troff, which define structured data, are not usually considered programming languages. Programming languages may, however, share the syntax with markup languages if a computational semantics is defined. XSLT, for example, is a Turing complete XML dialect. Moreover, LaTeX, which is mostly used for structuring documents, also contains a Turing complete subset.

The term *computer language* is sometimes used interchangeably with programming language. However, the usage of both terms varies among authors, including the exact scope of each. One usage describes programming languages as a subset of computer languages. In this vein, languages used in computing that have a different goal than expressing computer programs are generically designated computer languages. For instance, markup languages are sometimes referred to as computer languages to emphasize that they are not meant to be used for programming.

Another usage regards programming languages as theoretical constructs for programming abstract machines, and computer languages as the subset thereof that runs on physical computers, which have finite hardware resources. John C. Reynolds emphasizes that formal specification languages are just as much programming languages as are the languages intended for execution. He also argues that textual and even graphical input formats that affect the behavior of a computer are programming languages, despite the fact they are commonly not Turing-complete, and remarks that ignorance of programming language concepts is the reason for many flaws in input formats.

History

Early Developments

The earliest computers were often programmed without the help of a programming language, by writing programs in absolute machine language. The programs, in decimal or binary form, were read in from punched cards or magnetic tape or toggled in on switches on the front panel of the computer. Absolute machine languages were later termed *first-generation programming languages* (1GL).

The next step was development of so-called *second-generation programming languages* (2GL) or assembly languages, which were still closely tied to the instruction set architecture of the specific computer. These served to make the program much more human-readable and relieved the programmer of tedious and error-prone address calculations.

The first *high-level programming languages*, or *third-generation programming languages* (3GL), were written in the 1950s. An early high-level programming language to be designed for a computer was Plankalkül, developed for the German Z3 by Konrad Zuse between 1943 and 1945. However, it was not implemented until 1998 and 2000.

John Mauchly's Short Code, proposed in 1949, was one of the first high-level languages ever developed for an electronic computer. Unlike machine code, Short Code statements represented mathematical expressions in understandable form. However, the program had to be translated into machine code every time it ran, making the process much slower than running the equivalent machine code.

The Manchester Mark 1 ran programs written in Autocode from 1952.

At the University of Manchester, Alick Glennie developed Autocode in the early 1950s. A programming language, it used a compiler to automatically convert the language into machine code. The first code and compiler was developed in 1952 for the Mark 1 computer at the University of Manchester and is considered to be the first compiled high-level programming language.

The second autocode was developed for the Mark 1 by R. A. Brooker in 1954 and was called the "Mark 1 Autocode". Brooker also developed an autocode for the Ferranti Mercury in the 1950s in conjunction with the University of Manchester. The version for the EDSAC 2 was devised by D. F. Hartley of University of Cambridge Mathematical Laboratory in 1961. Known as EDSAC 2 Autocode, it was a straight development from Mercury Autocode adapted for local circumstances and was noted for its object code optimisation and source-language diagnostics which were advanced for the time. A contemporary but separate thread of development, Atlas Autocode was developed for the University of Manchester Atlas 1 machine.

In 1954, FORTRAN was invented at IBM by John Backus. It was the first widely used high-level general purpose programming language to have a functional implementation, as opposed to just a design on paper. It is still popular language for high-performance computing and is used for programs that benchmark and rank the world's fastest supercomputers.

Another early programming language was devised by Grace Hopper in the US, called FLOW-MATIC. It was developed for the UNIVAC I at Remington Rand during the period from 1955 until 1959. Hopper found that business data processing customers were uncomfortable with mathematical notation, and in early 1955, she and her team wrote a specification for an English programming language and implemented a prototype. The FLOW-MATIC compiler became publicly available in early 1958 and was substantially complete in 1959. Flow-Matic was a major influence in the design of COBOL, since only it and its direct descendant AIMACO were in actual use at the time.

Refinement

The increased use of high-level languages introduced a requirement for *low-level programming languages* or *system programming languages*. These languages, to varying degrees, provide facilities between assembly languages and high-level languages and can be used to perform tasks which require direct access to hardware facilities but still provide higher-level control structures and error-checking.

The period from the 1960s to the late 1970s brought the development of the major language paradigms now in use:

- APL introduced *array programming* and influenced functional programming.

- ALGOL refined both *structured procedural programming* and the discipline of language specification; the "Revised Report on the Algorithmic Language ALGOL 60" became a model for how later language specifications were written.

- Lisp, implemented in 1958, was the first dynamically typed *functional programming* language.

- In the 1960s, Simula was the first language designed to support *object-oriented programming*; in the mid-1970s, Smalltalk followed with the first "purely" object-oriented language.

- C was developed between 1969 and 1973 as a system programming language for the Unix operating system and remains popular.

- Prolog, designed in 1972, was the first *logic programming* language.

- In 1978, ML built a polymorphic type system on top of Lisp, pioneering *statically typed functional programming* languages.

Each of these languages spawned descendants, and most modern programming languages count at least one of them in their ancestry.

The 1960s and 1970s also saw considerable debate over the merits of *structured programming*, and whether programming languages should be designed to support it. Edsger Dijkstra, in a famous 1968 letter published in the Communications of the ACM, argued that GOTO statements should be eliminated from all "higher level" programming languages.

Consolidation and Growth

A selection of textbooks that teach programming, in languages both popular and obscure. These are only a few of the thousands of programming languages and dialects that have been designed in history.

The 1980s were years of relative consolidation. C++ combined object-oriented and systems programming. The United States government standardized Ada, a systems programming language derived from Pascal and intended for use by defense contractors. In Japan and elsewhere, vast sums were spent investigating so-called "fifth generation" languages that incorporated logic programming constructs. The functional languages community moved to standardize ML and Lisp. Rather than inventing new paradigms, all of these movements elaborated upon the ideas invented in the previous decades.

One important trend in language design for programming large-scale systems during the 1980s was an increased focus on the use of *modules* or large-scale organizational units of code. Modula-2, Ada, and ML all developed notable module systems in the 1980s, which were often wedded to generic programming constructs.

The rapid growth of the Internet in the mid-1990s created opportunities for new languages. Perl, originally a Unix scripting tool first released in 1987, became common in dynamic websites. Java came to be used for server-side programming, and bytecode virtual machines became popular again in commercial settings with their promise of "Write once, run anywhere" (UCSD Pascal had been popular for a time in the early 1980s). These developments were not fundamentally novel, rather they were refinements of many existing languages and paradigms (although their syntax was often based on the C family of programming languages).

Programming language evolution continues, in both industry and research. Current directions include security and reliability verification, new kinds of modularity (mixins, delegates, aspects), and database integration such as Microsoft's LINQ.

Fourth-generation programming languages (4GL) are a computer programming languages which aim to provide a higher level of abstraction of the internal computer hardware details than 3GLs. *Fifth generation programming languages* (5GL) are programming languages based on solving problems using constraints given to the program, rather than using an algorithm written by a programmer.

Elements

All programming languages have some primitive building blocks for the description of data and the processes or transformations applied to them (like the addition of two numbers or the selection of an item from a collection). These primitives are defined by syntactic and semantic rules which describe their structure and meaning respectively.

Syntax

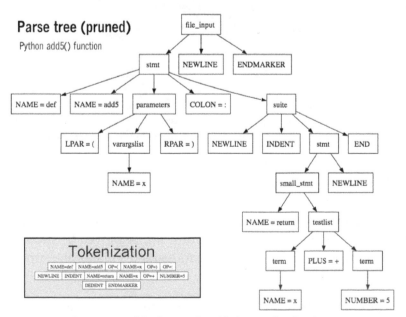

Parse tree of Python code with inset tokenization.

```
def add5(x):
    return x+5

def dotwrite(ast):
    nodename = getNodename()
    label=symbol.sym_name.get(int(ast[0]),ast[0])
    print '    %s [label="%s' % (nodename, label),
    if isinstance(ast[1], str):
        if ast[1].strip():
            print '= %s"];' % ast[1]
        else:
            print '"]'
    else:
        print '"];'
        children = []
        for in n, childenumerate(ast[1:]):
            children.append(dotwrite(child))
        print ,'    %s -> {' % nodename
        for in :namechildren
            print '%s' % name,
```

Syntax highlighting is often used to aid programmers in recognizing elements of source code.
The language above is Python.

A programming language's surface form is known as its syntax. Most programming languages are purely textual; they use sequences of text including words, numbers, and punctuation, much like written natural languages. On the other hand, there are some programming languages which are more graphical in nature, using visual relationships between symbols to specify a program.

The syntax of a language describes the possible combinations of symbols that form a syntactically correct program. The meaning given to a combination of symbols is handled by semantics (either formal or hard-coded in a reference implementation). Since most languages are textual, this article discusses textual syntax.

Programming language syntax is usually defined using a combination of regular expressions (for lexical structure) and Backus–Naur form (for grammatical structure). Below is a simple grammar, based on Lisp:

```
expression ::= atom | list

atom  ::= number | symbol

number ::= [+-]?['0'-'9']+

symbol ::= ['A'-'Z''a'-'z'].*

list  ::= '(' expression* ')'
```

This grammar specifies the following:

- an *expression* is either an *atom* or a *list*;

- an *atom* is either a *number* or a *symbol*;

- a *number* is an unbroken sequence of one or more decimal digits, optionally preceded by a plus or minus sign;

- a *symbol* is a letter followed by zero or more of any characters (excluding whitespace); and

- a *list* is a matched pair of parentheses, with zero or more *expressions* inside it.

The following are examples of well-formed token sequences in this grammar: `12345,` `()` and `(a b c232 (1))`.

Not all syntactically correct programs are semantically correct. Many syntactically correct programs are nonetheless ill-formed, per the language's rules; and may (depending on the language specification and the soundness of the implementation) result in an error on translation or execution. In some cases, such programs may exhibit undefined behavior. Even when a program is well-defined within a language, it may still have a meaning that is not intended by the person who wrote it.

Using natural language as an example, it may not be possible to assign a meaning to a grammatically correct sentence or the sentence may be false:

- "Colorless green ideas sleep furiously." is grammatically well-formed but has no generally accepted meaning.

- "John is a married bachelor." is grammatically well-formed but expresses a meaning that cannot be true.

The following C language fragment is syntactically correct, but performs operations that are not semantically defined (the operation *p >> 4 has no meaning for a value having a complex type and p->im is not defined because the value of p is the null pointer):

```
complex *p = NULL;

complex abs_p = sqrt(*p >> 4 + p->im);
```

If the type declaration on the first line were omitted, the program would trigger an error on compilation, as the variable "p" would not be defined. But the program would still be syntactically correct since type declarations provide only semantic information.

The grammar needed to specify a programming language can be classified by its position in the Chomsky hierarchy. The syntax of most programming languages can be specified using a Type-2 grammar, i.e., they are context-free grammars. Some languages, including Perl and Lisp, contain constructs that allow execution during the parsing phase. Languages that have constructs that allow the programmer to alter the behavior of the parser make syntax analysis an undecidable problem, and generally blur the distinction between parsing and execution. In contrast to Lisp's macro system and Perl's BEGIN blocks, which may contain general computations, C macros are merely string replacements and do not require code execution.

Semantics

The term *semantics* refers to the meaning of languages, as opposed to their form (syntax).

Static Semantics

The static semantics defines restrictions on the structure of valid texts that are hard or impossible to express in standard syntactic formalisms. For compiled languages, static semantics essentially include those semantic rules that can be checked at compile time. Examples include checking that every identifier is declared before it is used (in languages that require such declarations) or that the labels on the arms of a case statement are distinct. Many important restrictions of this type, like checking that identifiers are used in the appropriate context (e.g. not adding an integer to a function name), or that subroutine calls have the appropriate number and type of arguments, can be enforced by defining them as rules in a logic called a type system. Other forms of static analyses like data flow analysis may also be part of static semantics. Newer programming languages like Java and C# have definite assignment analysis, a form of data flow analysis, as part of their static semantics.

Dynamic Semantics

Once data has been specified, the machine must be instructed to perform operations on the data. For example, the semantics may define the strategy by which expressions are evaluated to values, or the manner in which control structures conditionally execute statements. The *dynamic semantics* (also known as *execution semantics*) of a language defines how and when the various constructs of a language should produce a program behavior. There are many ways of defining execution semantics. Natural language is often used to specify the execution semantics of languages commonly used in practice. A significant amount of academic research went into formal semantics of programming languages, which allow execution semantics to be specified in a formal manner. Results from this field of research have seen limited application to programming language design and implementation outside academia.

Type System

A type system defines how a programming language classifies values and expressions into *types*, how it can manipulate those types and how they interact. The goal of a type system is to verify and usually enforce a certain level of correctness in programs written in that language by detecting certain incorrect operations. Any decidable type system involves a trade-off: while it rejects many incorrect programs, it can also prohibit some correct, albeit unusual programs. In order to bypass this downside, a number of languages have *type loopholes*, usually unchecked casts that may be used by the programmer to explicitly allow a normally disallowed operation between different types. In most typed languages, the type system is used only to type check programs, but a number of languages, usually functional ones, infer types, relieving the programmer from the need to write type annotations. The formal design and study of type systems is known as *type theory*.

Typed Versus Untyped Languages

A language is *typed* if the specification of every operation defines types of data to which the operation is applicable, with the implication that it is not applicable to other types. For example, the data represented by `"this text between the quotes"` is a string, and in many programming languages dividing a number by a string has no meaning and will be rejected by the compilers. The invalid operation may be detected when the program is compiled ("static" type checking) and will be rejected by the compiler with a compilation error message, or it may be detected when the program is run ("dynamic" type checking), resulting in a run-time exception. Many languages allow a function called an exception handler to be written to handle this exception and, for example, always return "-1" as the result.

A special case of typed languages are the *single-type* languages. These are often scripting or mark-up languages, such as REXX or SGML, and have only one data type—most commonly character strings which are used for both symbolic and numeric data.

In contrast, an *untyped language*, such as most assembly languages, allows any operation to be performed on any data, which are generally considered to be sequences of bits of various lengths. High-level languages which are untyped include BCPL, Tcl, and some varieties of Forth.

In practice, while few languages are considered typed from the point of view of type theory (verifying or rejecting *all* operations), most modern languages offer a degree of typing. Many production languages provide means to bypass or subvert the type system, trading type-safety for finer control over the program's execution.

Static Versus Dynamic Typing

In *static typing*, all expressions have their types determined prior to when the program is executed, typically at compile-time. For example, 1 and (2+2) are integer expressions; they cannot be passed to a function that expects a string, or stored in a variable that is defined to hold dates.

Statically typed languages can be either *manifestly typed* or *type-inferred*. In the first case, the programmer must explicitly write types at certain textual positions (for example, at variable declarations). In the second case, the compiler *infers* the types of expressions and declarations based on context. Most mainstream statically typed languages, such as C++, C# and Java, are manifestly typed. Complete type inference has traditionally been associated with less mainstream languages, such as Haskell and ML. However, many manifestly typed languages support partial type inference; for example, Java and C# both infer types in certain limited cases. Additionally, some programming languages allow for some types to be automatically converted to other types; for example, an int can be used where the program expects a float.

Dynamic typing, also called *latent typing*, determines the type-safety of operations at run time; in other words, types are associated with *run-time values* rather than *textual expressions*. As with type-inferred languages, dynamically typed languages do not require the programmer to write explicit type annotations on expressions. Among other things, this may permit a single variable to refer to values of different types at different points in the program execution. However, type errors cannot be automatically detected until a piece of code is actually executed, potentially making debugging more difficult. Lisp, Smalltalk, Perl, Python, JavaScript, and Ruby are all examples of dynamically typed languages.

Weak and Strong Typing

Weak typing allows a value of one type to be treated as another, for example treating a string as a number. This can occasionally be useful, but it can also allow some kinds of program faults to go undetected at compile time and even at run time.

Strong typing prevents the above. An attempt to perform an operation on the wrong type of value raises an error. Strongly typed languages are often termed *type-safe* or *safe*.

An alternative definition for "weakly typed" refers to languages, such as Perl and JavaScript, which permit a large number of implicit type conversions. In JavaScript, for example, the expression 2 * x implicitly converts x to a number, and this conversion succeeds even if x is `null`, `undefined`, an `Array`, or a string of letters. Such implicit conversions are often useful, but they can mask programming errors. *Strong* and *static* are now generally considered orthogonal concepts, but usage in the literature differs. Some use the term *strongly typed* to mean *strongly, statically typed*, or, even more confusingly, to mean simply *statically typed*. Thus C has been called both strongly typed and weakly, statically typed.

It may seem odd to some professional programmers that C could be "weakly, statically typed". However, notice that the use of the generic pointer, the void* pointer, does allow for casting of pointers to other pointers without needing to do an explicit cast. This is extremely similar to somehow casting an array of bytes to any kind of datatype in C without using an explicit cast, such as `(int)` or `(char)`.

Standard Library and Run-time System

Most programming languages have an associated core library (sometimes known as the 'standard library', especially if it is included as part of the published language standard), which is conventionally made available by all implementations of the language. Core libraries typically include definitions for commonly used algorithms, data structures, and mechanisms for input and output.

The line between a language and its core library differs from language to language. In some cases, the language designers may treat the library as a separate entity from the language. However, a language's core library is often treated as part of the language by its users, and some language specifications even require that this library be made available in all implementations. Indeed, some languages are designed so that the meanings of certain syntactic constructs cannot even be described without referring to the core library. For example, in Java, a string literal is defined as an instance of the java.lang.String class; similarly, in Smalltalk, an anonymous function expression (a "block") constructs an instance of the library's BlockContext class. Conversely, Scheme contains multiple coherent subsets that suffice to construct the rest of the language as library macros, and so the language designers do not even bother to say which portions of the language must be implemented as language constructs, and which must be implemented as parts of a library.

Design and Implementation

Programming languages share properties with natural languages related to their purpose as vehicles for communication, having a syntactic form separate from its semantics, and showing *language families* of related languages branching one from another. But as artificial constructs, they also differ in fundamental ways from languages that have evolved through usage. A significant difference is that a programming language can be fully described and studied in its entirety, since it has a precise and finite definition. By contrast, natural languages have changing meanings given by their users in different communities. While constructed languages are also artificial languages designed from the ground up with a specific purpose, they lack the precise and complete semantic definition that a programming language has.

Many programming languages have been designed from scratch, altered to meet new needs, and combined with other languages. Many have eventually fallen into disuse. Although there have been attempts to design one "universal" programming language that serves all purposes, all of them have failed to be generally accepted as filling this role. The need for diverse programming languages arises from the diversity of contexts in which languages are used:

- Programs range from tiny scripts written by individual hobbyists to huge systems written by hundreds of programmers.

- Programmers range in expertise from novices who need simplicity above all else, to experts who may be comfortable with considerable complexity.

- Programs must balance speed, size, and simplicity on systems ranging from microcontrollers to supercomputers.

- Programs may be written once and not change for generations, or they may undergo continual modification.

- Programmers may simply differ in their tastes: they may be accustomed to discussing problems and expressing them in a particular language.

One common trend in the development of programming languages has been to add more ability to solve problems using a higher level of abstraction. The earliest programming languages were tied very closely to the underlying hardware of the computer. As new programming languages have developed, features have been added that let programmers express ideas that are more remote from simple translation into underlying hardware instructions. Because programmers are less tied to the complexity of the computer, their programs can do more computing with less effort from the programmer. This lets them write more functionality per time unit.

Natural language programming has been proposed as a way to eliminate the need for a specialized language for programming. However, this goal remains distant and its benefits are open to debate. Edsger W. Dijkstra took the position that the use of a formal language is essential to prevent the introduction of meaningless constructs, and dismissed natural language programming as "foolish". Alan Perlis was similarly dismissive of the idea. Hybrid approaches have been taken in Structured English and SQL.

A language's designers and users must construct a number of artifacts that govern and enable the practice of programming. The most important of these artifacts are the language *specification* and *implementation*.

Specification

The specification of a programming language is an artifact that the language users and the implementors can use to agree upon whether a piece of source code is a valid program in that language, and if so what its behavior shall be.

A programming language specification can take several forms, including the following:

- An explicit definition of the syntax, static semantics, and execution semantics of the language. While syntax is commonly specified using a formal grammar, semantic definitions may be written in natural language (e.g., as in the C language), or a formal semantics (e.g., as in Standard ML and Scheme specifications).

- A description of the behavior of a translator for the language (e.g., the C++ and Fortran specifications). The syntax and semantics of the language have to be inferred from this description, which may be written in natural or a formal language.

- A *reference* or *model* implementation, sometimes written in the language being specified (e.g., Prolog or ANSI REXX). The syntax and semantics of the language are explicit in the behavior of the reference implementation.

Implementation

An *implementation* of a programming language provides a way to write programs in that language and execute them on one or more configurations of hardware and software. There are, broadly, two approaches to programming language implementation: *compilation* and *interpretation*. It is generally possible to implement a language using either technique.

The output of a compiler may be executed by hardware or a program called an interpreter. In some implementations that make use of the interpreter approach there is no distinct boundary between compiling and interpreting. For instance, some implementations of BASIC compile and then execute the source a line at a time.

Programs that are executed directly on the hardware usually run several orders of magnitude faster than those that are interpreted in software.

One technique for improving the performance of interpreted programs is just-in-time compilation. Here the virtual machine, just before execution, translates the blocks of bytecode which are going to be used to machine code, for direct execution on the hardware.

Proprietary Languages

Although most of the most commonly used programming languages have fully open specifications and implementations, many programming languages exist only as proprietary programming languages with the implementation available only from a single vendor, which may claim that such a proprietary language is their intellectual property. Proprietary programming languages are commonly domain specific languages or internal scripting languages for a single product; some proprietary languages are used only internally within a vendor, while others are available to external users.

Some programming languages exist on the border between proprietary and open; for example, Oracle Corporation asserts proprietary rights to some aspects of the Java programming language, and Microsoft's C# programming language, which has open implementations of most parts of the system, also has Common Language Runtime (CLR) as a closed environment.

Many proprietary languages are widely used, in spite of their proprietary nature; examples include MATLAB and VBScript. Some languages may make the transition from closed to open; for example, Erlang was originally an Ericsson's internal programming language.

Usage

Thousands of different programming languages have been created, mainly in the computing field. Software is commonly built with 5 programming languages or more.

Programming languages differ from most other forms of human expression in that they require a greater degree of precision and completeness. When using a natural language to communicate with other people, human authors and speakers can be ambiguous and make small errors, and still expect their intent to be understood. However, figuratively speaking, computers "do exactly what they are told to do", and cannot "understand" what code the programmer intended to write. The combination of the language definition, a program, and the program's inputs must fully specify the external behavior that occurs when the program is executed, within the domain of control of that program. On the other hand, ideas about an algorithm can be communicated to humans without the precision required for execution by using pseudocode, which interleaves natural language with code written in a programming language.

A programming language provides a structured mechanism for defining pieces of data, and the operations or transformations that may be carried out automatically on that data. A programmer uses the abstractions present in the language to represent the concepts involved in a computation. These concepts are represented as a collection of the simplest elements available (called primitives). *Programming* is the process by which programmers combine these primitives to compose new programs, or adapt existing ones to new uses or a changing environment.

Programs for a computer might be executed in a batch process without human interaction, or a user might type commands in an interactive session of an interpreter. In this case the "commands" are simply programs, whose execution is chained together. When a language can run its commands through an interpreter (such as a Unix shell or other command-line interface), without compiling, it is called a scripting language.

Measuring Language Usage

It is difficult to determine which programming languages are most widely used, and what usage means varies by context. One language may occupy the greater number of programmer hours, a different one have more lines of code, and a third may consume the most CPU time. Some languages are very popular for particular kinds of applications. For example, COBOL is still strong in the corporate data center, often on large mainframes; Fortran in scientific and engineering applications; Ada in aerospace, transportation, military, real-time and embedded applications; and C in embedded applications and operating systems. Other languages are regularly used to write many different kinds of applications.

Various methods of measuring language popularity, each subject to a different bias over what is measured, have been proposed:

- counting the number of job advertisements that mention the language

- the number of books sold that teach or describe the language

- estimates of the number of existing lines of code written in the language – which may underestimate languages not often found in public searches

- counts of language references (i.e., to the name of the language) found using a web search engine.

Combining and averaging information from various internet sites, langpop.com claims that in 2013 the ten most popular programming languages are (in descending order by overall popularity): C, Java, PHP, JavaScript, C++, Python, Shell, Ruby, Objective-C and C#.

Taxonomies

There is no overarching classification scheme for programming languages. A given programming language does not usually have a single ancestor language. Languages commonly arise by combining the elements of several predecessor languages with new ideas in circulation at the time. Ideas that originate in one language will diffuse throughout a family of related languages, and then leap suddenly across familial gaps to appear in an entirely different family.

The task is further complicated by the fact that languages can be classified along multiple axes. For example, Java is both an object-oriented language (because it encourages object-oriented organization) and a concurrent language (because it contains built-in constructs for running multiple threads in parallel). Python is an object-oriented scripting language.

In broad strokes, programming languages divide into *programming paradigms* and a classification by *intended domain of use,* with general-purpose programming languages distinguished from domain-specific programming languages. Traditionally, programming languages have been regarded as describing computation in terms of imperative sentences, i.e. issuing commands. These are generally called imperative programming languages. A great deal of research in programming languages has been aimed at blurring the distinction between a program as a set of instructions and a program as an assertion about the desired answer, which is the main feature of declarative programming. More refined paradigms include procedural programming, object-oriented programming, functional programming, and logic programming; some languages are hybrids of paradigms or multi-paradigmatic. An assembly language is not so much a paradigm as a direct model of an underlying machine architecture. By purpose, programming languages might be considered general purpose, system programming languages, scripting languages, domain-specific languages, or concurrent/distributed languages (or a combination of these). Some general purpose languages were designed largely with educational goals.

A programming language may also be classified by factors unrelated to programming paradigm. For instance, most programming languages use English language keywords, while a minority do not. Other languages may be classified as being deliberately esoteric or not.

Debugger

A debugger or debugging tool is a computer program that is used to test and debug other programs (the "target" program). The code to be examined might alternatively be running on an *instruction set simulator* (ISS), a technique that allows great power in its ability to halt when specific conditions are encountered, but which will typically be somewhat slower than executing the code directly on the appropriate (or the same) processor. Some debuggers offer two modes of operation, full or partial simulation, to limit this impact.

Winpdb debugging itself.

A "trap" occurs when the program cannot normally continue because of a programming bug or invalid data. For example, the program might have tried to use an instruction not available on the current version of the CPU or attempted to access unavailable or protected memory. When the program "traps" or reaches a preset condition, the debugger typically shows the location in the original code if it is a source-level debugger or symbolic debugger, commonly now seen in integrated development environments. If it is a low-level debugger or a machine-language debugger it shows the line in the disassembly (unless it also has online access to the original source code and can display the appropriate section of code from the assembly or compilation).

Features

Typically, debuggers offer a query processor, a symbol resolver, an expression interpreter, and a debug support interface at its top level. Debuggers also offer more sophisticated functions such as running a program step by step (single-stepping or program animation), stopping (breaking) (pausing the program to examine the current state) at some event or specified instruction by means of a breakpoint, and tracking the values of variables. Some debuggers have the ability to modify program state while it is running. It may also be possible to continue execution at a different location in the program to bypass a crash or logical error.

The same functionality which makes a debugger useful for eliminating bugs allows it to be used as a software cracking tool to evade copy protection, digital rights management, and other software protection features. It often also makes it useful as a general verification tool, fault coverage, and performance analyzer, especially if instruction path lengths are shown.

Most mainstream debugging engines, such as gdb and dbx, provide console-based command line interfaces. Debugger front-ends are popular extensions to debugger engines that provide IDE integration, program animation, and visualization features.

Reverse Debugging

Some debuggers include a feature called "reverse debugging", also known as "historical debugging" or "backwards debugging". These debuggers make it possible to step a program's execution backwards in time. Various debuggers include this feature. Microsoft Visual Studio (2010 Ultimate edition, 2012 Ultimate, 2013 Ultimate, and 2015 Enterprise edition) offers IntelliTrace reverse debugging for C#, Visual Basic .NET, and some other languages, but not C++. Reverse debuggers also exist for C, C++, Java, Python, Perl, and other languages. Some are open source; some are proprietary commercial software. Some reverse debuggers slow down the target by orders of magnitude, but the best reverse debuggers cause a slowdown of 2× or less. Reverse debugging is very useful for certain types of problems, but is still not commonly used yet.

Language Dependency

Some debuggers operate on a single specific language while others can handle multiple languages transparently. For example, if the main target program is written in COBOL but calls assembly language subroutines and PL/1 subroutines, the debugger may have to dynamically switch modes to accommodate the changes in language as they occur.

Memory Protection

Some debuggers also incorporate memory protection to avoid storage violations such as buffer overflow. This may be extremely important in transaction processing environments where memory is dynamically allocated from memory 'pools' on a task by task basis.

Hardware Support for Debugging

Most modern microprocessors have at least one of these features in their CPU design to make debugging easier:

- Hardware support for single-stepping a program, such as the trap flag.

- An instruction set that meets the Popek and Goldberg virtualization requirements makes it easier to write debugger software that runs on the same CPU as the software being debugged; such a CPU can execute the inner loops of the program under test at full speed, and still remain under debugger control.

- In-system programming allows an external hardware debugger to reprogram a system under test (for example, adding or removing instruction breakpoints). Many systems with such ISP support also have other hardware debug support.

- Hardware support for code and data breakpoints, such as address comparators and data value comparators or, with considerably more work involved, page fault hardware.

- JTAG access to hardware debug interfaces such as those on ARM architecture processors or using the Nexus command set. Processors used in embedded systems typically have extensive JTAG debug support.

- Micro controllers with as few as six pins need to use low pin-count substitutes for JTAG, such as BDM, Spy-Bi-Wire, or debugWIRE on the Atmel AVR. DebugWIRE, for example, uses bidirectional signaling on the RESET pin.

Debugger Front-ends

Some of the most capable and popular debuggers implement only a simple command line interface (CLI)—often to maximize portability and minimize resource consumption. Developers typically consider debugging via a graphical user interface (GUI) easier and more productive. This is the reason for visual front-ends, that allow users to monitor and control subservient CLI-only debuggers via graphical user interface. Some GUI debugger front-ends are designed to be compatible with a variety of CLI-only debuggers, while others are targeted at one specific debugger.

List of Debuggers

Some widely used debuggers are:

- Firefox JavaScript debugger

- GDB - the GNU debugger

- LLDB

- Microsoft Visual Studio Debugger

- Valgrind

- WinDbg

- Eclipse debugger API used in a range of IDEs: Eclipse IDE (Java) Nodeclipse (JavaScript)

- WDW, the OpenWatcom debugger

Earlier minicomputer debuggers include:

- Dynamic debugging technique (DDT)

- On-line Debugging Tool (ODT)

Earlier Mainframe debuggers include (in date of release order):

- 1985 CA/EZTEST

- 1990 XPEDITER and Expediter CICS

Current mainframe debuggers:

- Debug Tool for z/OS

- XPEDITER and Expediter CICS

- z/XDC

Program Debugging

Important Commands of gdb

- `break [file:] function` : Set a breakpoint at the beginning of `function` (in file).

- `break [file:] #n` : Set a breakpoint at line #n (`in file`).

- `run [arglist]` : Start your program (with command line `arglist`, if any).

- next : Execute next line of the program (after stopping). That is, executes `next` line completely, including function calls (if any). It is called step over any function calls in the line.

- `c` : Continue executing the program (after stopping) till next breakpoint, if any.

- `print expr` : Display the value of an expression.

- `list [ file : ] function` : Type the text of the program in the vicinity of where it is presently stopped.

- `step` : Execute next program line (after stopping). It there is any function call present in the next program line, it goes into 1st line of that function. It is called step into any function calls in the line.

- `quit` : Exit from GDB.

- `q` : Exit from GDB.

- `help` : Show information about GDB commands.

- `help [name]` : Show information about GDB command `name`.

Palindrome Probelm

- A palindrome is a string that reads same in either direction. A palindrome can be string, phrase, numbers, or any sequence of symbols.

- We debug the following program (`palindrome.c`) which takes a string as command linc argument and tests whether it is a palindrome or not.

- Compile the program `gcc -g -o palindrome palindrome.c`

- It generates a executable program named `palindrome`.

- Start the debugger with the name of executable program to be debugged. In our case, command is `gdb palindrome`

- The debugger out puts its prompt (gdb)

  $ gdb `palindrome` (gdb)

- We keep first break point at the first instruction of the main function, that is the line 7, to stop the execution immediately after started.

  (gdb) `break main`

  Breakpoint 1 at 0x80483da: file palindrome.c, line 7.

  (gdb)

- Start the execution by the command *run madam*

  (gdb) *run madam*

  Starting program: palindrome madam

  Breakpoint 1, main (argc=2, argv=0xafb79394) at

  palindrome.c:7

  7   if (argc != 2) {

  (gdb)

- Program is stopped at the line 7.

- Now we can keep more break points or execute the program step by step.

- We will go for keeping more break points. We have to decide where to keep break points?

- To see the part of the code around the breakpoint use the command list. It displays 10 lines around the current breakpoint.

(gdb) list

```
    2.          #include<string.h>

    3.        main(int argc, char *argv[])

    4.            {

    5.                int i,length, mid;

    6.

    7.                if (argc != 2) {

    8.                    printf(«Error in

  input.\n");

    9.                        exit(1);

   10.            }

   11.
```

(gdb)

It may not be necessary to keep the break point in the above part of the program. So we will see the code around line 15.

(gdb) list 15

```
10.        }

11.

12.        length = strlen(argv[1]);

13.        mid = length/2;

14.        for (i=0; i<=mid; ++i){

15.            if (argv [1] [i] != argv [1] [lengthi]){

16.                    printf(«\»%s\»  is  not  a  palindrome.\n",
       argv [1]);

17.                    exit(0);

18.                }

19.        }
```

(gdb)

- There could be an error in the for loop. So, keep break point at the line 15.

  (gdb) `break 15`

  ```
  Breakpoint 2 at 0x8048435: file palindrome.c, line 15.
  ```

  (gdb)

  • Continue execution using the command c .

  (gdb) c

  ```
  Continuing.

  Breakpoint 2, main (argc=2, argv=0xafb79394) at
  palindrome.c:15

  15              if (argv [1] [i] != argv[1] length-i]){
  ```

- **(gdb)**

- Program giving wrong output, that it is executing lines 16 and 17, which is in the if part.

- We have to check why if condition is satisfied?

- Use the `print` command to display the values stored in variables or expression.

  (gdb) `print length`

  ```
  $1 = 5
  ```

  (gdb)

- Length of the input string "madam" is correct. Check other variables.

        (gdb) print mid

        $2 = 2

        (gdb)

- Value stored in mid also correct. Check left and right expression of the if condition.

    (gdb) print argv [1] [i]

    $3 = 109 'm'

    (gdb) print argv [1] [length-i]

    $4 = 0 '\0'

    (gdb)

The left expression is 'm' and the right expression is '\0' which are not equal!

- Why ? It is comparing 'm' and '\0'. It is suppose to compare 'm' and 'm' , which are first and last character of the input string. Check indexes used to compare? That is, i and length - i.

        (gdb) print i

        $5 = 0

        (gdb) print length-i

        $6 = 5

        (gdb)

- Index of an array of length 5 varies between 0 and 4. But we are comparing the character stored in the indexes 0 and 5, which is not correct.

- Index should be used in the right expression should be length-i-1.

- Quit the gdb.

    (gdb) q

    The program is running. Exit anyway? (y or n) y

    $

- Edit the program, compile, and execute.

- Now, the program works correctly.

Run Time Errors

- Correcting run time errors are easier than correcting logical errors.

- We discusses most important run time errors.

- Segmentation fault : It occurs when a program try to access a memory location that it is not allowed to access.

  ○ This location may part of the operating system, other user, or other processes.

- Divide by zero: Many operating systems report message `Floating point exception` , when there is expression which denominator of the division is 0.

- Stack Over flow: Most of the cases it happen, when there is infinite recursion. In recursive function calls, program has to store various environment variables, before start executing the calling function. It can also happen when there are many big temporary arrays.

- Whenever these errors occurs, program execution stops with appropriate error message.

- These errors also can be debugged using `gdb` .

References

- Whitten, Jeffrey L.; Lonnie D. Bentley, Kevin C. Dittman. (2003). Systems Analysis and Design Methods. 6th edition. ISBN 0-256-19906-X

- Dean, Tom (2002). "Programming Robots". Building Intelligent Robots. Brown University Department of Computer Science. Retrieved 23 September 2006

- Suryanarayana, Girish (2015). "Software Process versus Design Quality: Tug of War?". IEEE Software. 32 (4): 7–11. doi:10.1109/MS.2015.87

- In mathematical terms, this means the programming language is Turing-complete MacLennan, Bruce J. (1987). Principles of Programming Languages. Oxford University Press. p. 1. ISBN 0-19-511306-3

- Oetiker, Tobias; Partl, Hubert; Hyna, Irene; Schlegl, Elisabeth (June 20, 2016). "The Not So Short Introduction to LATEX 2ε" (Version 5.06). tobi.oetiker.ch. pp. 1–157. Retrieved April 16, 2017

- Michael Sipser (1996). Introduction to the Theory of Computation. PWS Publishing. ISBN 0-534-94728-X. Section 2.2: Pushdown Automata, pp.101–114

- "HPL - A Portable Implementation of the High-Performance Linpack Benchmark for Distributed-Memory Computers". Retrieved 2015-02-21

- Lübke, Daniel; van Lessen, Tammo (2016). "Modeling Test Cases in BPMN for Behavior-Driven Development". IEEE Software. 33 (5): 15–21. doi:10.1109/MS.2016.117

- Dykes, Lucinda; Tittel, Ed (2005). XML For Dummies, 4th Edition. Wiley. p. 20. ISBN 0-7645-8845-1. ...it's a markup language, not a programming language

Permissions

We would like to thank the editorial team for lending their expertise to make the book truly unique. They have played a crucial role in the development of this book. Without their invaluable contributions this book wouldn't have been possible. They have made vital efforts to compile up to date information on the varied aspects of this subject to make this book a valuable addition to the collection of many professionals and students.

This book was conceptualized with the vision of imparting up-to-date and integrated information in this field. To ensure the same, a matchless editorial board was set up. Every individual on the board went through rigorous rounds of assessment to prove their worth. After which they invested a large part of their time researching and compiling the most relevant data for our readers.

The editorial board has been involved in producing this book since its inception. They have spent rigorous hours researching and exploring the diverse topics which have resulted in the successful publishing of this book. They have passed on their knowledge of decades through this book. To expedite this challenging task, the publisher supported the team at every step. A small team of assistant editors was also appointed to further simplify the editing procedure and attain best results for the readers.

Apart from the editorial board, the designing team has also invested a significant amount of their time in understanding the subject and creating the most relevant covers. They scrutinized every image to scout for the most suitable representation of the subject and create an appropriate cover for the book.

The publishing team has been an ardent support to the editorial, designing and production team. Their endless efforts to recruit the best for this project, has resulted in the accomplishment of this book. They are a veteran in the field of academics and their pool of knowledge is as vast as their experience in printing. Their expertise and guidance has proved useful at every step. Their uncompromising quality standards have made this book an exceptional effort. Their encouragement from time to time has been an inspiration for everyone.

The publisher and the editorial board hope that this book will prove to be a valuable piece of knowledge for students, practitioners and scholars across the globe.

Index